PAST & PRESENT

DENVER

OPPOSITE: Pre–World War II Denver felt like the big city to residents, but this c. 1948 aerial photograph reveals it as a sleepy regional hub, with only one building over 12 stories high and no skyscrapers. That would change. Denverites were proud of their expansive, green Civic Center, stretching from the capitol to the City and County Building, center. (Author's collection.)

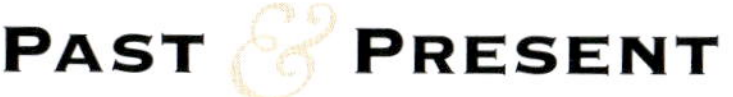

DENVER

Mark A. Barnhouse

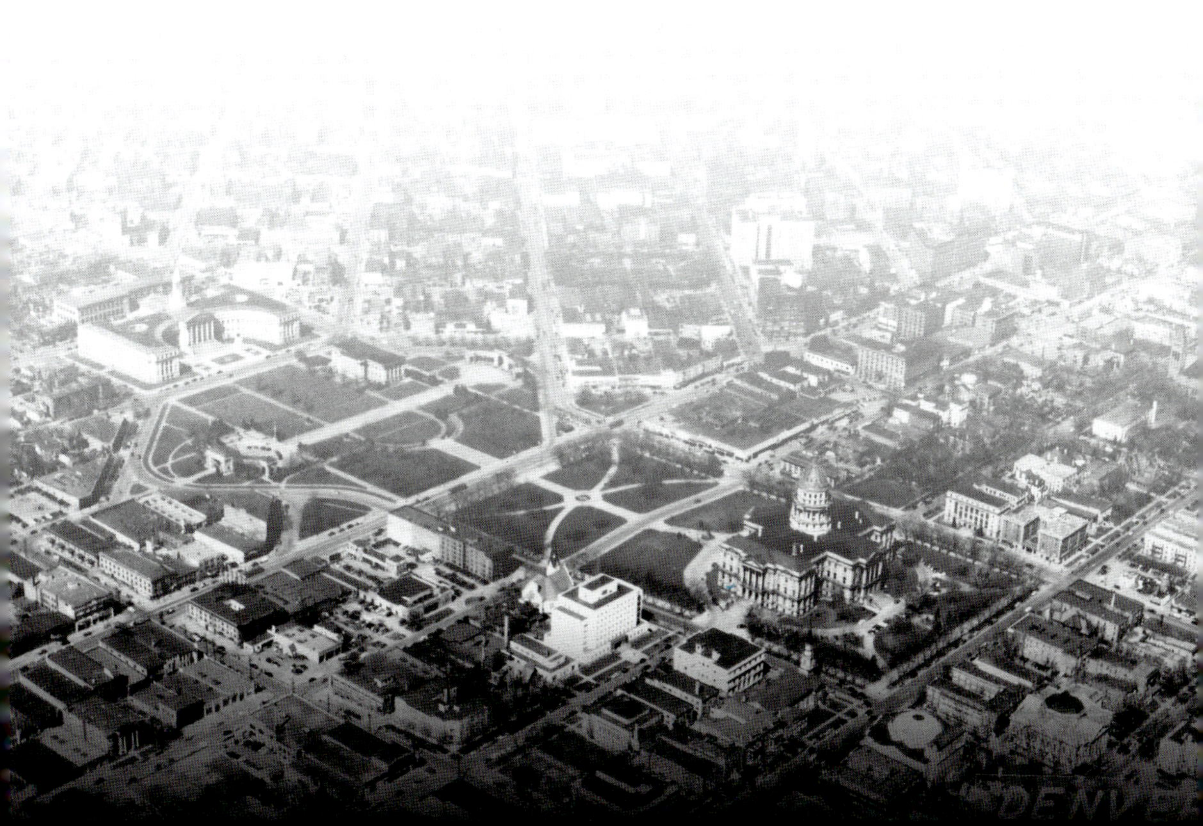

ISBN 978-1-4671-0905-5

Library of Congress Control Number: 2022944481

Published by Arcadia Publishing
Charleston, South Carolina

Printed in the United States of America

For all general information, please contact Arcadia Publishing:
Telephone 843-853-2070
Fax 843-853-0044
E-mail sales@arcadiapublishing.com
For customer service and orders:
Toll-Free 1-888-313-2665

Visit us on the Internet at www.arcadiapublishing.com

On the Front Cover: The 1400 block of Larimer Street, saved as Larimer Square by preservationist Dana Crawford beginning in 1963, formed a portion of Denver's first main street, running from Cherry Creek and city hall to the Windsor Hotel at Nineteenth Street. Long derided (or celebrated, by Jack Kerouac) as a "skid road," Larimer Street was down-at-heels by the time of this c. 1957 photograph, although some legitimate businesses remained, including Fred Mueller Saddles (left). (Past, Thomas J. Noel Collection; present, author.)

On the Back Cover: Fifteenth Street, seen in this Louis Charles McClure photograph looking northwest from Champa Street, once bustled with activity thanks to the presence of numerous streetcar lines and the Denver Tramway Company's Central Loop transfer point on Fifteenth between Arapahoe and Lawrence Streets. Fifteenth Street's most prominent building, the *Old Miner* statue-topped Mining Exchange, now demolished, is visible in the distance. (Denver Public Library, MCC-920.)

CONTENTS

ACKNOWLEDGMENTS

Having spent decades staring at old photographs and postcards of Denver, writing a book like this one has been great fun for me. It has given me a chance to do what I love when I am with other people walking through Denver's cityscape, to say, "this used to be . . ." and "so-and-so lived there." For this fine opportunity, I am grateful to Arcadia Publishing's Stacia Bannerman and Lindsey Givens.

While some images in this book are from my own collection, the vast majority came from two great institutions: Denver Public Library's Western History and Genealogy Collection and History Colorado's Stephen H. Hart Research Center. I thank Kellen Cutsforth at the Denver Public Library and Jori Johnson, Viviana Guajardo, and Poppie Gullett at History Colorado for their assistance. I also thank Keith Fessenden, archivist/historian at the National Western Stock Show, and Rev. Hugh M. Guentner, OSM, at Our Lady of Mount Carmel Church (in 2011) for their help.

Additionally, I thank the following people for their service or inspiration in other ways: Paul Cloyd, Sandra Dallas, Jan and Steve Davis, Ray Defa, the late Dennis Gallagher, Terri Gentry, Leslie Mohr Krupa, Steven Romeis, and Tom and Laurie Simmons. For years of friendship, generosity, and advice, along with front cover's Larimer Street photograph, I am grateful to my old professor and mentor, "Dr. Colorado," Thomas Jacob Noel. Finally, no list of acknowledgments is complete without Matt Wallington, who is always supportive, thoughtful, and wise.

Author's note: All present-day photographs are by the author, taken with a Nikon D3400 camera. In most cases, I tried to match the time of day of the original photograph, but in others, it made more sense to shoot at a different hour. Historic photograph sources are noted in each caption. DPL is short for Denver Public Library, Western History and Genealogy Collection. HC is short for History Colorado's collection. I have included call numbers or scan numbers for both of these sources.

Introduction

Photography has been around longer than Denver, a city founded in 1858, and we are fortunate to have a visual record going back to nearly the beginning. William Gunnison Chamberlain, William Henry Jackson, Louis Charles McClure, and Harry Mellon Rhoads, among others, documented Denver's early decades as it grew from a frontier outpost to an urbane metropolis, their work augmented by anonymous photographers whose work resides at Denver Public Library and History Colorado. Today's sprawling Denver metropolitan area, home to nearly three million people, bears little resemblance to the cow town of yore, but fragments of an earlier Mile High City continue to imbue today's Denver with a sense of its past. The intent of this volume is to remind readers that history remains all around us.

The first chapter is called "Main Streets" in the plural because Denver has never boasted a street called "Main," and several thoroughfares have claimed the honorary title during different eras. In the 1860s, F Street, today's Fifteenth, from Larimer to Wazee Streets was home to leading businesses, centering on the still-standing Wells Fargo depot at F and McGaa (Market) Streets; across Cherry Creek in Auraria, Ferry Street, now Eleventh, served a similar purpose. Larimer Street, with its connection to Auraria via a Cherry Creek–spanning bridge and home to city hall, subsequently claimed "Main Street" status, but this lasted only until the 1880s, when Sixteenth Street emerged as Denver's most important thoroughfare, home to its central post office, county courthouse, leading department stores, and smaller shops, along with office buildings and some banks. Parades, always an indicator of a street's importance, often ran down Sixteenth Street from Larimer Street to Broadway. Yet nearby Seventeenth Street, "Wall Street of the Rockies," home to many banks and brokerages, and Fifteenth Street, a major streetcar spine anchored by the Central Loop between Arapahoe and Lawrence Streets, vied with Sixteenth Street in importance. As Denver grew and diversified, neighborhood main streets served streetcar suburbs and racial and ethnic minority communities on the west and north sides and in Five Points. In the 20th and 21st centuries, partisans liked to proclaim both Broadway and Colfax Avenue as "Denver's Main Street," although both really serve more as automobile strips, with some interesting, more urban sections lined with shops and restaurants.

Denver's earliest leaders, not unlike today's capitalists, were absorbed by commerce and industry, the second chapter's focus. The city's relative isolation from the rest of the country inspired an independent spirit: Denver would make what it needed, even automobiles, and would prove its worth to the eastern and British capitalists who bankrolled its aspirations. As the most important city in a thousand-mile radius, it became an entrepôt, a hub for goods and services serving a vast hinterland. Downtown would never have grown as it did without this extraterritorial income. Agriculture and meat processing were also economic drivers—Denver was called a "cow town" with good reason. Yet Denverites knew how to have fun, too, and avidly patronized theaters, amusement parks (then called "summer resorts"), and other attractions, highlighted in the third chapter.

Early Denver was all business, but by the early 20th century, leaders realized their dusty burg wanted amenities on par with eastern cities. Following early acquisitions of parkland, Mayor Robert Walter Speer, who served between 1904 and 1912 and again from 1916 to 1918, advocated a "City Beautiful," planning parkways and Civic Center, graced by imposing Neoclassical embellishments, and building the Municipal Auditorium (now Ellie Caulkins Opera House), christened by the 1908 Democratic National Convention, the first presidential convention for either major party west of the Mississippi. The fourth chapter documents some of these, along with other public amenities and municipal points of pride. Yet private institutions also desired to contribute to the overall wellbeing and sense that Denver had come of age: some of these, including churches, fraternal orders, and private clubs, fill the fifth chapter.

This volume's final chapter explores the diversity of early Denver's housing stock, although given that poorer residents could not afford to have their homes commercially photographed, the selection leans toward the higher end, homes for the wealthy and upper-middle class, including some nationally famous names. Multifamily apartment buildings emerged as early as the 1880s, and a few of these close out this comparative look at Denver's past and present.

CHAPTER 1

Main Streets

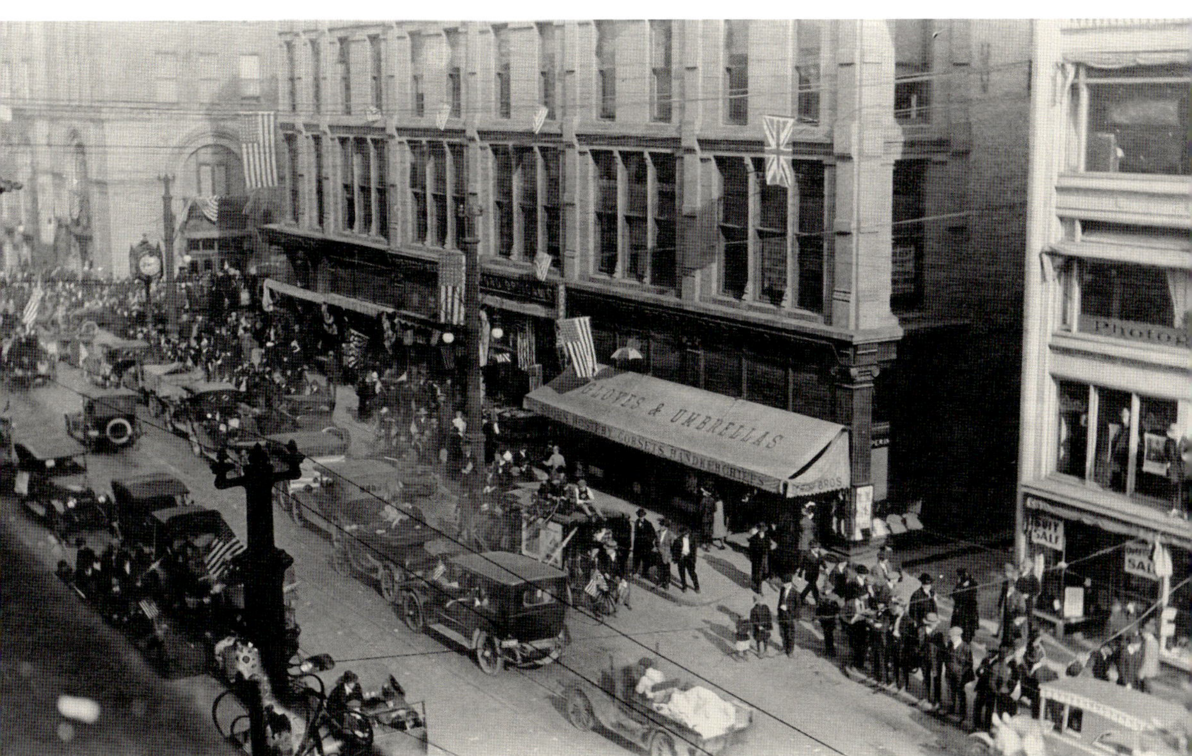

The Daniels and Fisher Tower (base visible at left) still stands on Sixteenth and Arapahoe Streets, but the Jacobson (center) and America Theater (right) Buildings fell to urban renewal. From the Tabor Theater's fourth floor, an anonymous photographer captured boisterous, patriotic crowds celebrating Armistice Day, November 11, 1918, at the natural place for congregating, Denver's "Main Street," Sixteenth Street. (Author's collection.)

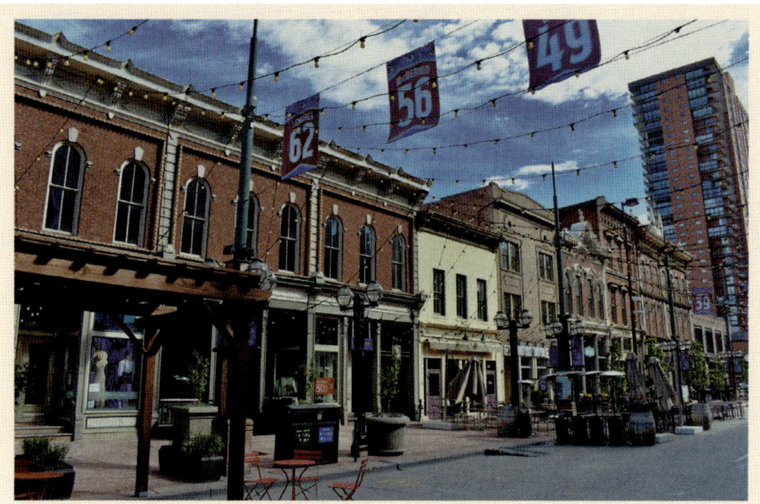

Denver's future was uncertain when William Chamberlain photographed the northwestern side of Larimer Street in 1861, including his studio (left). Next door was an early theater, Apollo Hall, and a few doors down was Denver's first bookstore, Woolworth & Moffat's News Depot, which included the post office. Graham's City Drug anchored the F (Fifteenth) Street corner. Larimer Street was already beginning to assume its main street persona, although these buildings would mostly succumb to the great fire of April 19, 1863. (DPL, X-19271.)

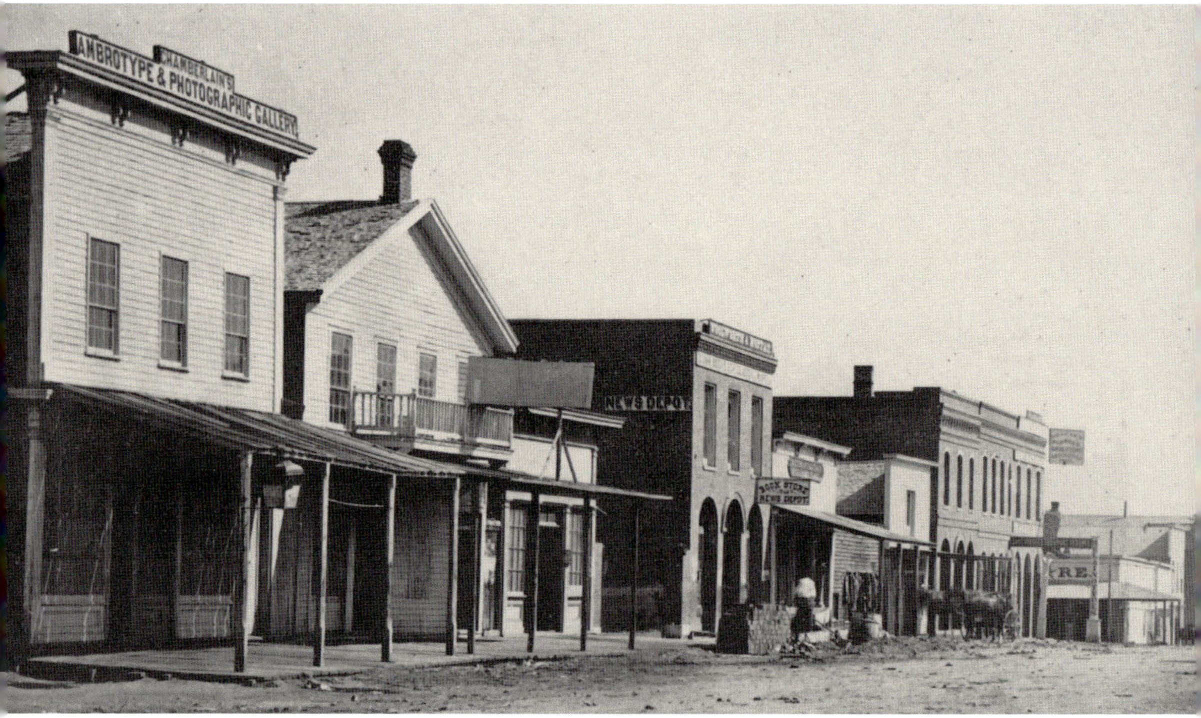

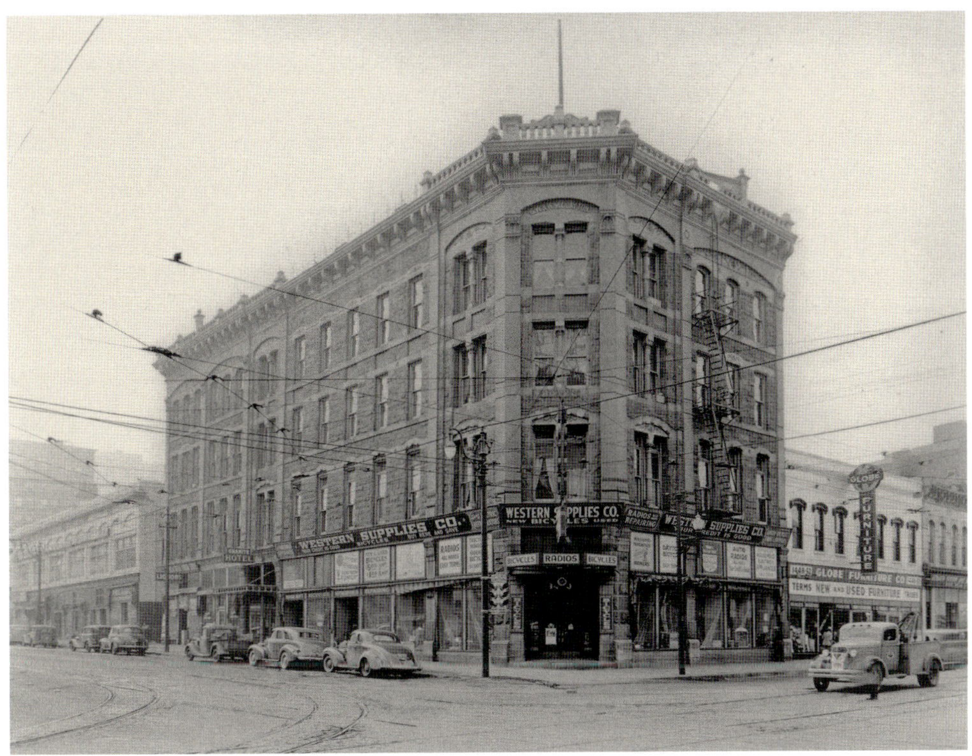

Denver founder Gen. William Larimer built his log cabin in 1858 at what became Fifteenth and Larimer Streets. Brothers William H. and George Washington Clayton acquired the property, erected a two-story structure, and subsequently demolished it in 1882 to build this four-story granite and rhyolite edifice by architect John W. Roberts housing Michael J. McNamara's department store. After McNamara moved uptown in 1889, it became the Granite Hotel, and today, it is Larimer Square's Granite Building. (HC, 10026585.)

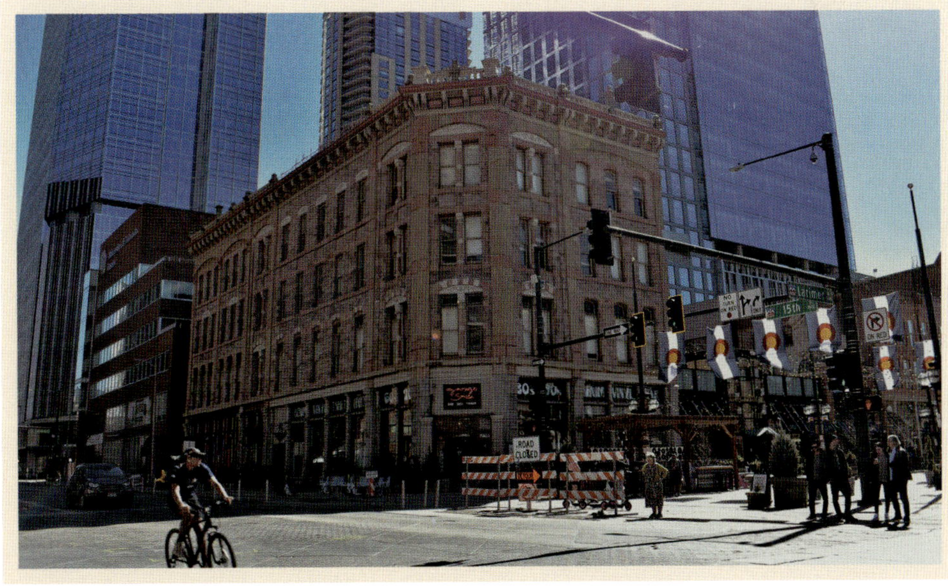

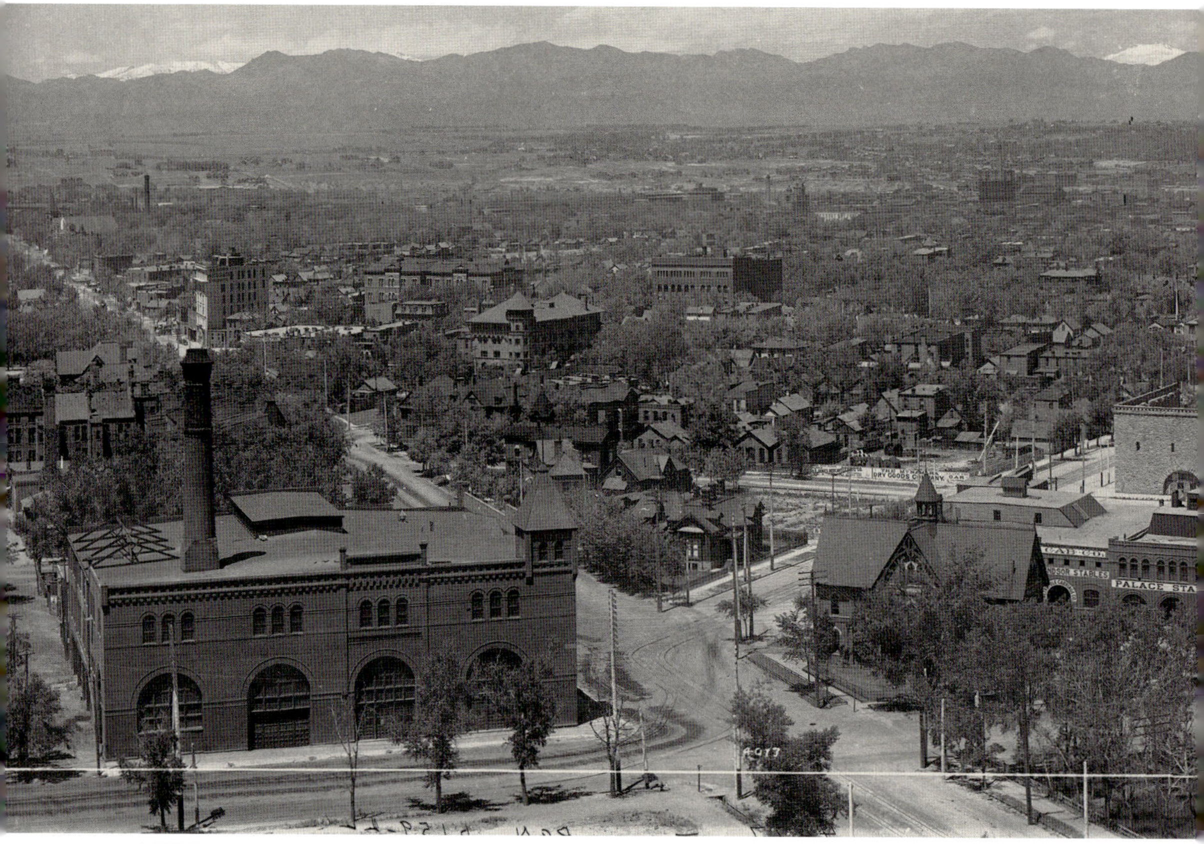

William Henry Jackson captured three of Denver's main streets in this c. 1890 view from the capitol dome: Broadway (running across the bottom), Colfax Avenue, and Fifteenth Street. The large brick powerhouse with smokestack (left), built by the Denver Electric & Cable Railway in 1887, served three short-lived cable-driven streetcar lines that ran south on Broadway, east on Colfax Avenue, and northwest on Fifteenth Street. Later converted to offices, it was demolished in 1912 to clear land for Civic Center. (HC, 10025120.)

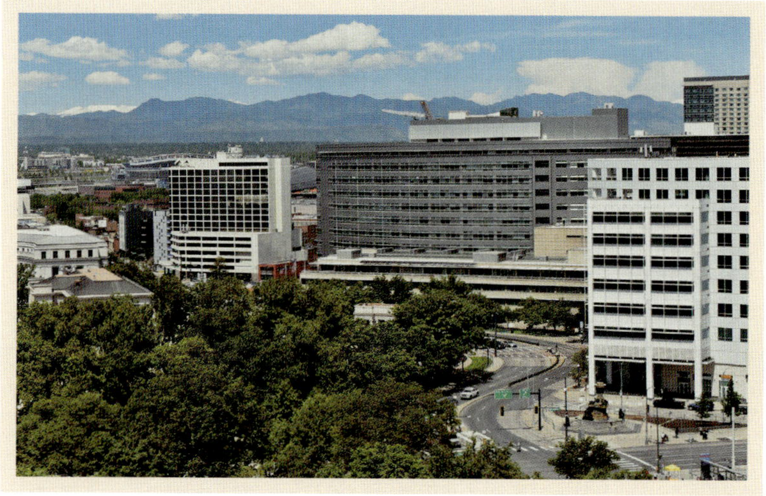

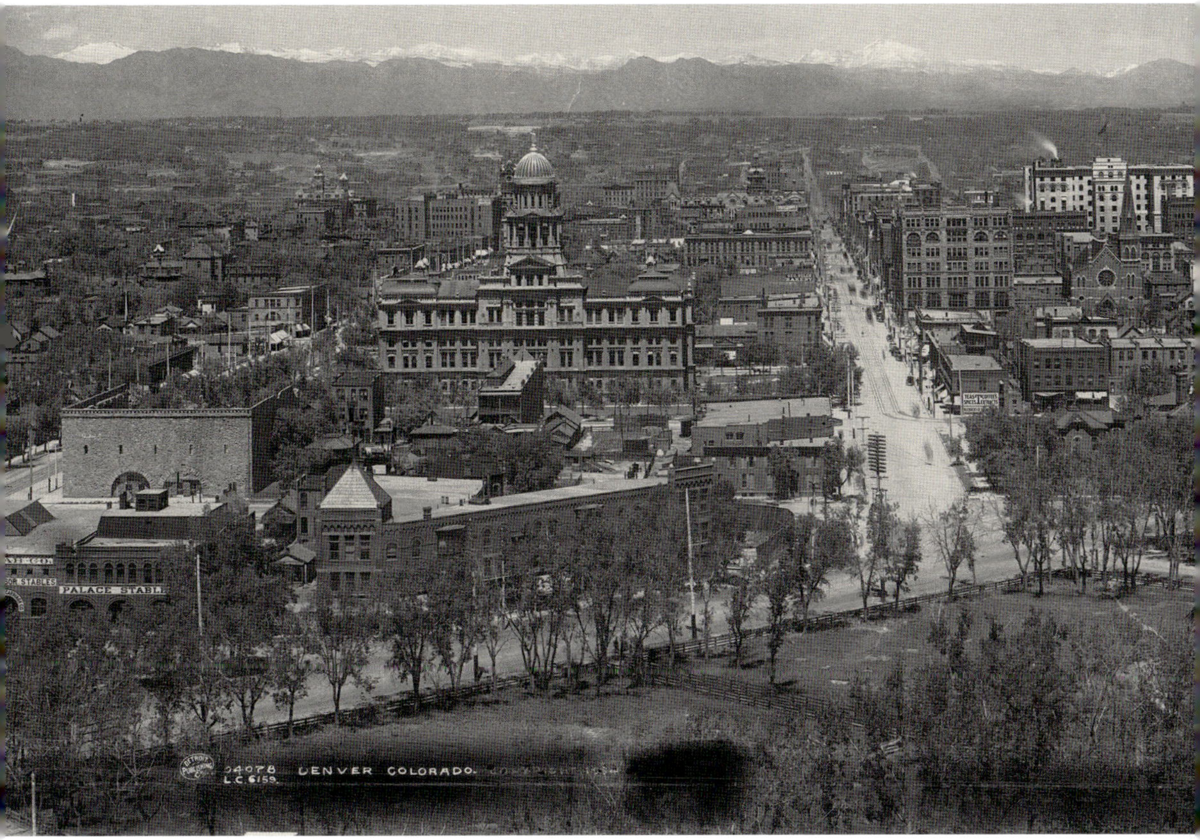

Jackson continued his panorama, moving northwest to capture Sixteenth Street, which served as Denver's main street from the 1880s through the 1950s. The prominent Arapahoe (later Denver) County Courthouse stood at Sixteenth Street and Court Place from 1882 until 1933, when, rendered obsolete by the new City & County Building, Mayor George Begole ordered its demolition. The seven-story Kittredge Building (right), at Sixteenth Street and Glenarm Place, was brand new and remains an ornament to Sixteenth Street today. (HC, 10025121.)

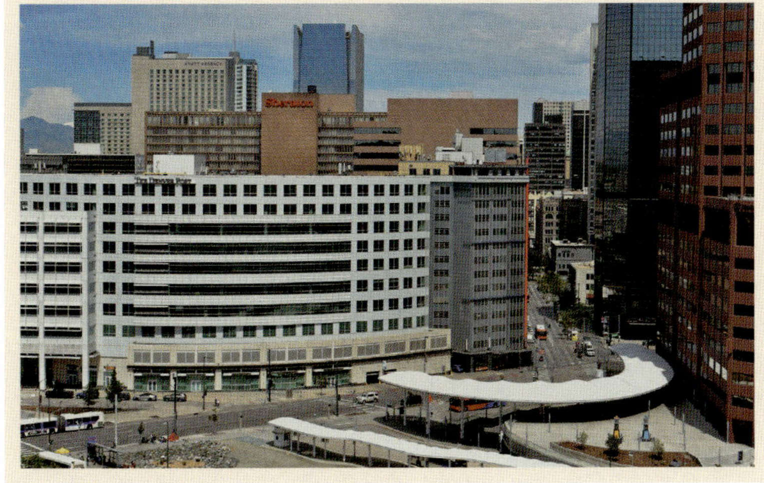

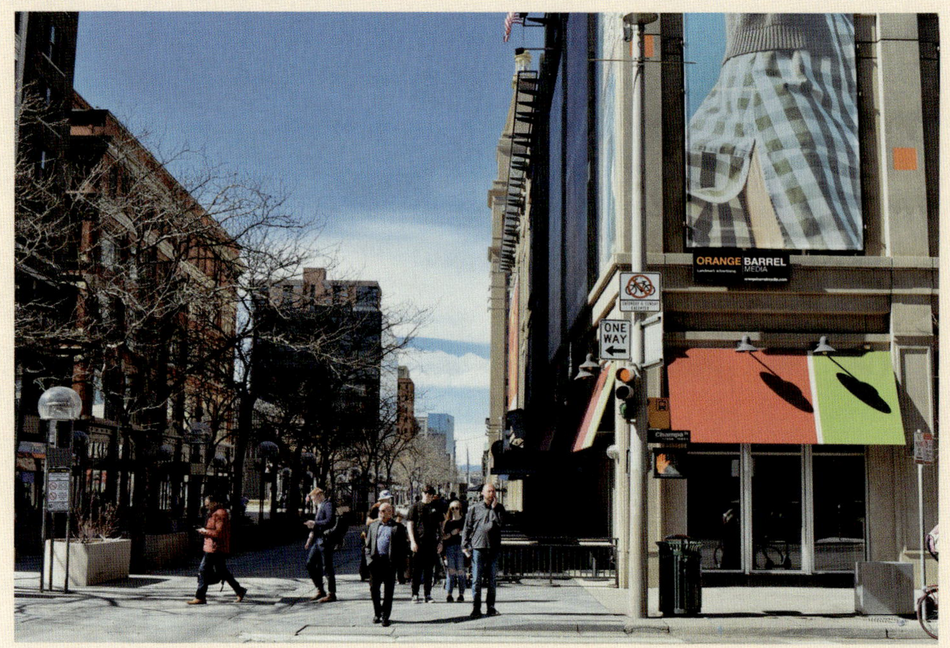

While much is gone, some of old Denver remains in this c. 1954 view of Sixteenth Street looking northwest from Champa Street. The University Building (far left) and Joslin's department store form a portion of a four-block stretch of historic buildings running from Curtis Street to Welton Street, and the Daniels and Fisher Tower (right) still watches over Sixteenth Street. Yet the Tabor Theater (left) and May Company (right) have been gone for more than half a century. (DPL, X-23059.)

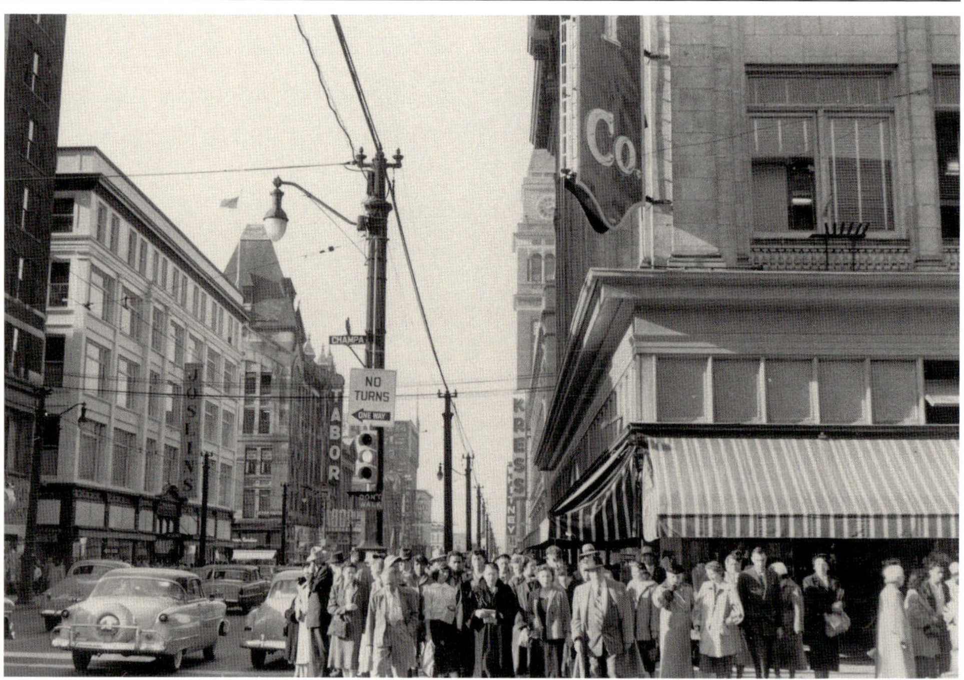

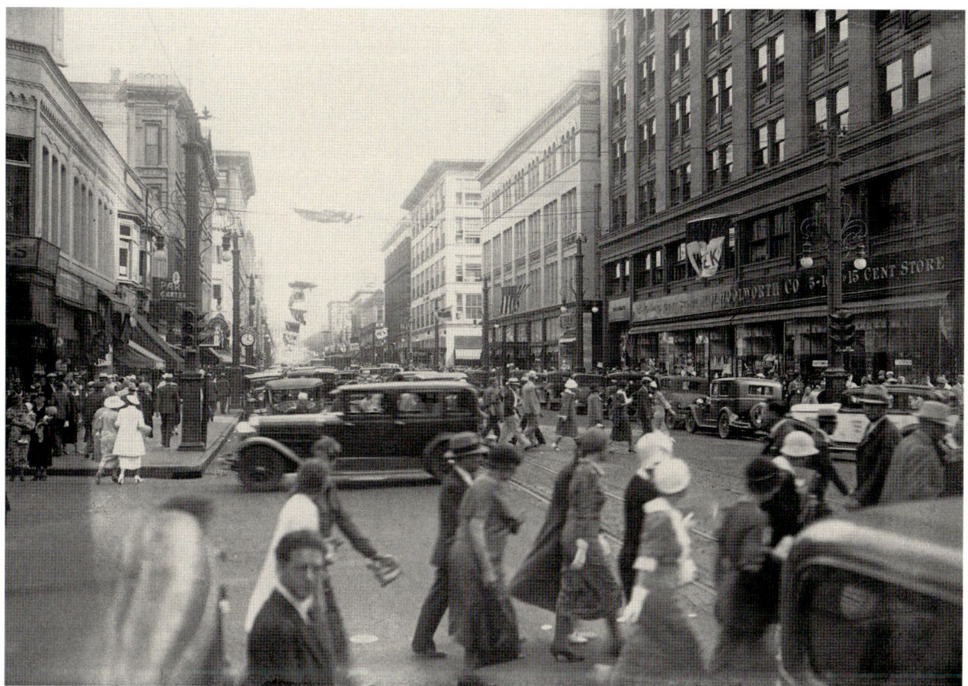

The remainder of the unbroken Curtis-to-Welton stretch of Sixteenth Street's historic buildings is seen in this c. 1934 photograph looking southeast from Champa Street. The Symes Building (right) housed F.W. Woolworth; this store would grow into adjacent buildings after World War II to become the world's largest Woolworth. Beyond it are the A.T. Lewis, Neusteter Company, Denver Dry Goods Company, McClintock, and Steel (now Sage) Buildings. (DPL, X-23350.)

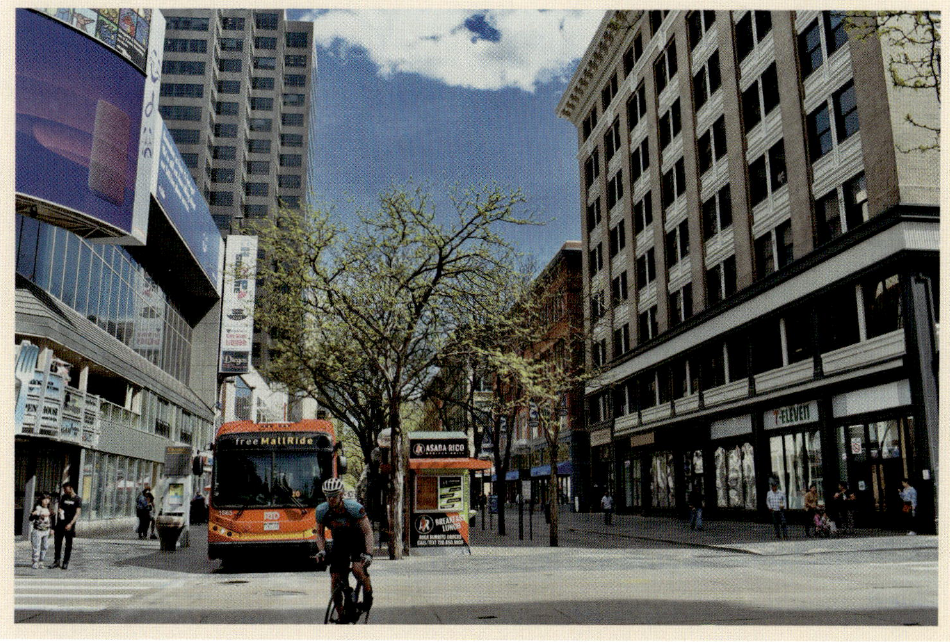

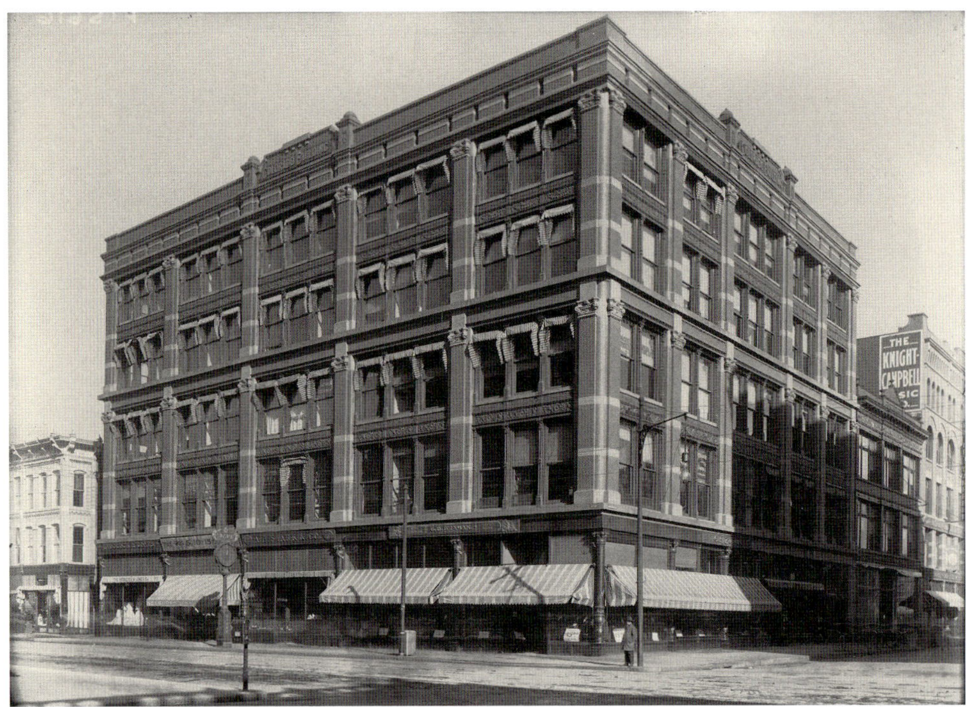

Some historic gems still stand on Sixteenth Street's northeastern side. Victorian commercial was John W. Roberts's style when he designed what initially was named the Hayden, Dickinson, and Feldhauser Building in 1891. When Charles Boettcher bought it in 1902, he renamed it the Colorado Building, and in 1909, he hired Frank E. Edbrooke to give it two more floors. In 1935, it gained a Jules Jacques Benoit Benedict–designed art deco mask that transformed it into a unique Victorian-deco hybrid. (DPL, X-24943.)

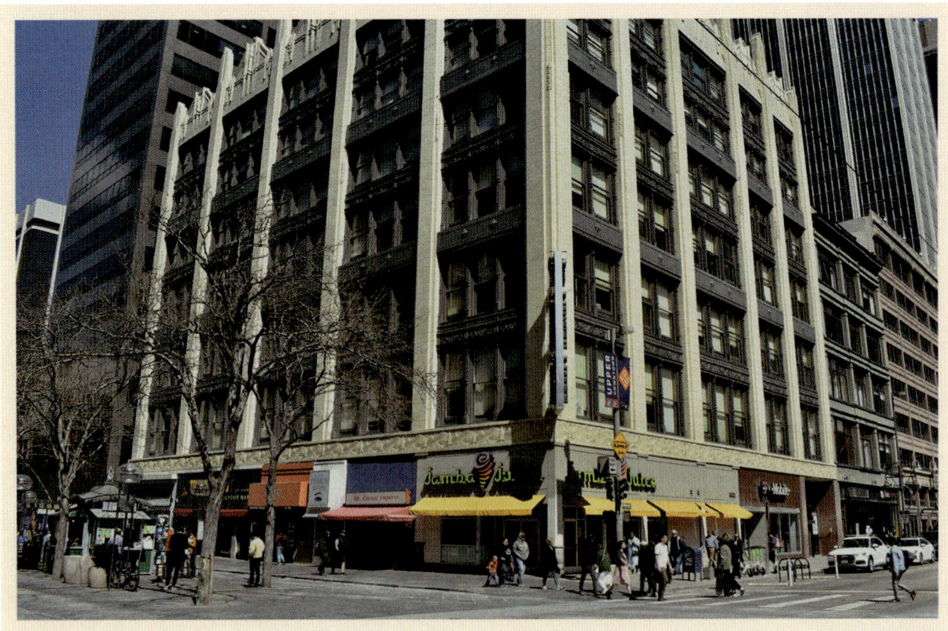

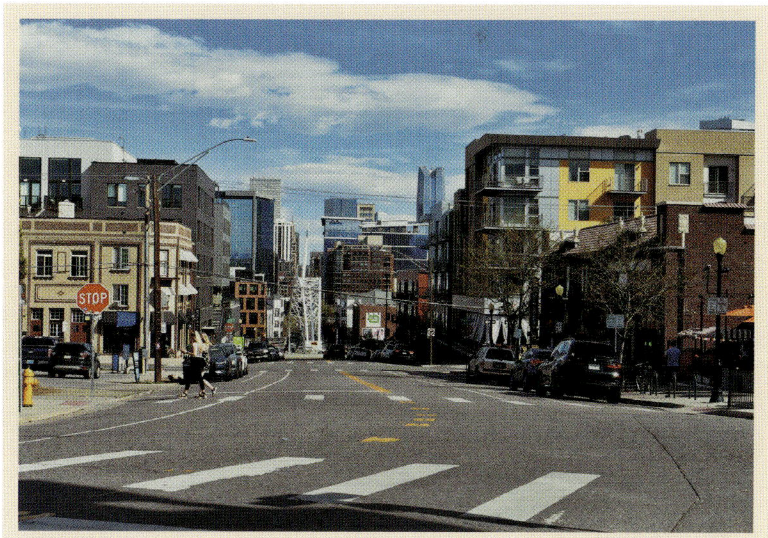

Two miles long, Sixteenth Street stretches from Broadway and Sixteenth Avenue to West Thirtieth Avenue and Tejon Street in the Highland neighborhood. This c. 1955 view from Tejon Street encompasses the Sixteenth Street viaduct, demolished in 1993, crossing railroad tracks, the South Platte River, and Interstate 25. At right is George Olinger's mortuary, now renovated into a dining, shopping, and ice cream destination by Paul Tamburello. Rubber-tired trolley coaches (right) and diesel buses (left) coexisted, but not for long. (HC, 10036957.)

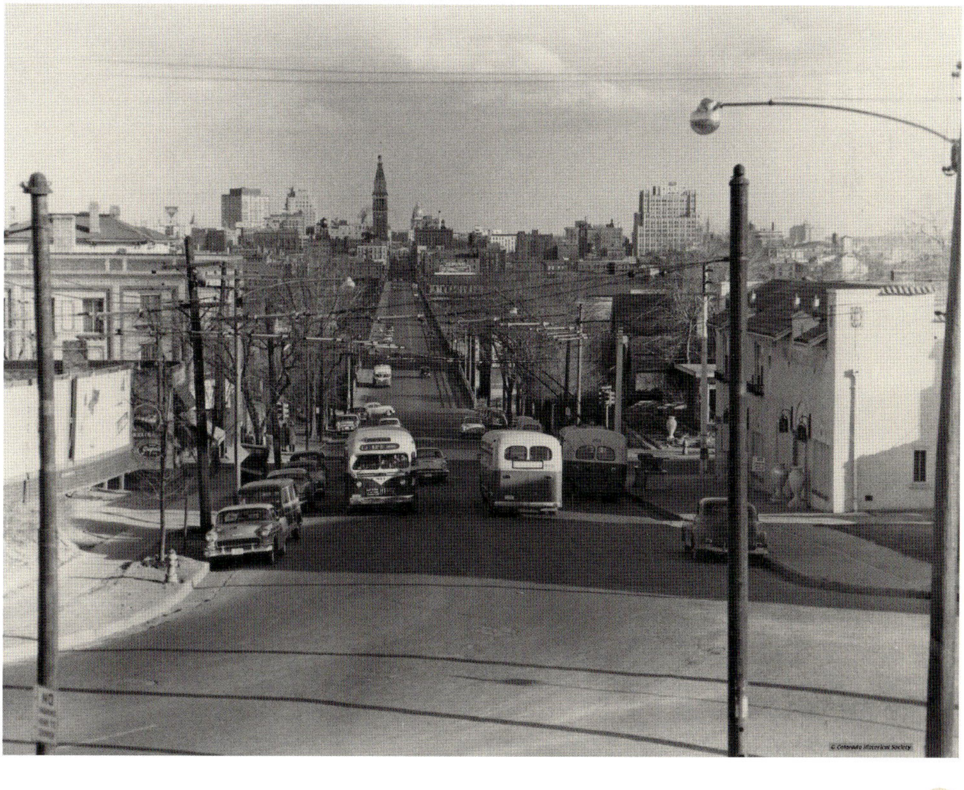

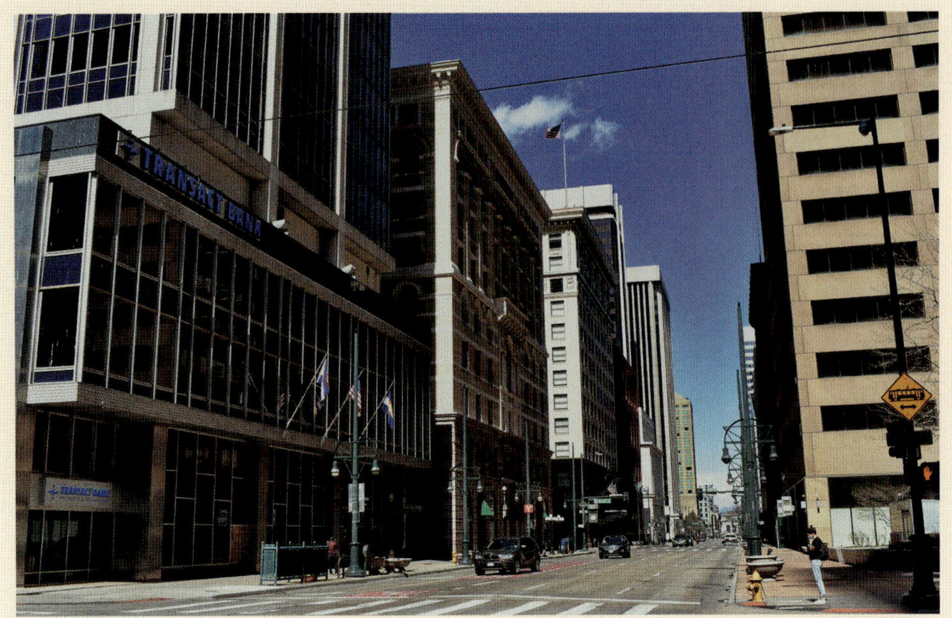

Bankers and brokers might have argued that Seventeenth Street, not Sixteenth, was Denver's main street, and from their perspective, it was. This c. 1900 Joseph Collier photograph looking northwest from California Street encompasses the Frank Edbrooke–designed California Building (left) and Denver's most elegant office structure, the Equitable Building (Andrews, Jacques, and Rantoul, 1893). Farther down are the Boston and Ernest and Cranmer Buildings, while the Albany Hotel's bay windows peek out on the right. (DPL, C-174.)

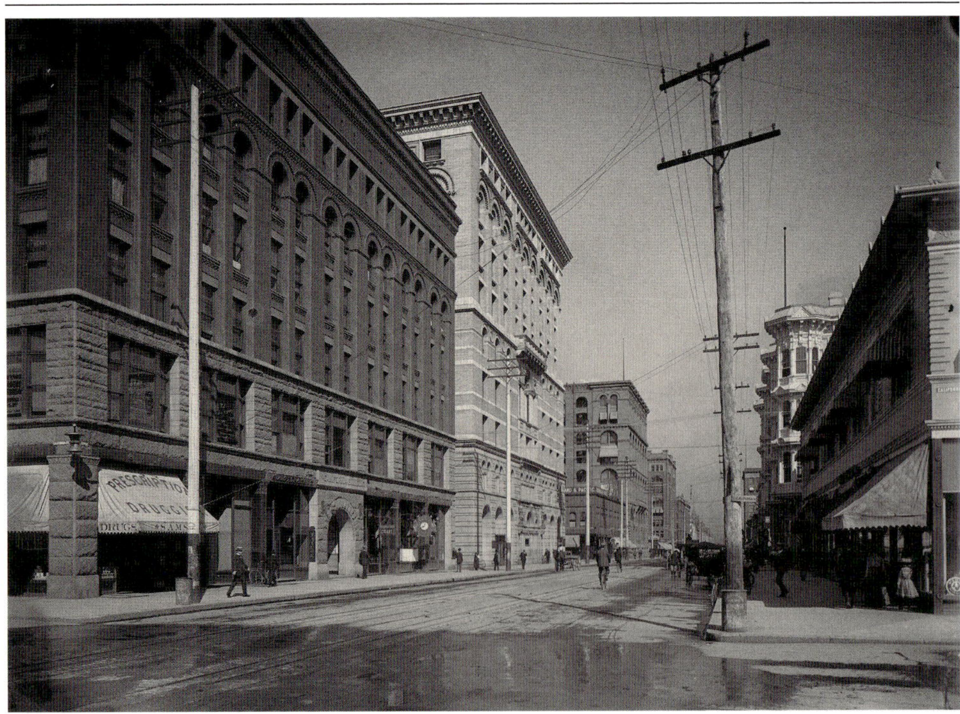

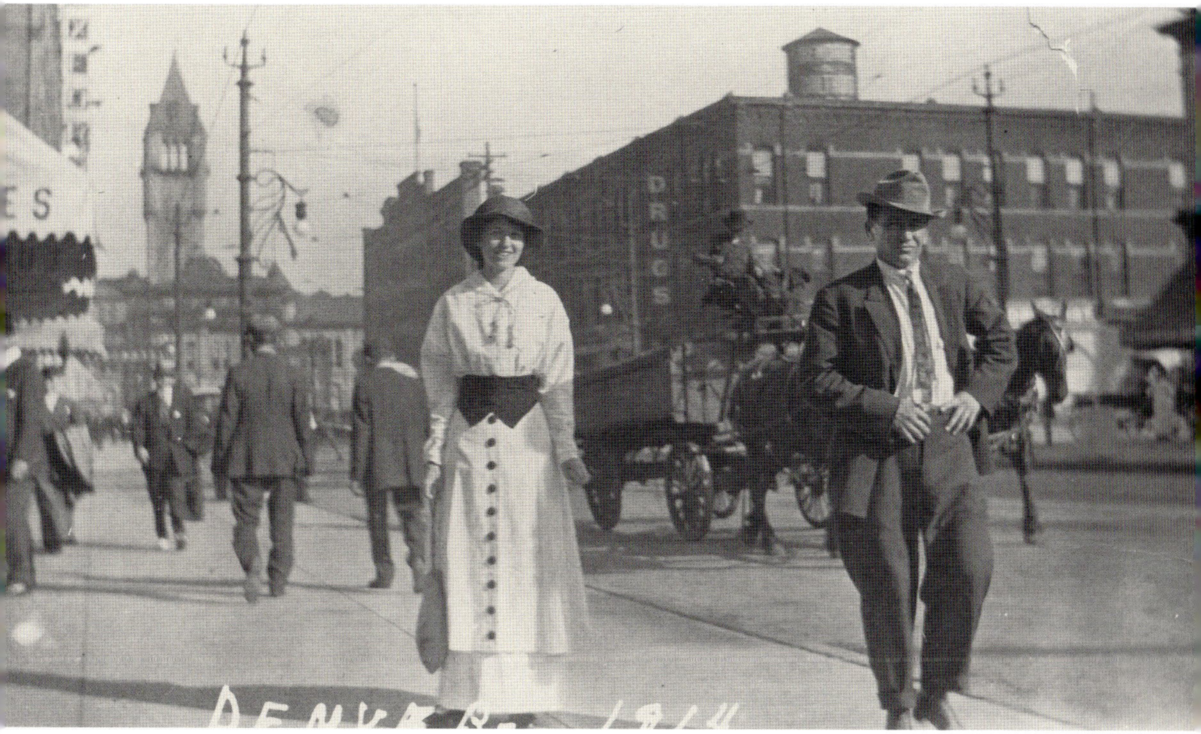

Seventeenth Street was the first view Denver visitors encountered upon arriving at Union Station. Between 1895 and 1914, the train depot sported a prominent tower (left). Travelers could commission photographers for postcards, as this young woman in a white dress did, to send back home. After describing a planned trip to Silver Plume, she wrote "I never saw the 'other fellow' before or after. Everyone wonders who he is." The view, sans tower, remains little changed today. (Author's collection.)

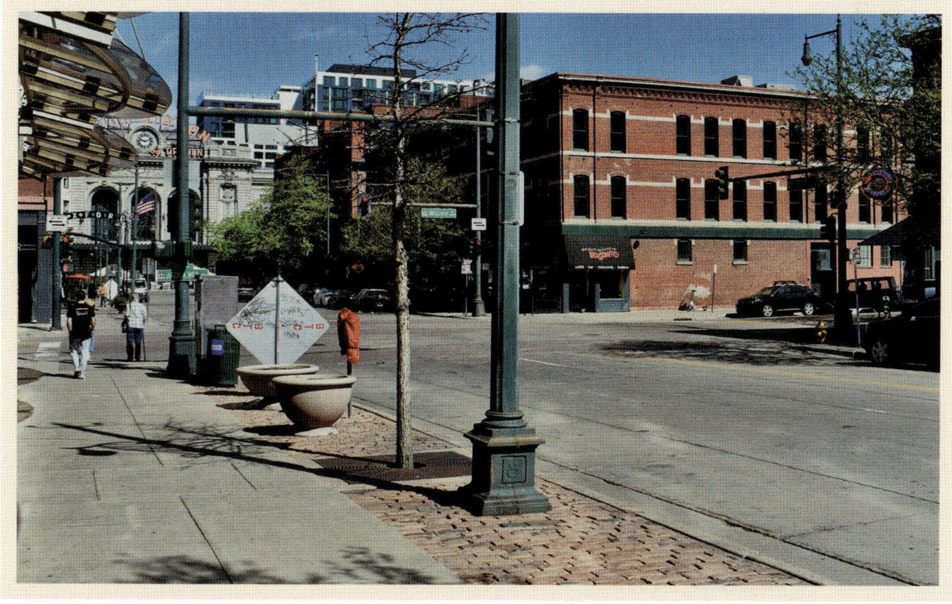

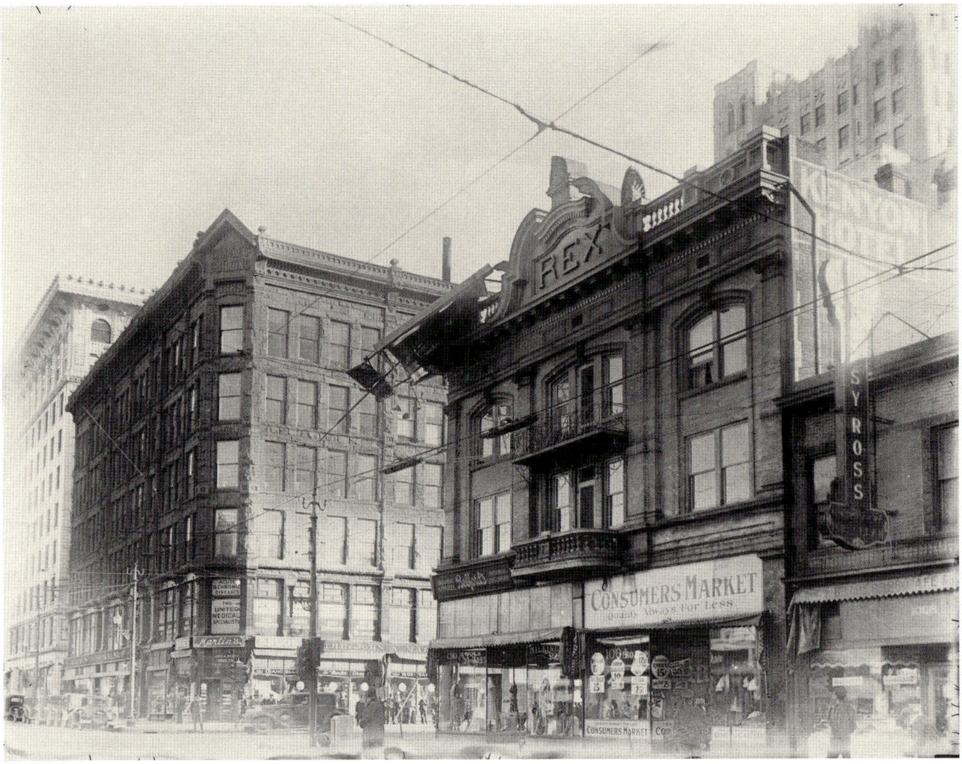

The Denver Gas and Electric (far left) and Mountain States Telephone & Telegraph (far right) Buildings remain, but the Charles Building (left) and Rex Hotel (right) have disappeared from this stretch of Fifteenth Street at Curtis Street. The Charles, built in 1889 by John Quincy Charles, was designed by Leonard Cutshaw and once housed the *Denver Times*. It came down in 1939 for parking, and 20 years later, Mountain States Telephone & Telegraph expanded its facilities to Fifteenth Street; the glass facade dates to 2021. (DPL, Rh-408.)

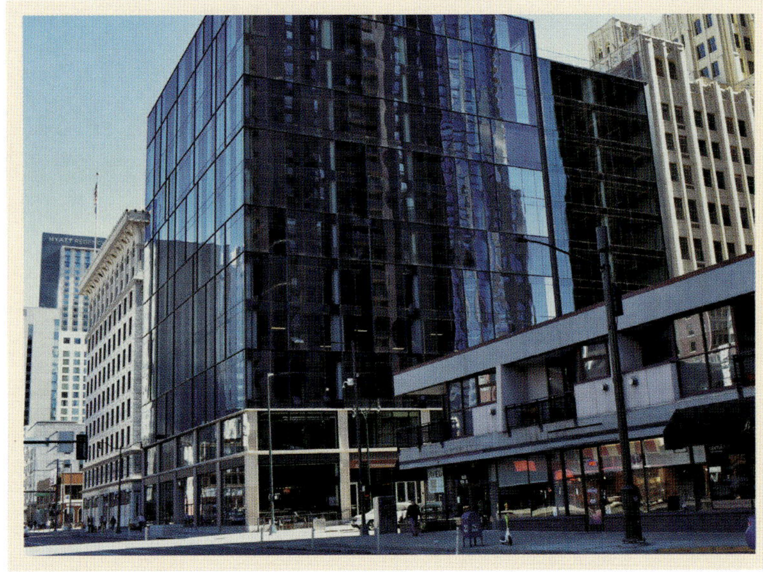

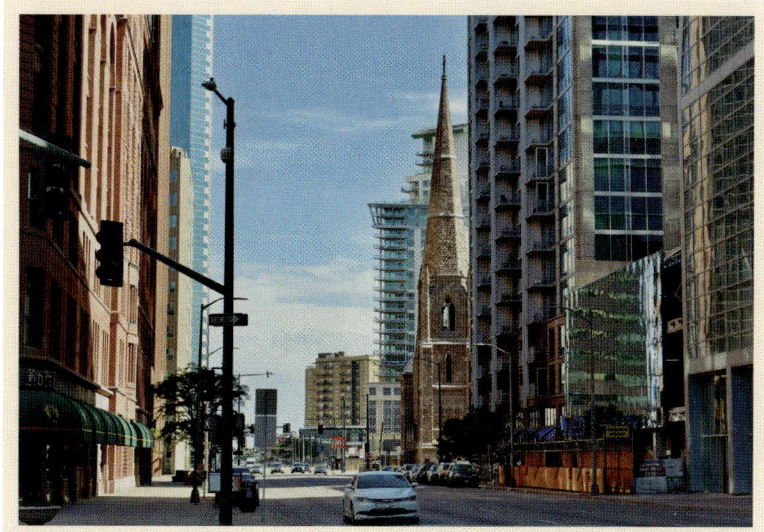

Broadway, running south from downtown, has a "Main Street" quality in several locations, particularly between Seventeenth and Eighteenth Avenues, where the Brown Palace Hotel (left) once faced the Hotel Metropole (right), both designed by Frank E. Edbrooke, with the latter housing the ornate Broadway Theatre, once Denver's finest. Robert S. Roeschlaub's masterpiece, Trinity Methodist Church, anchors the Eighteenth Avenue corner, and the Brown remains, but the Metropole, later incorporated into the Cosmopolitan Hotel, disappeared in 1984. (HC, 10039006.)

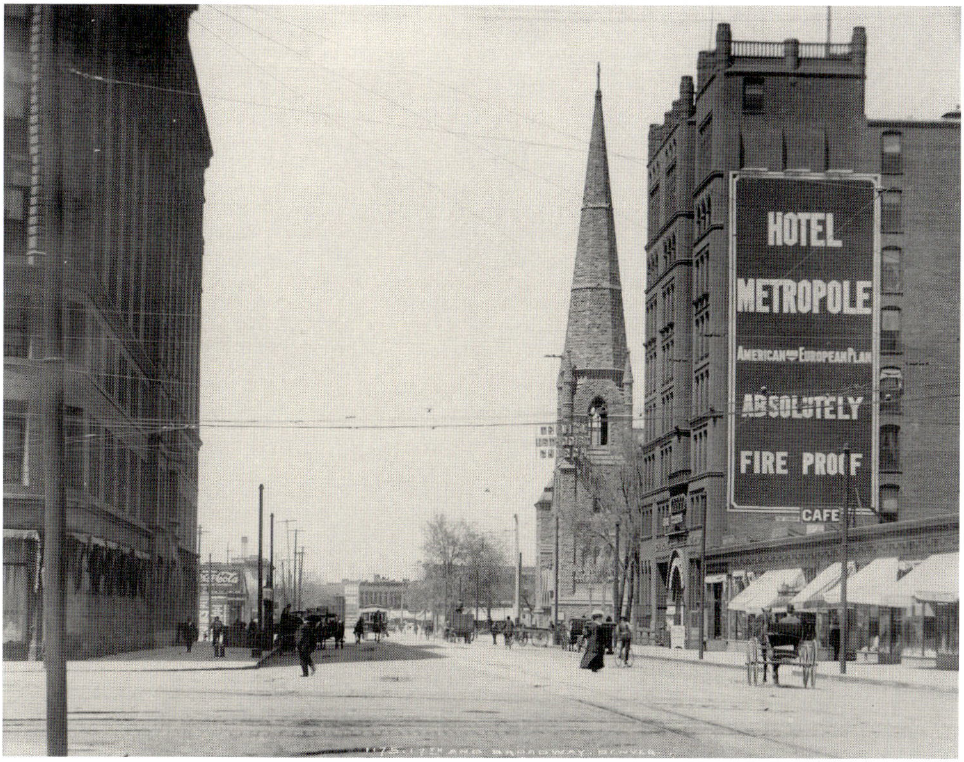

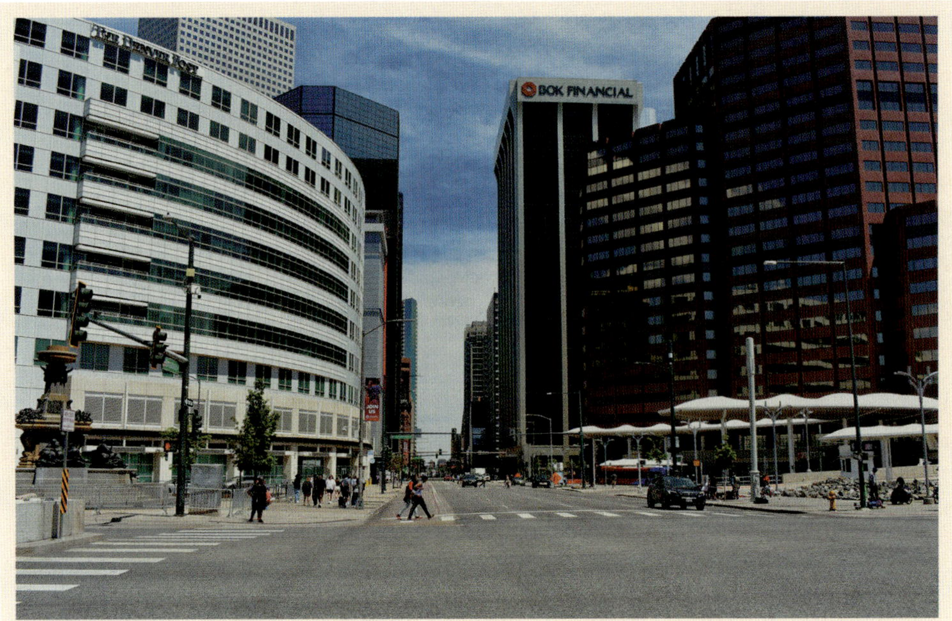

Streetcar lines once ran for miles on Broadway, with automobiles coexisting. At Colfax Avenue, the city replaced an early fire station with the 1911 Pioneer Fountain (left) marking the historic Smoky Hill Trail's terminus. Sculptor Frederick MacMonnies originally intended for a Native American to crown the fountain, but business interests, who were funding it, objected, so he sculpted Kit Carson atop a horse instead. In 2020, the city, citing Carson's mixed legacy, removed the statue. (HC, 10039006.)

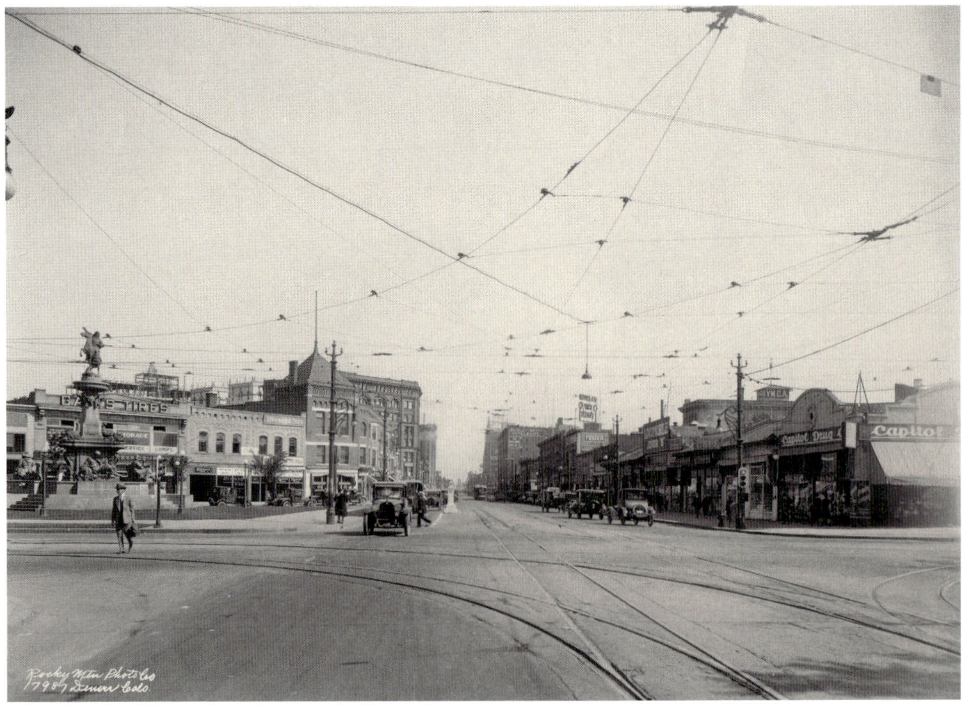

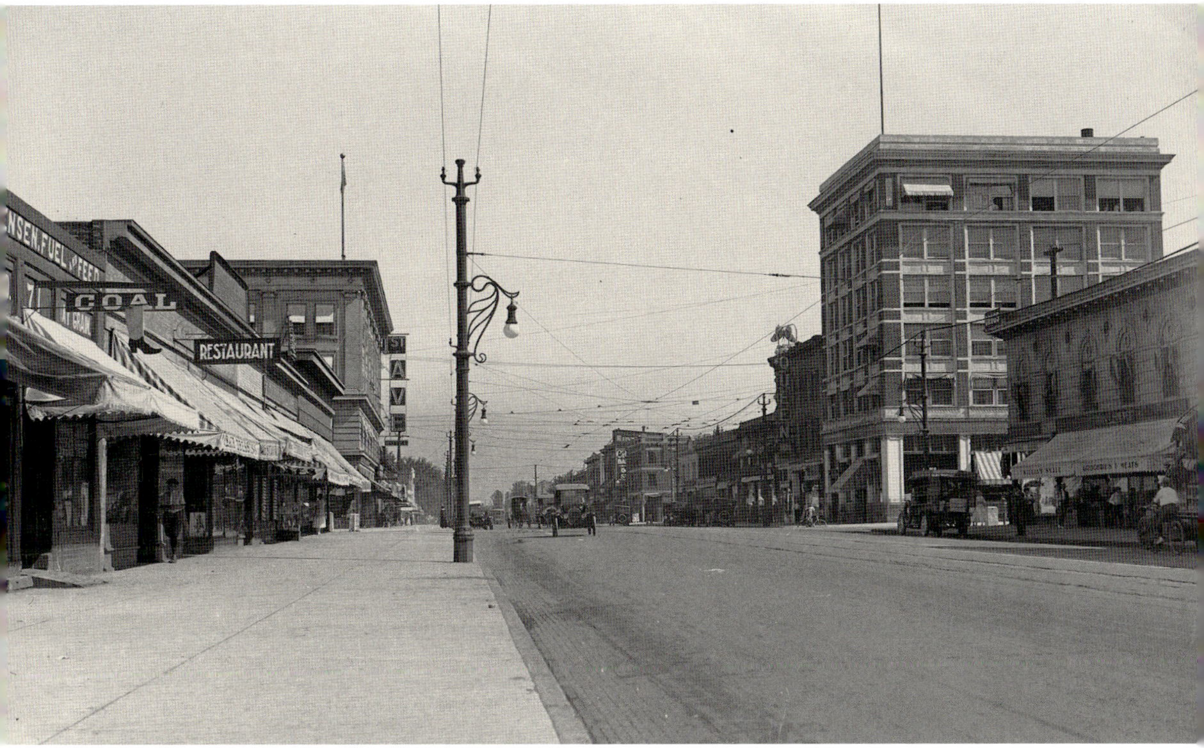

South of Cherry Creek, Broadway developed a "Miracle Mile" character, a hub away from downtown, as seen in this Oscar Lindevall photograph. At First Avenue arose the First Avenue Hotel (left, Charles Quayle, 1906), renovated in 2020–2021 into affordable housing. In 1914, Broadway National Bank, later Union Bank, built a six-story headquarters (right) designed by William and Arthur Fisher. Willis Marean and Albert Norton designed the two-story building across from it (far right), the Stuart Hotel, in 1909. (HC, 20007745.)

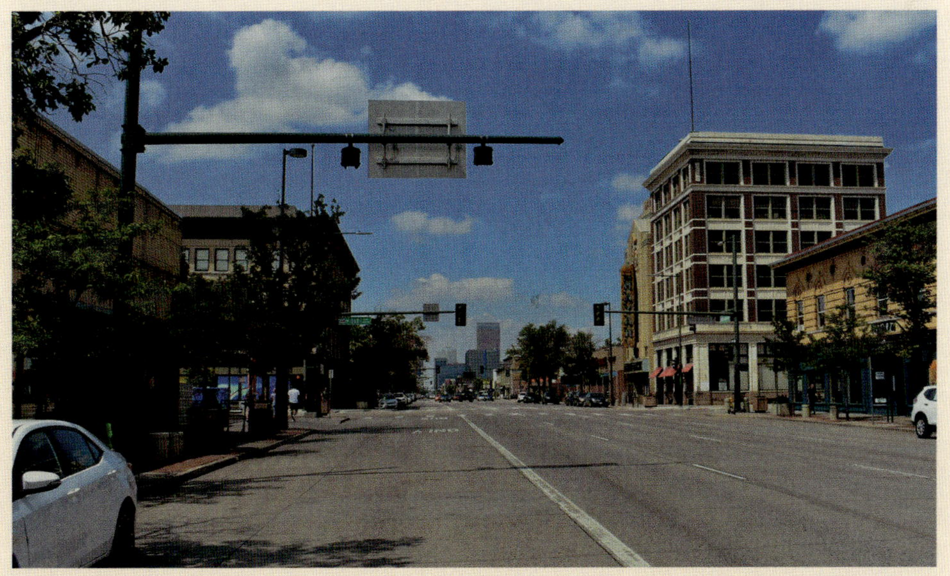

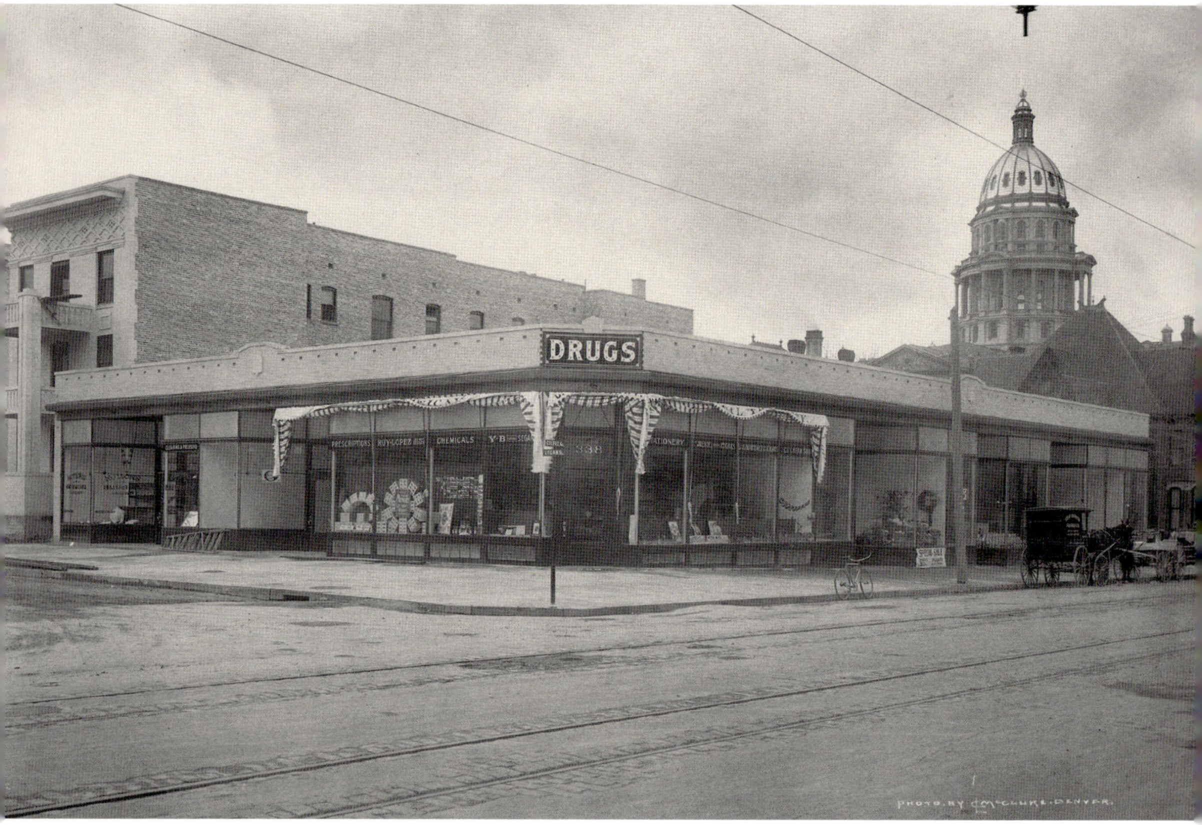

Colfax partisans refer to the avenue as Denver's "Main Street," as it stretches such a vast distance, from Bennett to Golden. Designated US Highway 40 before World War II, it developed into a classic automobile-oriented strip, lined with motels. Between Colorado Boulevard and Broadway, however, it retains most of its urban character, with sidewalk-fronting structures such as this one-story commercial block at Logan Street, once housing Christian Van Zandt's Cathedral Pharmacy. (DPL, MCC-3466; photograph by Louis Charles McClure.)

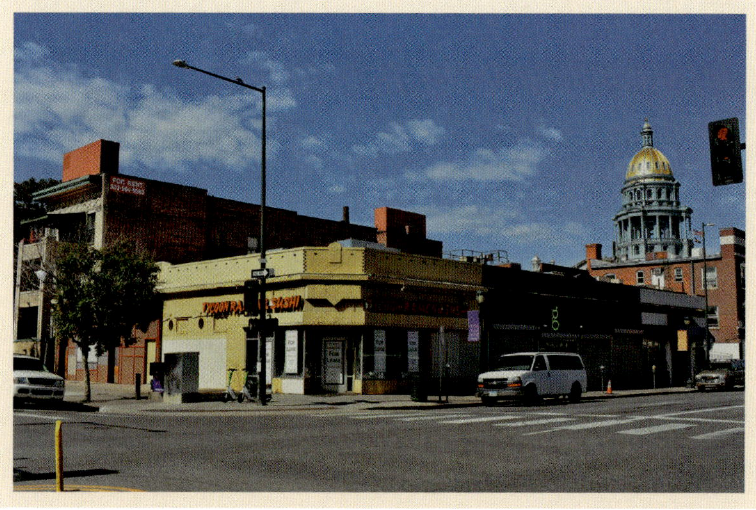

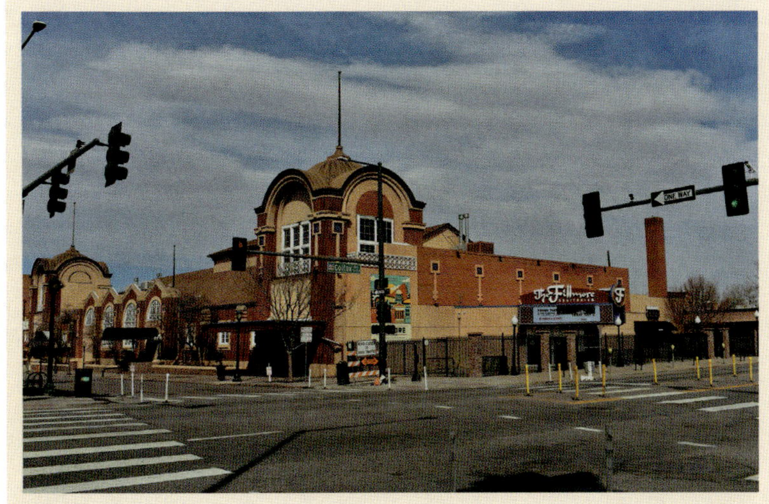

No Denver building has a more diverse history than Mammoth Gardens (left). In 1907, Albert Ross-Lewin opened Mammoth Gardens Roller-Skating Rink on Clarkson Street near Colfax Avenue. In 1911, Oliver Fritchle converted it to an electric automobile and battery factory, ceasing production in 1920. Subsequently it served as a garage, ice-skating rink, casino, dance hall, warehouse, concert hall, farmer's market, and sports venue. In 1999, it became the Fillmore Auditorium; the adjacent Clarko Hotel (right) came down in 1990. (DPL, X-24875.)

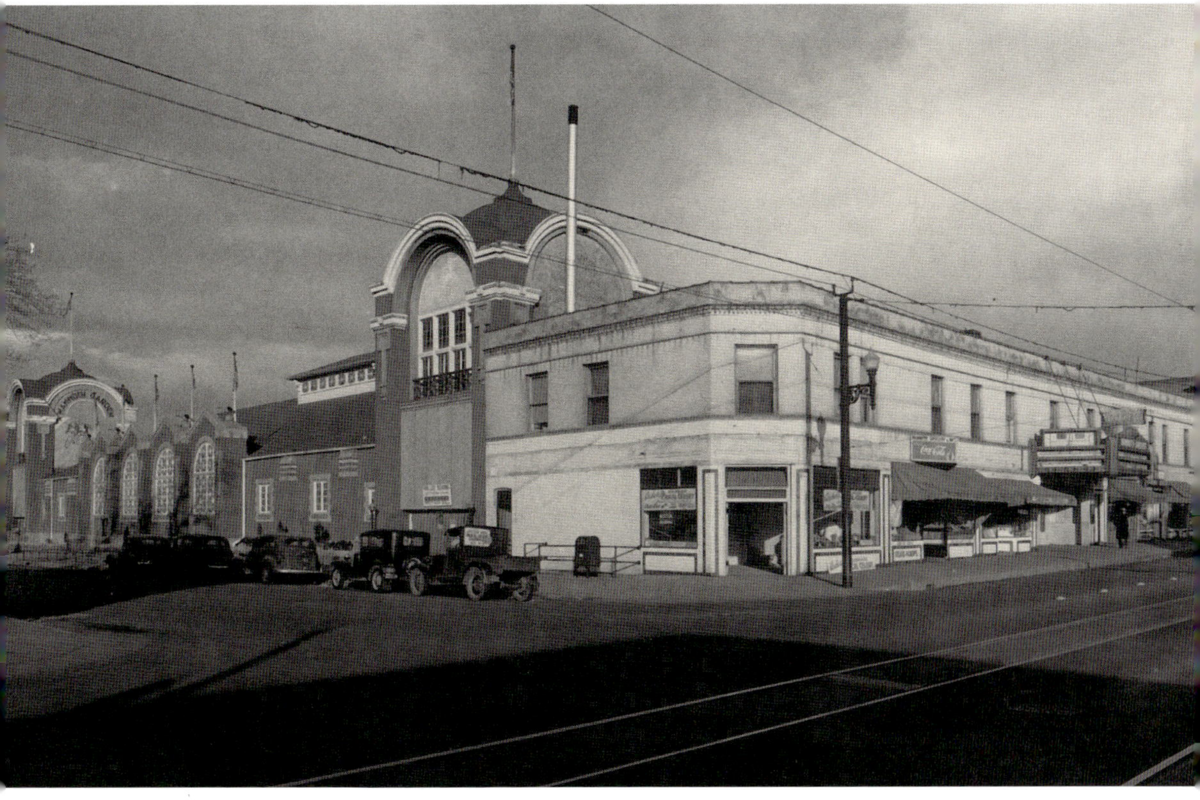

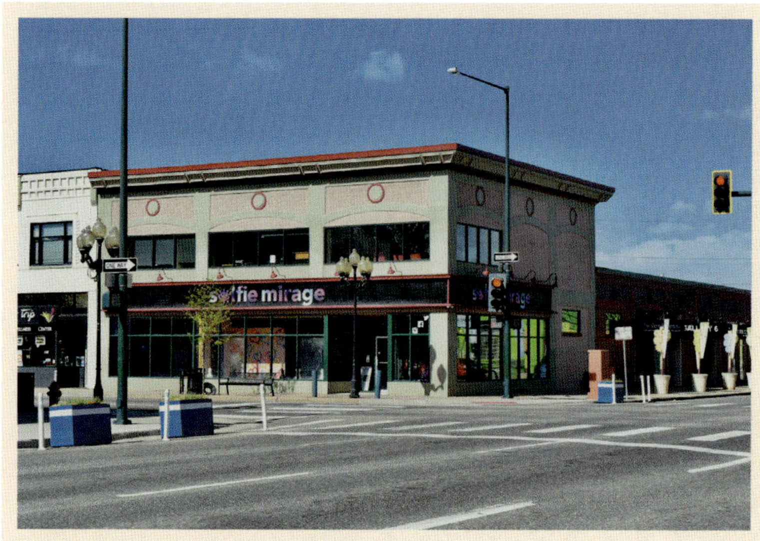

Santa Fe Drive represents a different kind of main street, that of a non-majority community. Named for its eventual terminus, Santa Fe Drive emerged as a neighborhood strip in the 19th century, boasting white-owned businesses such as Harry Fisher Rhoads's hardware store at Eighth Avenue, photographed by his son Harry Mellon Rhoads in the 1910s after it became a Ford dealership. Santa Fe became West Side Hispanic Denver's main drag before transitioning into an arts district in the 2000s. (DPL, Rh-722.)

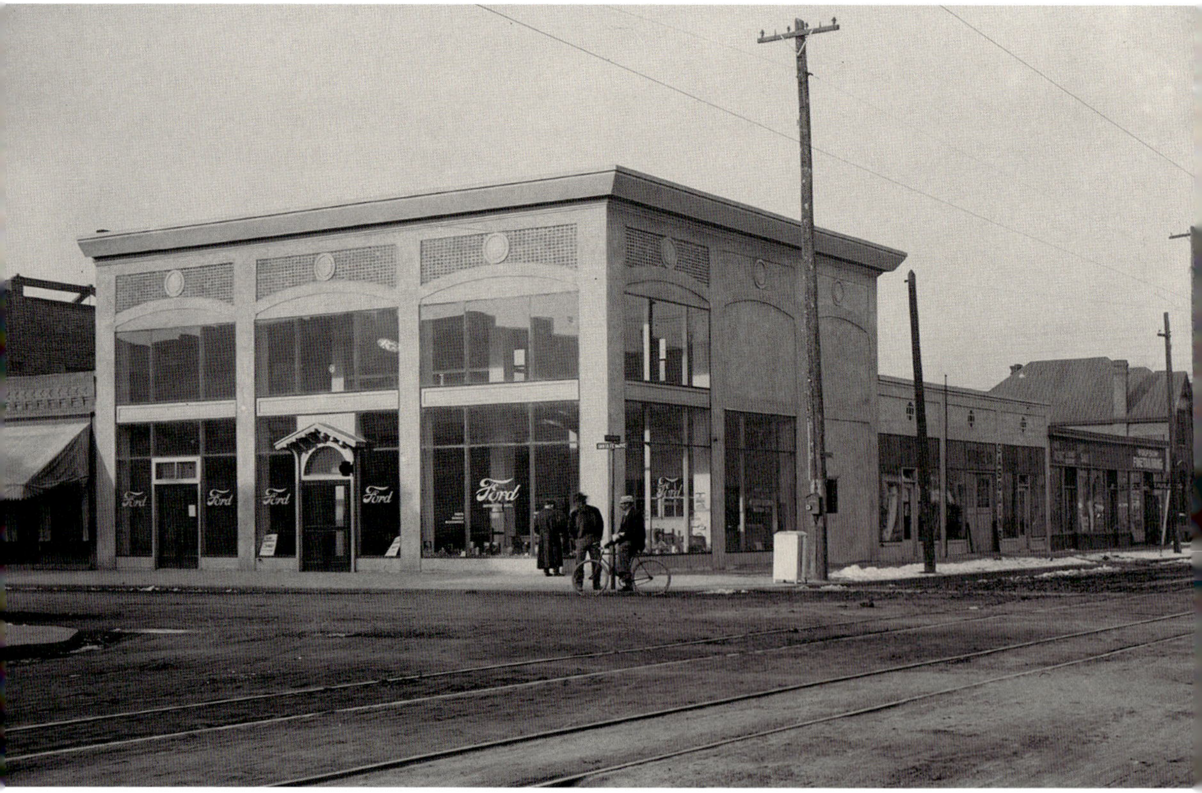

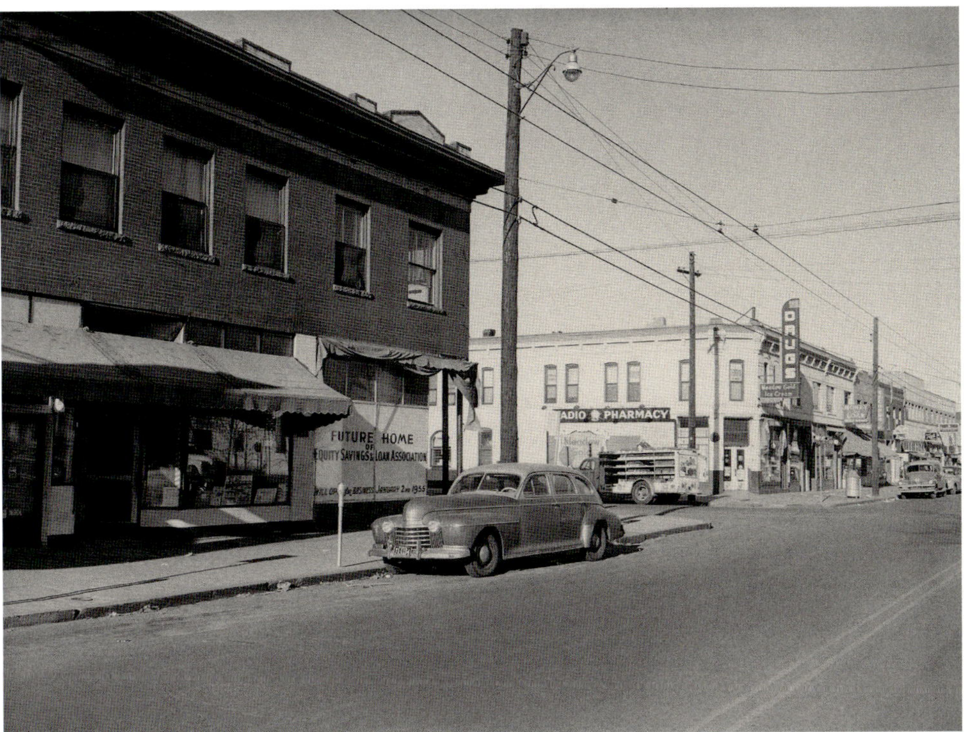

Welton Street in Five Points served as Black Denver's main street for several decades and remains important to the community today, still hosting annual Juneteenth celebrations, even as the neighborhood has gentrified. In this 1954 Burnis McCloud photograph, Black-owned Equity Savings and Loan had leased space in the two-story building at left owned by Charles Cousins Jr. Across Twenty-Sixth Street, pharmacist and activist Oglesvie "Sonny" Larson's Radio Pharmacy (right) dispensed medicine and served ice cream sodas to Five Points residents. (DPL, MC-52.)

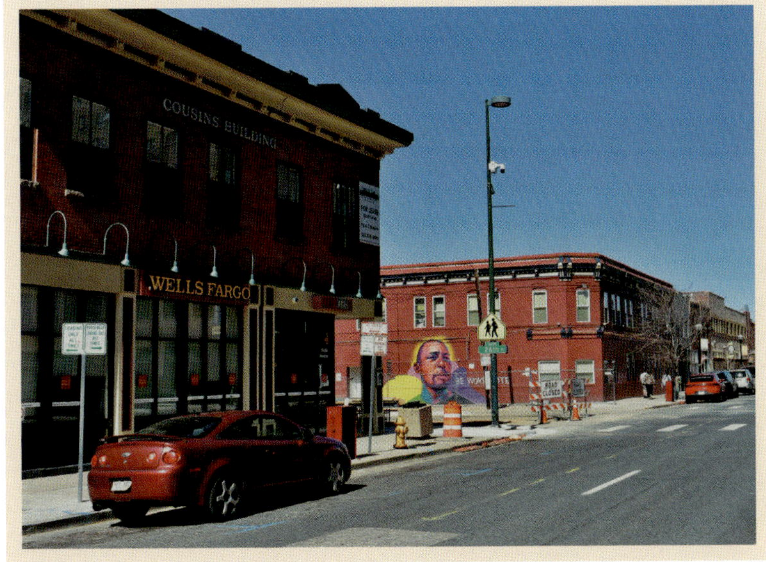

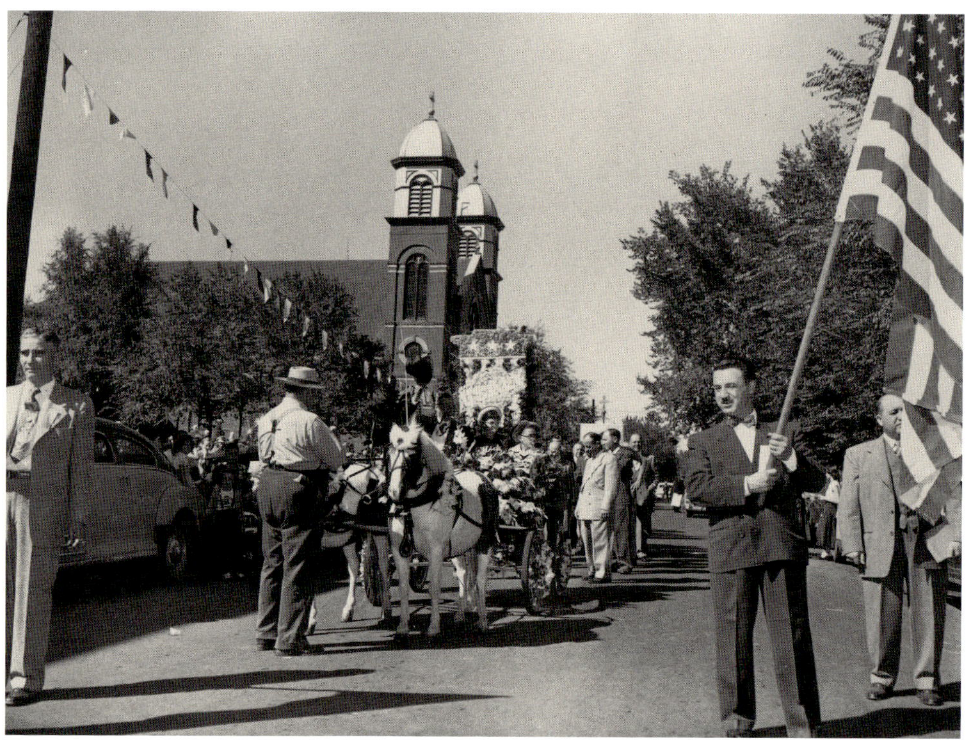

The Italian American community's main street was a three-block stretch of Navajo Street south of West Thirty-Eighth Avenue, centered on Our Lady of Mount Carmel Church, rebuilt in 1903 by Fr. Mariano Lepore after an 1898 fire destroyed the original. Every August, the church and the Società Nativi di Potenza Basilicata (Potenza Lodge) celebrates the Feast of San Rocco, including a neighborhood parade, as seen here around 1948. (Our Lady of Mount Carmel; photograph by Jerry Acierno.)

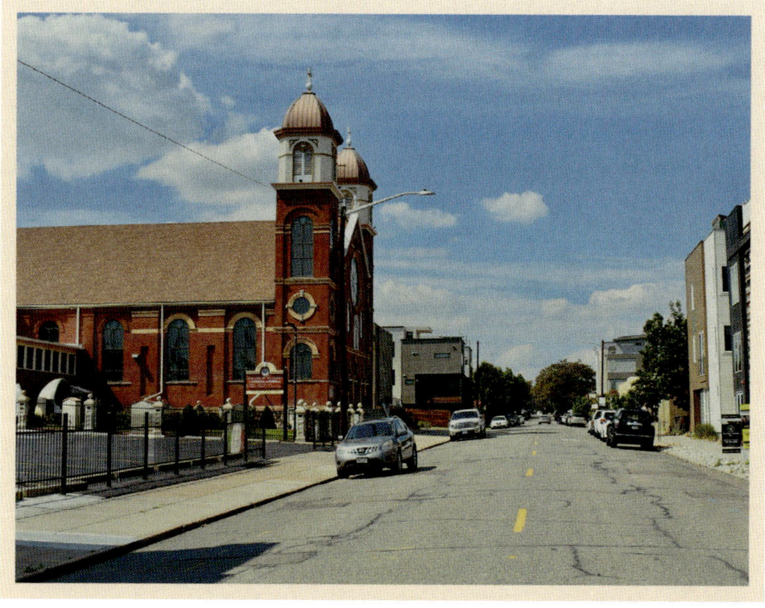

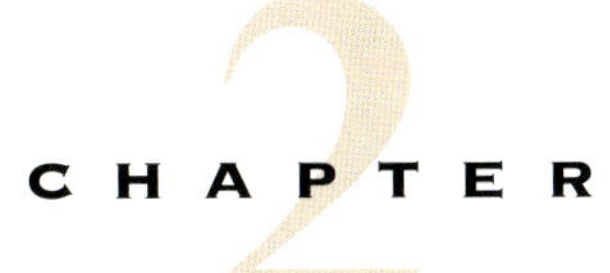

Commerce and Industry

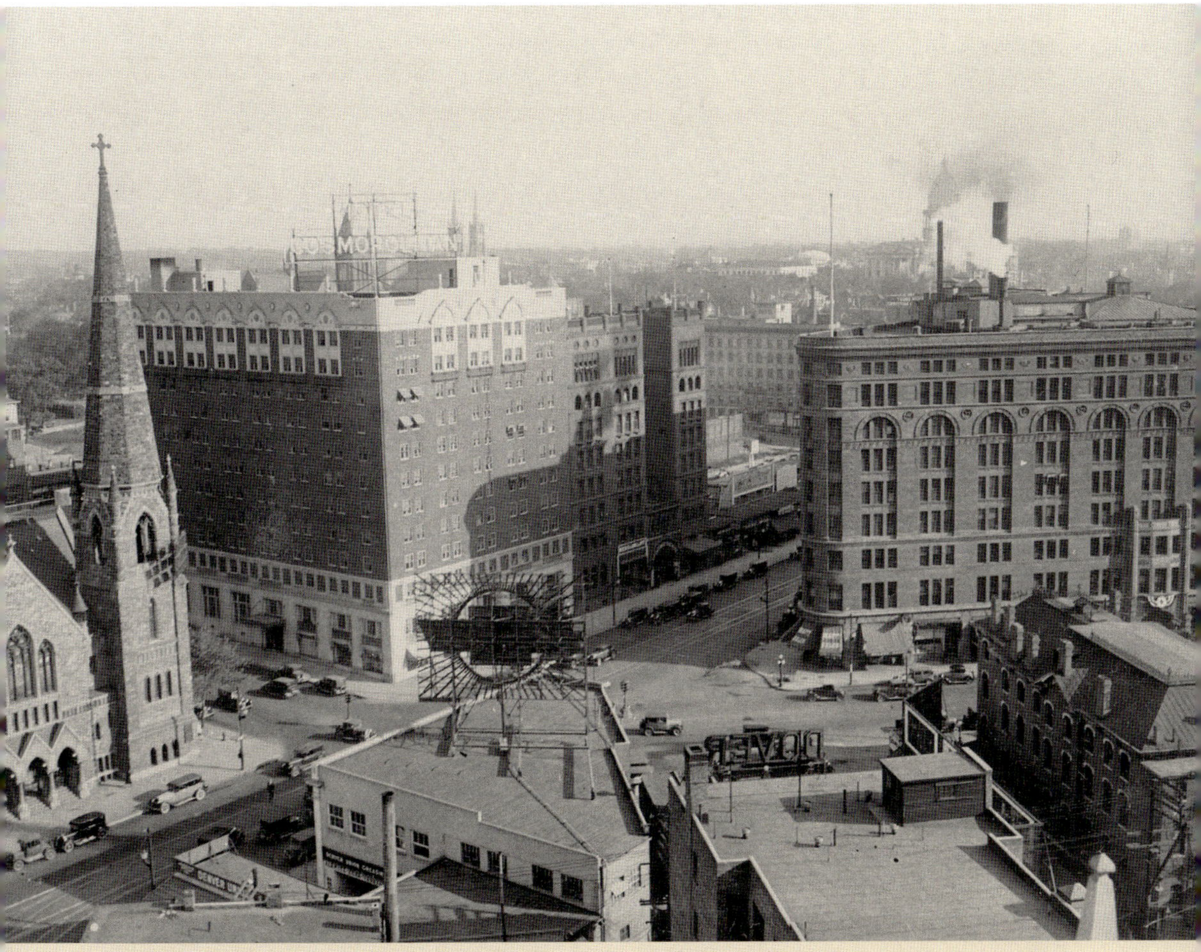

This late-1920s image taken from the now demolished Continental Oil Company Building at Eighteenth Street and Glenarm Place shows three of Denver's important hotels: the Brown Palace (right), the now demolished Cosmopolitan (left), and in the distance between them, the now demolished Shirley-Savoy. The Navarre (right) still stands proudly across from the Brown, as does Trinity Methodist Church (left). (DPL, X-22519.)

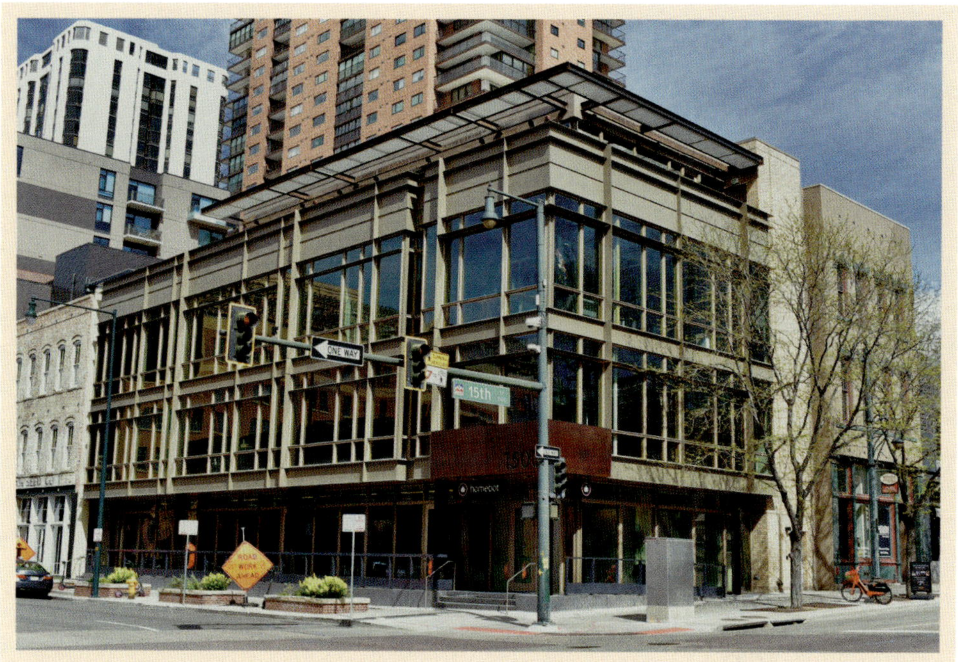

The neo-Gothic edifice erected by J.P. Fink in 1873 on the eastern corner of Fifteenth and Market Streets originally housed a private bank, Garson's Clothing Store, and the German Bank, with a Masonic lodge on the top floor. By the time Louis Charles McClure photographed it in the early 1930s, it was in the heart of Denver's wholesale food district. After decades as a parking lot, a David Tryba–designed steel and glass building arose in its place in 2017. (DPL, MCC-3665.)

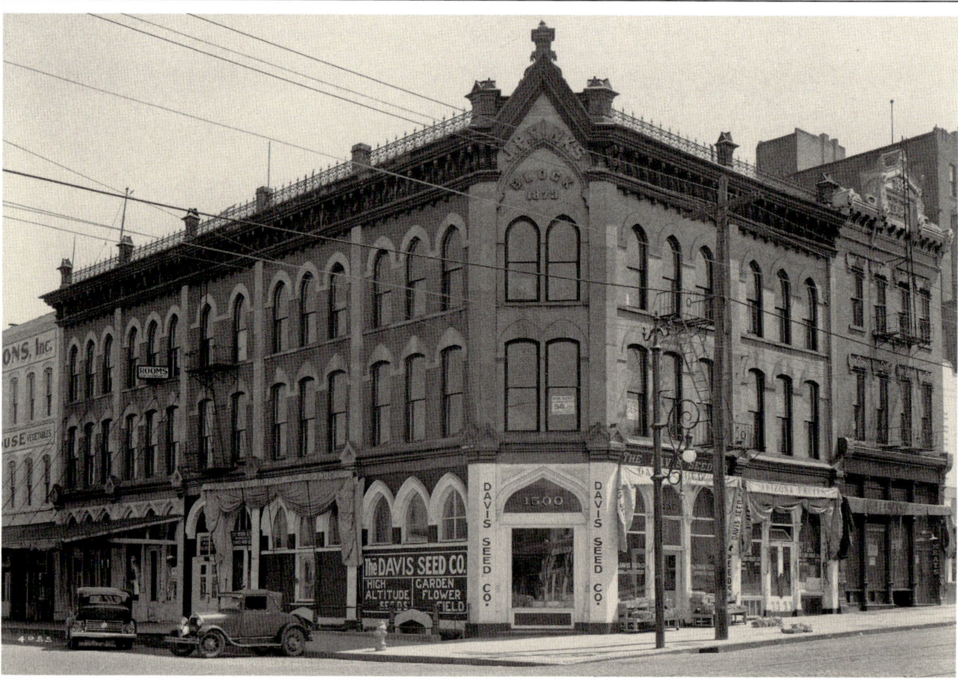

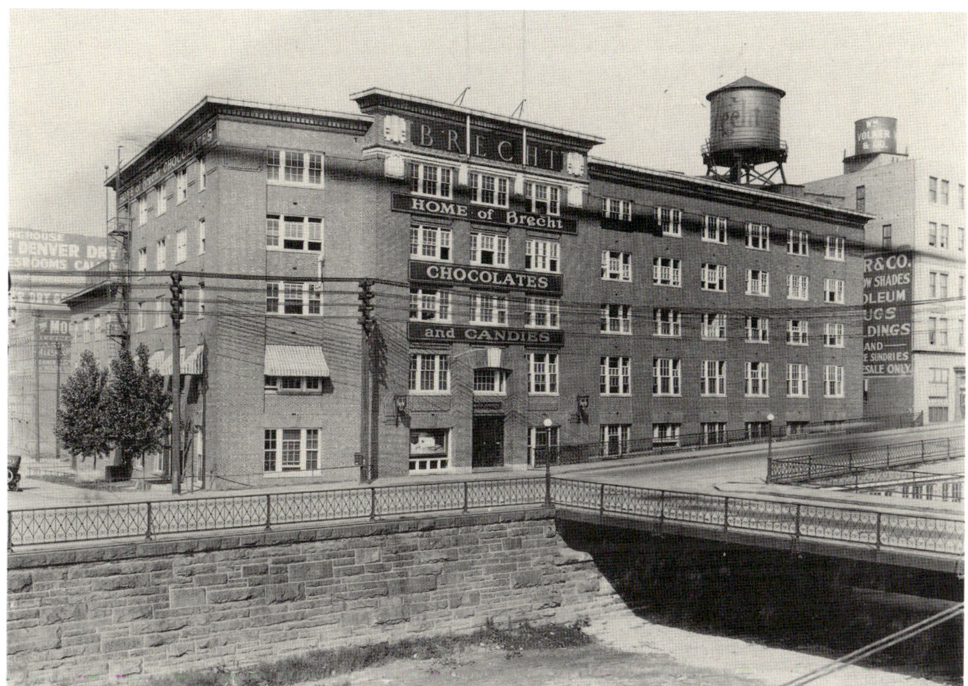

Overlooking Cherry Creek at Wazee Street, with the then Fourteenth Street viaduct rising at right, the 1909 Brecht Candy Company, designed by Maurice Biscoe and Henry Harwood Hewitt for German candy manufacturer Gustavius A. Von Brecht, became Acme Lofts in 1994 when Dana Crawford renovated it, preserving the name of a later occupant, Acme Upholstery Company. Brecht Candy employed over 200 people, producing up to three million pounds annually utilizing sugar from Colorado sugar beets. (DPL, X-23925.)

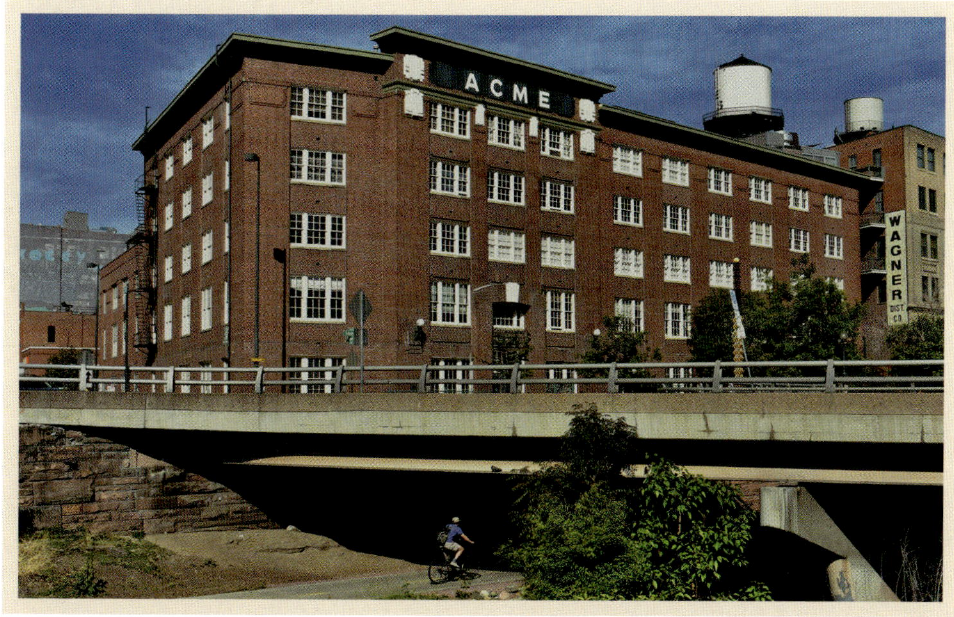

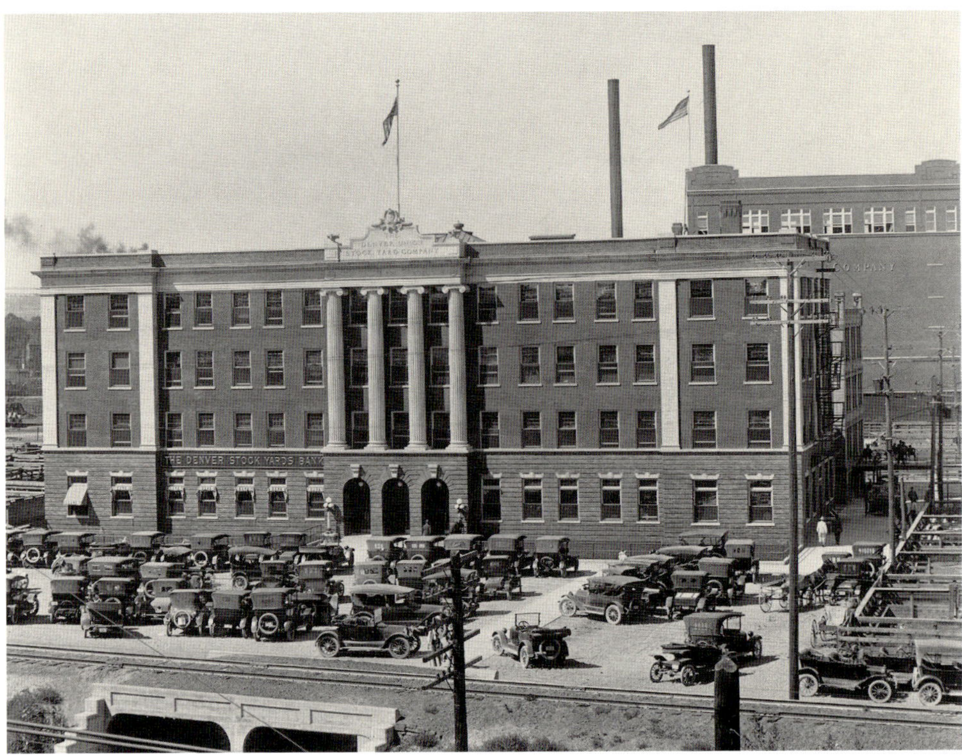

Denver cattle trading began early, leading to the Denver Union Stockyards' establishment in 1881 along the South Platte River north of East Forty-Sixth Avenue. Agents working in the Livestock Exchange Building, constructed in three phases (1898, 1916, and 1919), oversaw trading and the stockyards' vast network of pens. Today, the building is home to the Denver Stockyard Saloon, packed during the National Western Stock Show and Rodeo each January (since 1906) but open all year. (National Western Stock Show Archives.)

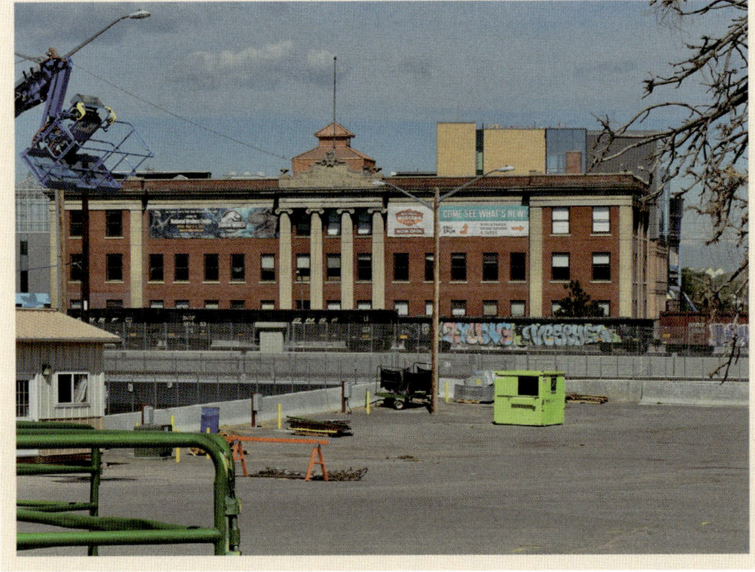

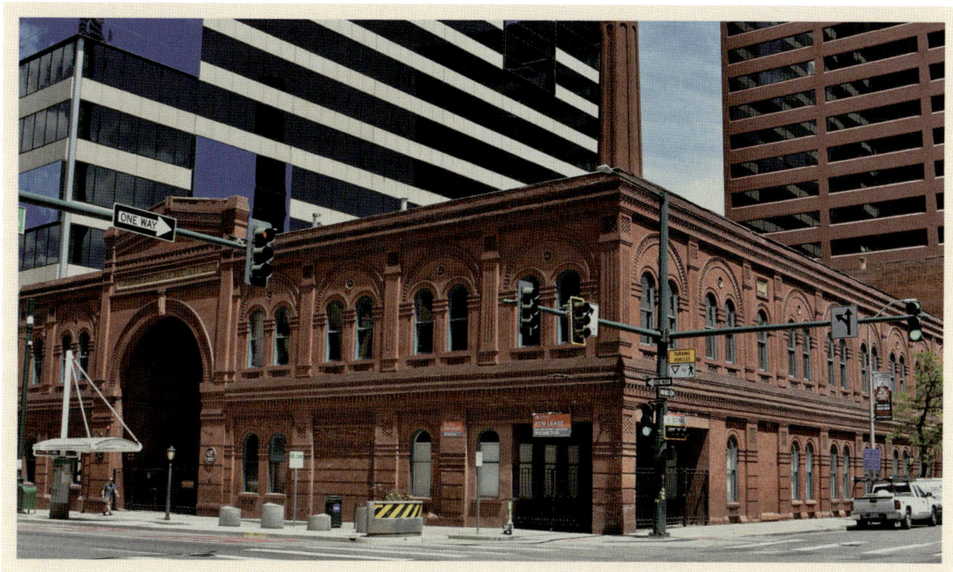

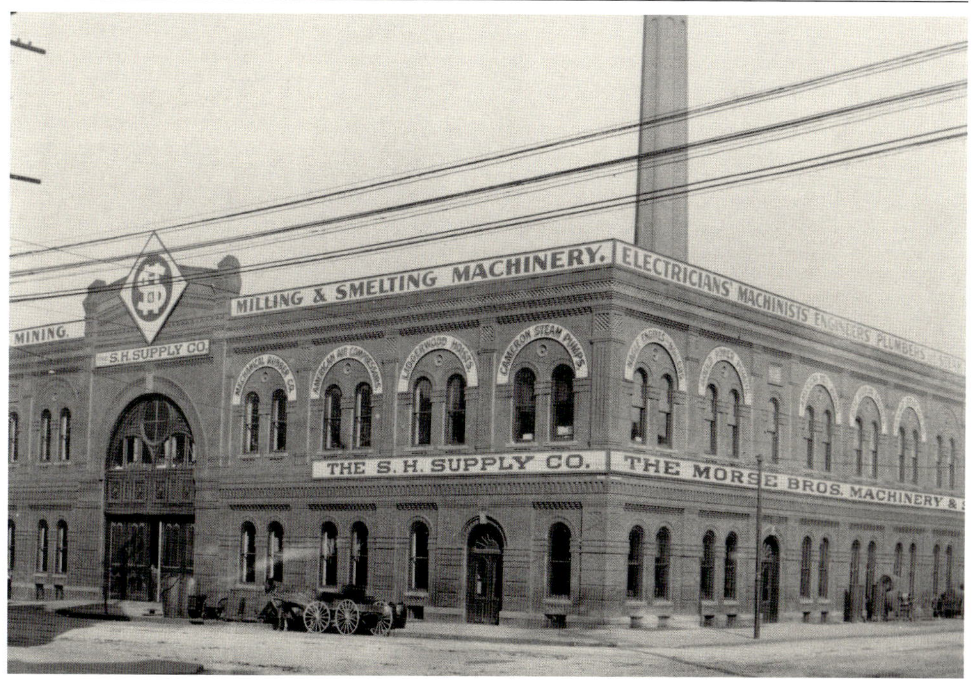

Denver City Cable Railway, an outgrowth of Denver's first horse-powered streetcar company, built this impressive two-story, Romanesque Revival powerhouse in 1889, capped by a 110-foot smokestack. The Panic of 1893 and technological changes led to its bankruptcy and merger with Denver Tramway Company in 1899. After decades serving other purposes and threatened with demolition, Historic Denver Inc.'s then president E. James Judd spearheaded its 1972 salvation; the Old Spaghetti Factory restaurant occupied the first floor from 1973 until 2018. (DPL, X-27853.)

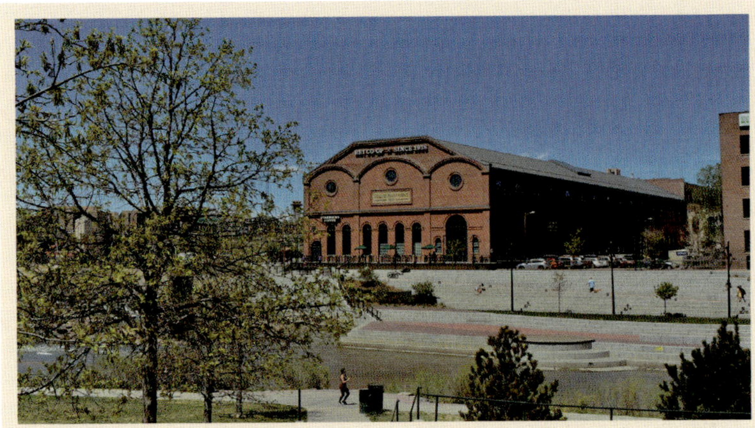

After consolidating with its competitors, each with their own powerhouses, Denver Tramway Company built this Stearns-Roger–designed powerhouse in 1901 for its 160 miles of streetcar lines. After electric operations ceased, it became a warehouse and later the Forney Museum of Transportation. In 2000, sporting goods co-op REI opened a 90,000-square-foot flagship store in the building. Confluence Park, centerpiece of the South Platte River Greenway and considered Denver's birthplace, was completed in 1975 and renovated in 2017–2019. (DPL, MCC-3966.)

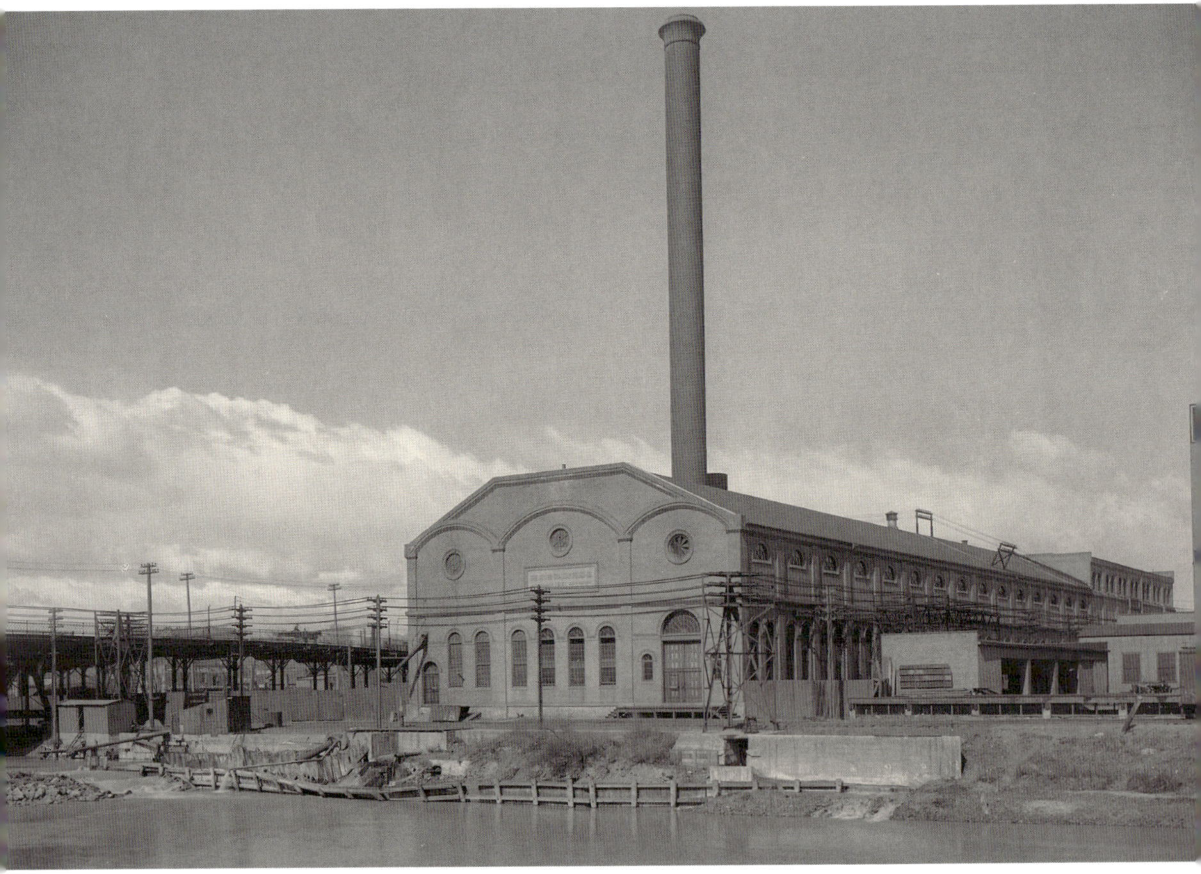

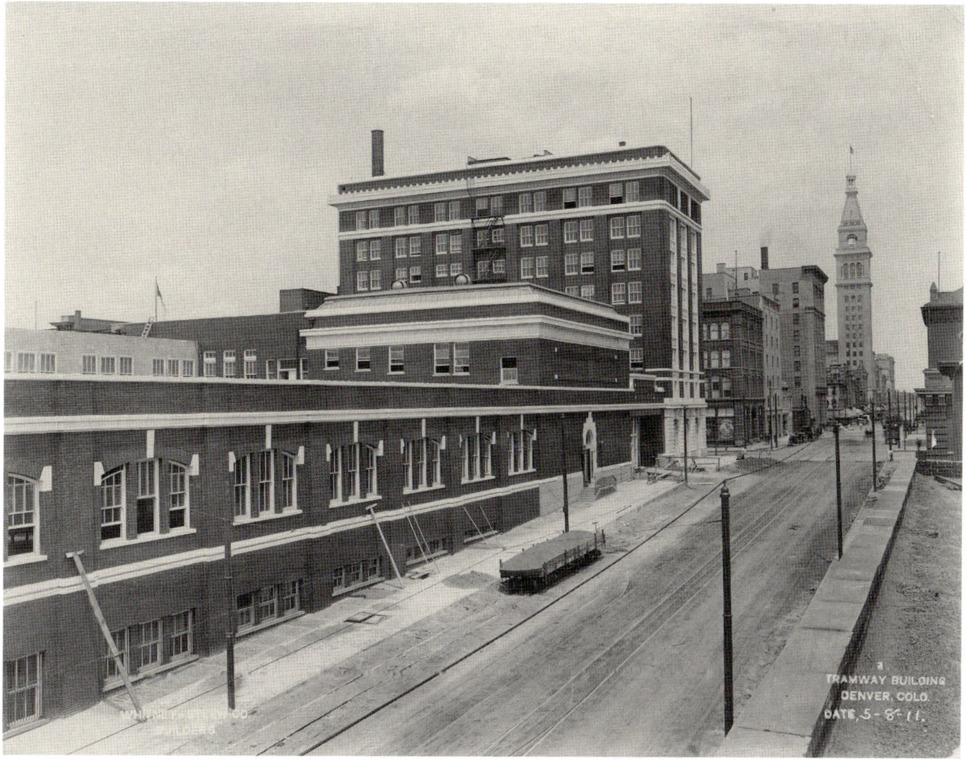

Denver Tramway's eight-story headquarters at Fifteenth and Arapahoe Streets is nearing completion in this 1911 photograph. The William and Arthur Fisher–designed tower and attached two-story carbarn, with street-level entrances on both floors thanks to the sloping site, served into the 1950s. In 1957, the University of Colorado took over, establishing a Denver extension of its Boulder campus. In 1999, the tower became Hotel Teatro; the carbarn, now with additional floors, houses Denver Center Theatre Company's operations. (HC, 10032337.)

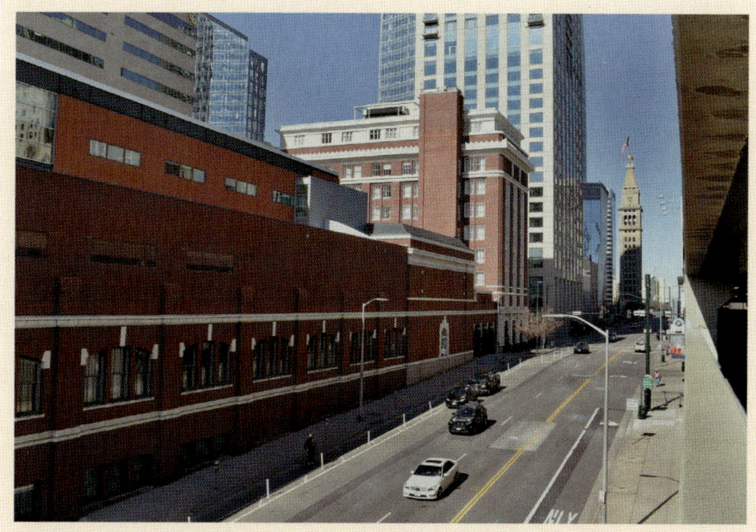

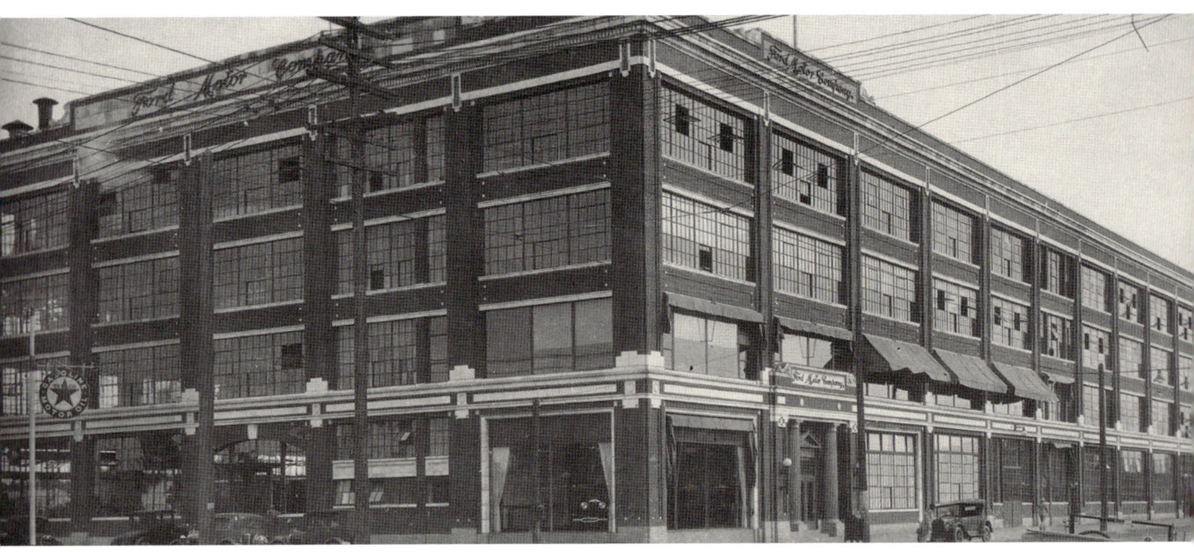

Two transportation eras are juxtaposed in the modern photograph at South Broadway and Interstate 25, as Regional Transportation District's light rail line crosses a bridge (underside visible at top left) in front of a Model T assembly plant built by Ford Motor Company in 1913. Ford assembled automobiles here until 1943, using parts shipped from factories elsewhere, before selling it to Gates Rubber Company, which renovated it as headquarters in 1978. It is now an office building and data center. (HC, 93-426-1.)

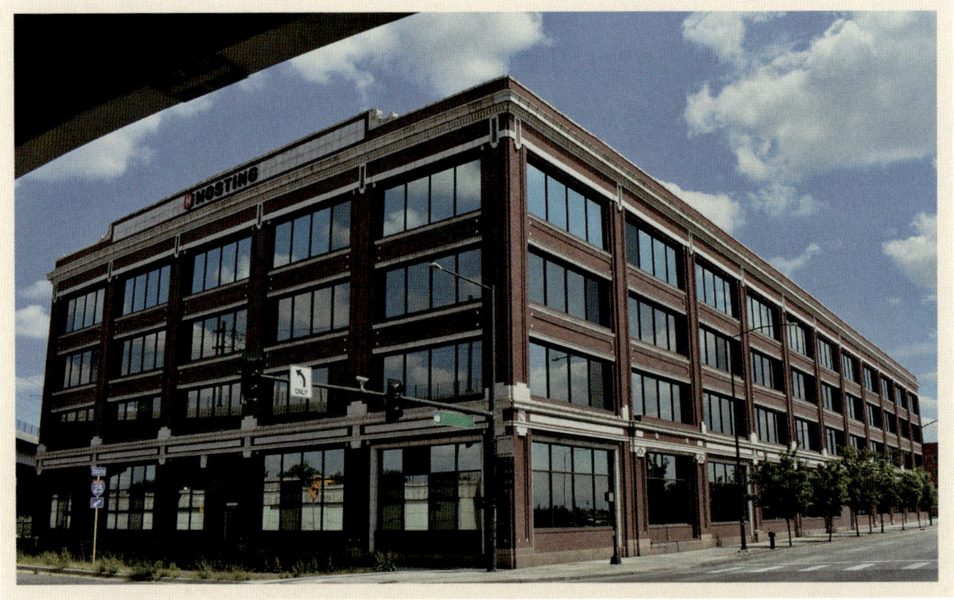

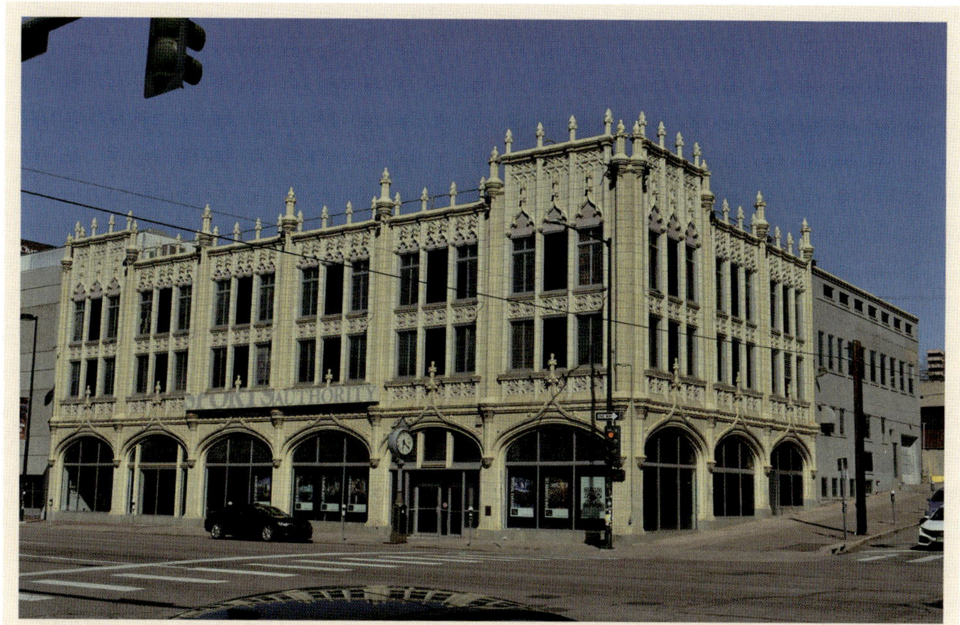

In the early 20th century, Broadway south of downtown became Denver's first auto row, with every make represented. In 1925, Frank Cullen and Ward Thompson hired Jules Jacques Benoit Benedict to design their French Gothic, multilevel Chrysler-Plymouth dealership, with floors linked by ramps, at Broadway and Tenth Avenue. In 1971, Gart Brothers Sporting Goods opened the Sports Castle in the building. Later owner Sports Authority closed it in 2016, and it now functions as an events venue. (DPL, X-23818.)

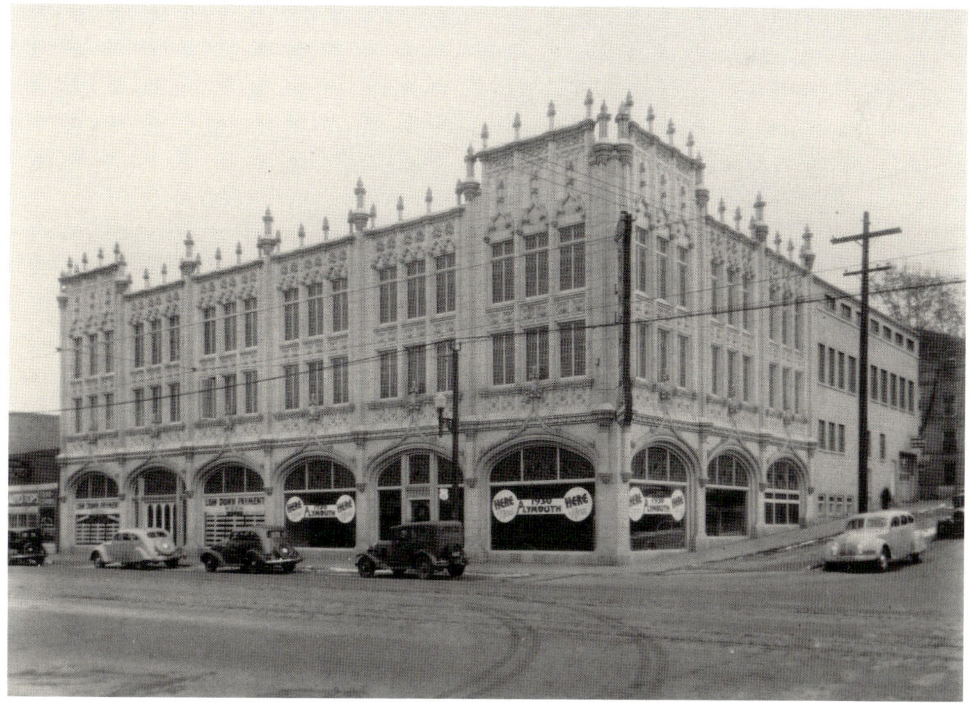

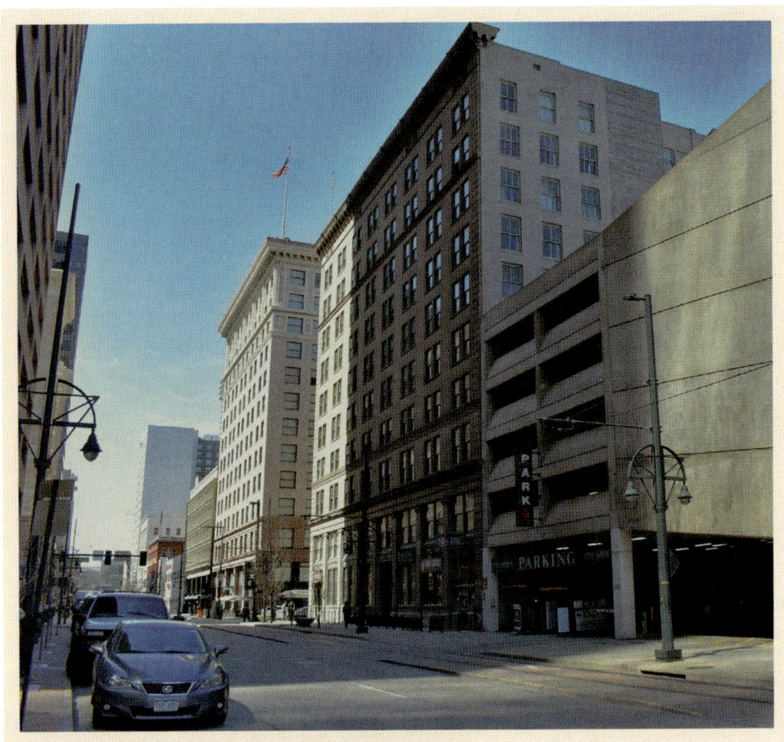

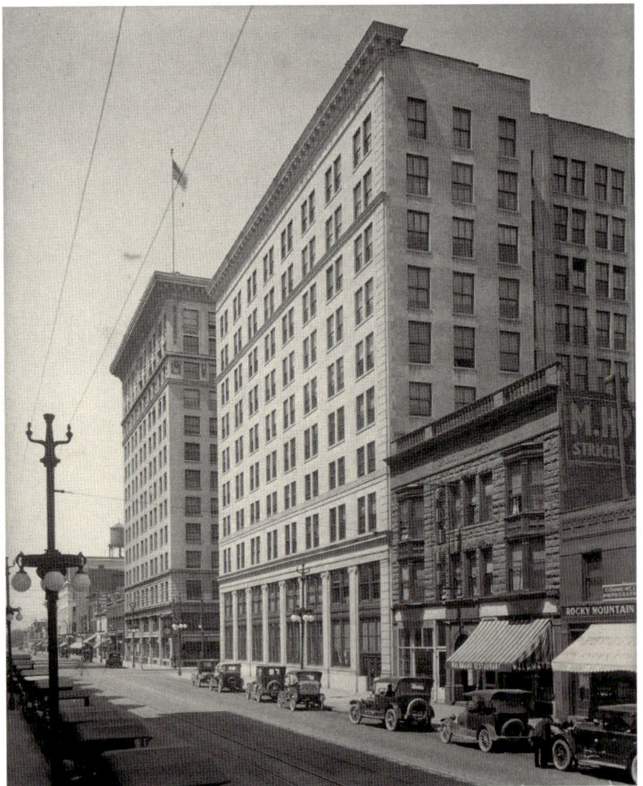

This view of Stout and Seventeenth Streets encompasses two of Denver's formerly largest banks, First National (left) and US National (center), conservatively designed in the Neoclassical style by Harry W.J. Edbrooke and the Fisher Brothers respectively. First National, then the largest west of the Mississippi, arose in 1911. Its original 14-story planned height proved controversial, engendering a height ordinance. US National followed in 1921. First National is now a hotel, and US National has become loft apartments. (DPL, X-22687.)

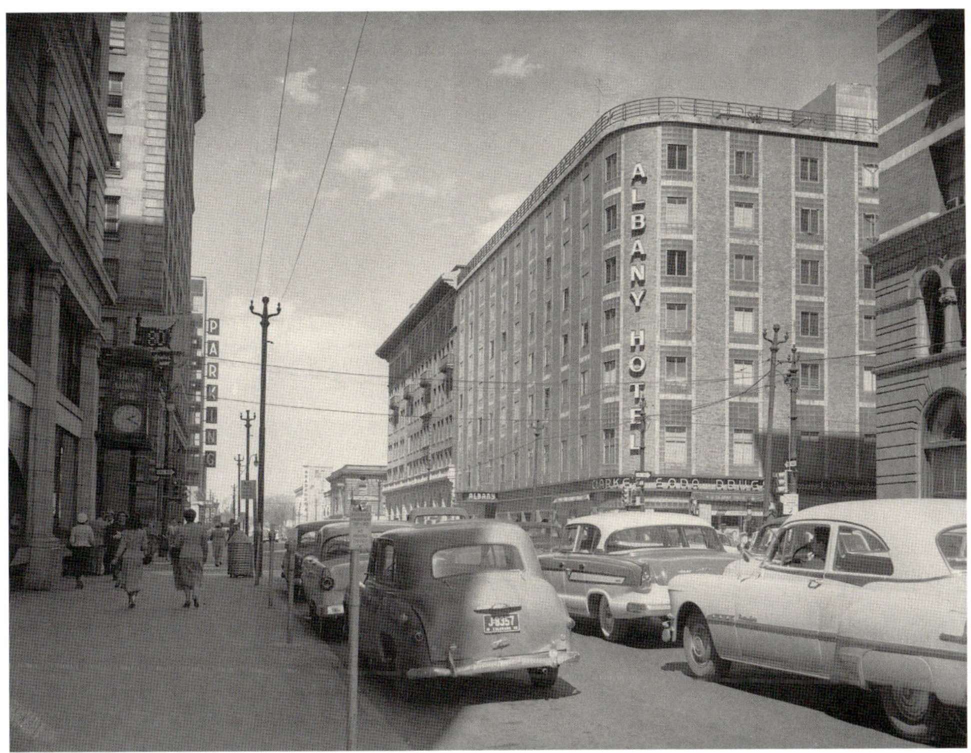

Across Stout Street from the two banks on the opposite page, the Albany Hotel (right) opened in 1885; an addition came in 1906. In 1908, deals done in an Albany smoke-filled room resulted in an unsuccessful William Jennings Bryan presidential candidacy. In 1937, the Albany's owners demolished the 1885 building for a Burnham Hoyt–designed replacement in the Art Moderne style. The entire hotel came down in 1977 for Energy Plaza, now Johns Manville Plaza. (DPL, X-29192.)

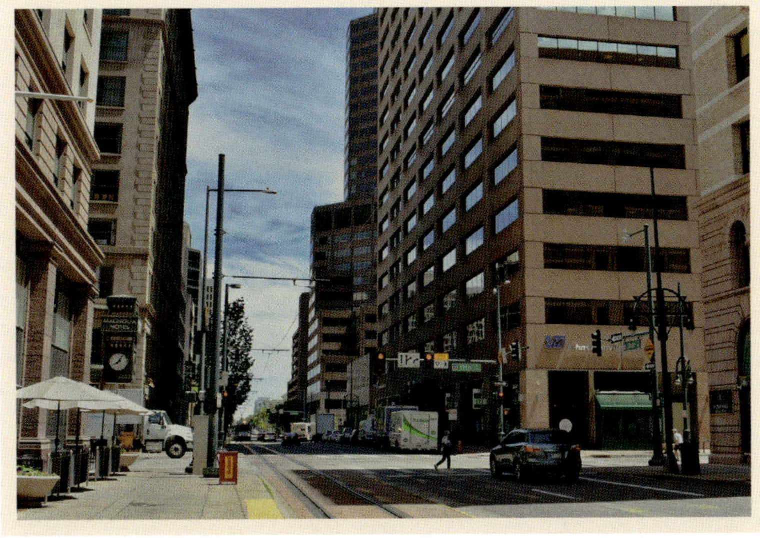

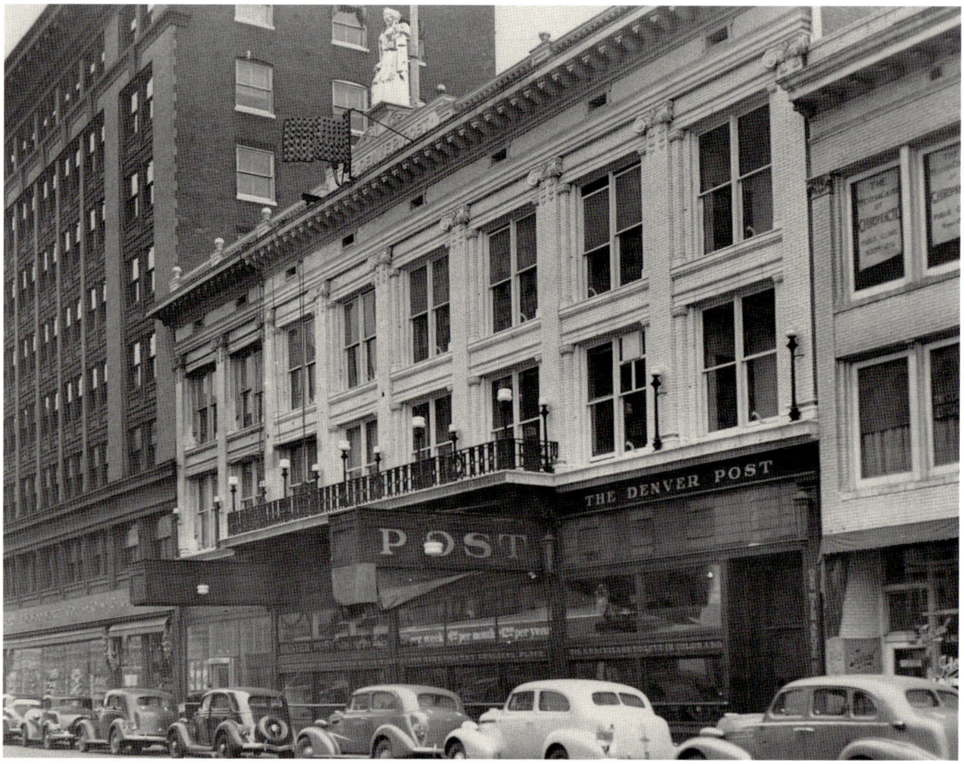

The 1906 Symes Building (left) still stands at Sixteenth and Champa Streets, but the Denver Post Building has been gone since 1951. Frederick Gilmer Bonfils and Harry Heye Tammen bought the failing journal, originally a Democratic party organ, in 1895 and turned it into Colorado's leading newspaper. In 1907, they built a new headquarters, topped by a statue, *Justice*, and it remained here until 1950. F.W. Woolworth, a Symes tenant, demolished it in 1951 to build an addition. (HC, 10035473.)

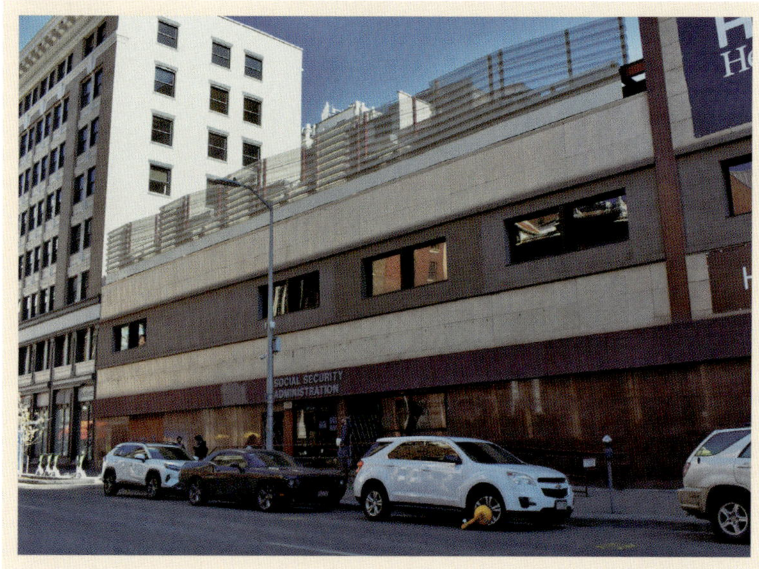

CHAPTER 3

AMUSEMENTS

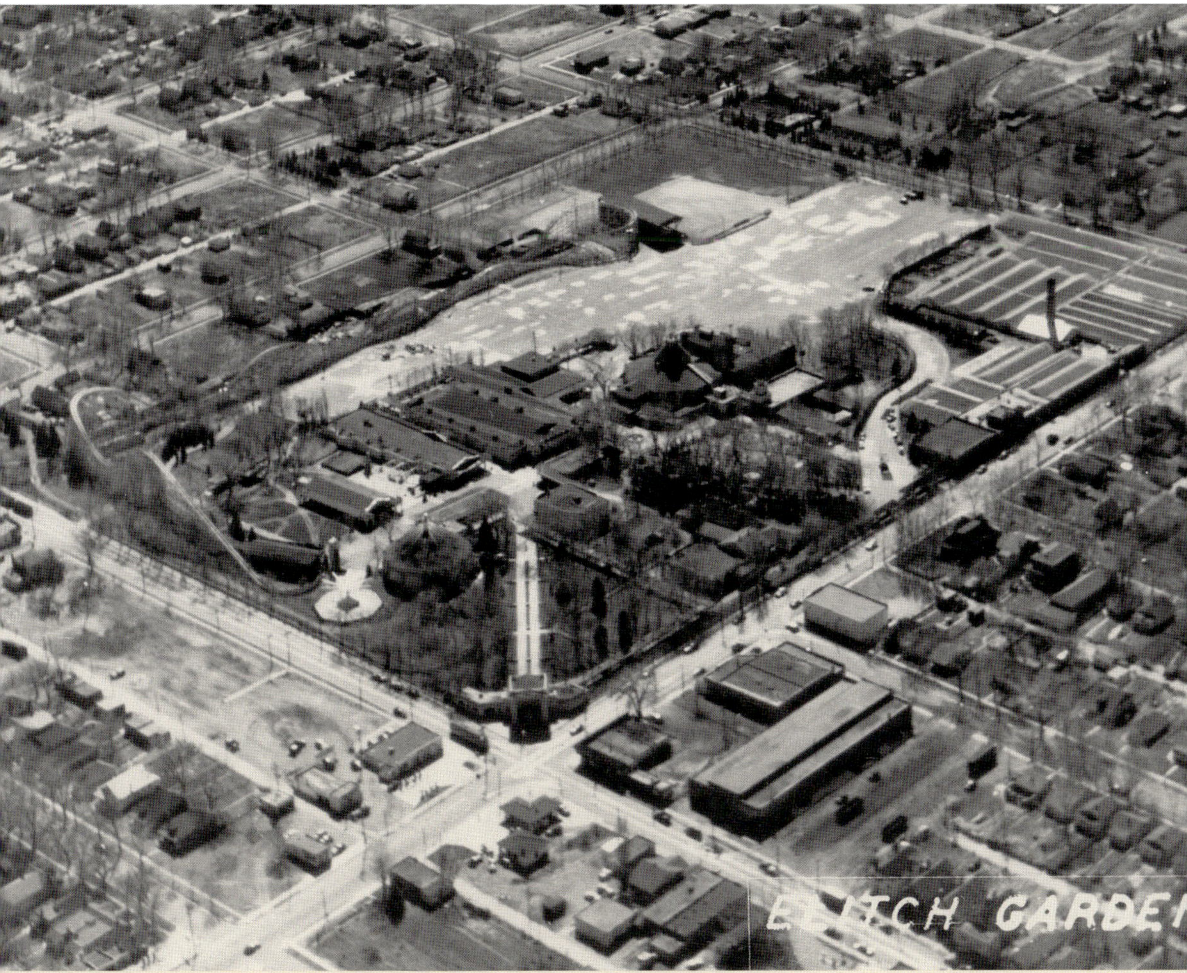

Mary and John Elitch founded their summertime resort, Elitch Gardens, at West Thirty-Eighth Avenue and Tennyson Street in 1890, and it was still going strong when this aerial photograph was taken around 1948. By this time, it had built substantial greenhouses (upper right) to grow carnations for sale and showier flowers for the park's extensive gardens. Elitch Gardens relocated in 1995. (Author's collection.)

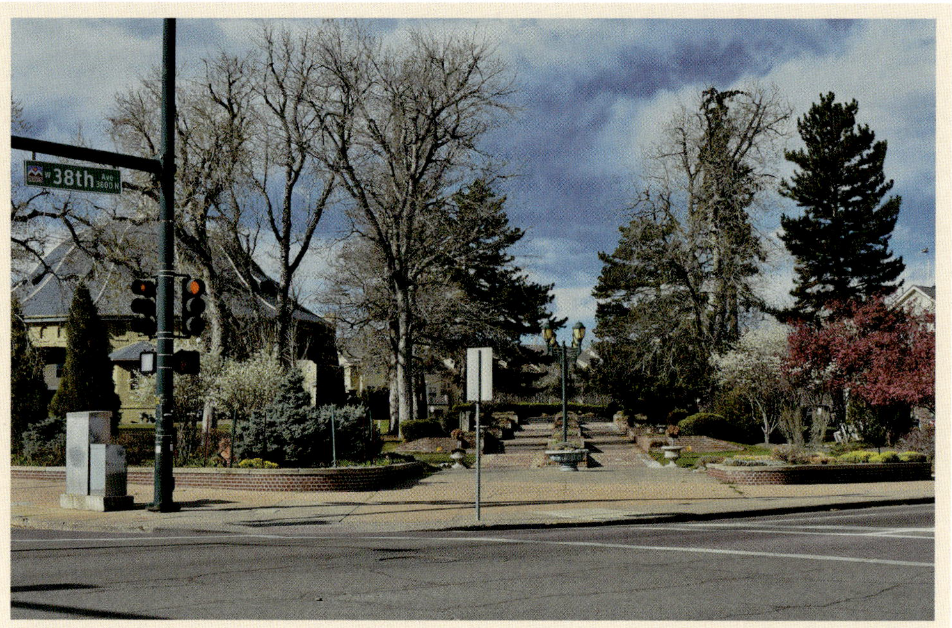

The original Elitch Gardens entrance was a log cabin–like structure, but in 1909, it was replaced by this Neoclassical entry, serving fun-seekers arriving by streetcar. Owner Mary Elitch-Long was likely reacting to the 1908 opening of nearby Lakeside, "The White City," a grand Neoclassical park inspired by the Chicago World's Fair. Louis Charles McClure captured the new entry, along with its flower shop (left). Today, the original walkway beyond the gate remains, passing near the former merry-go-round house (left). (DPL, MCC-1058.)

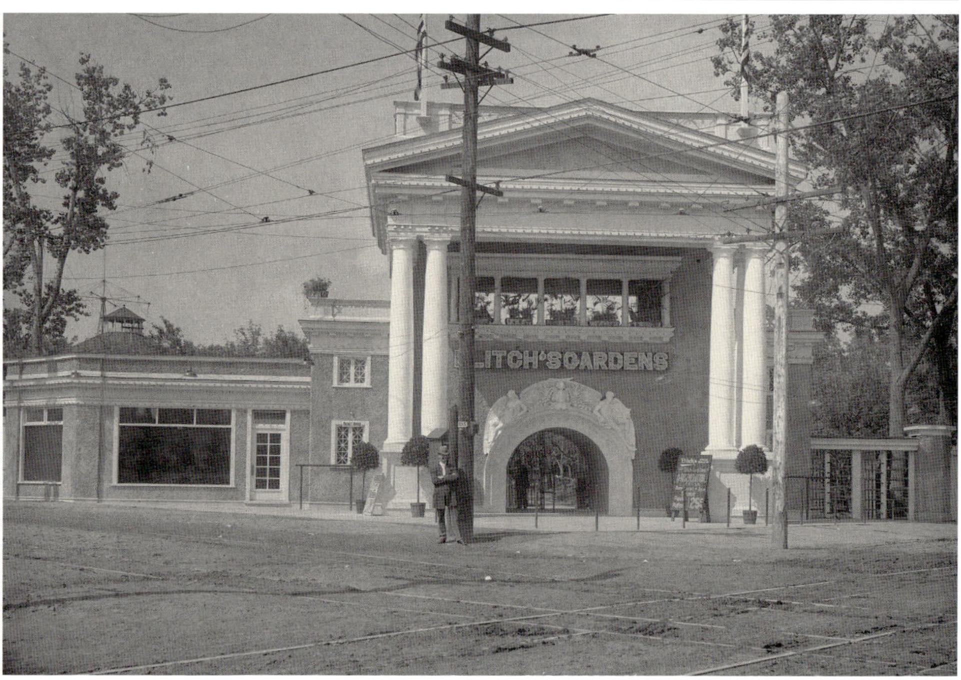

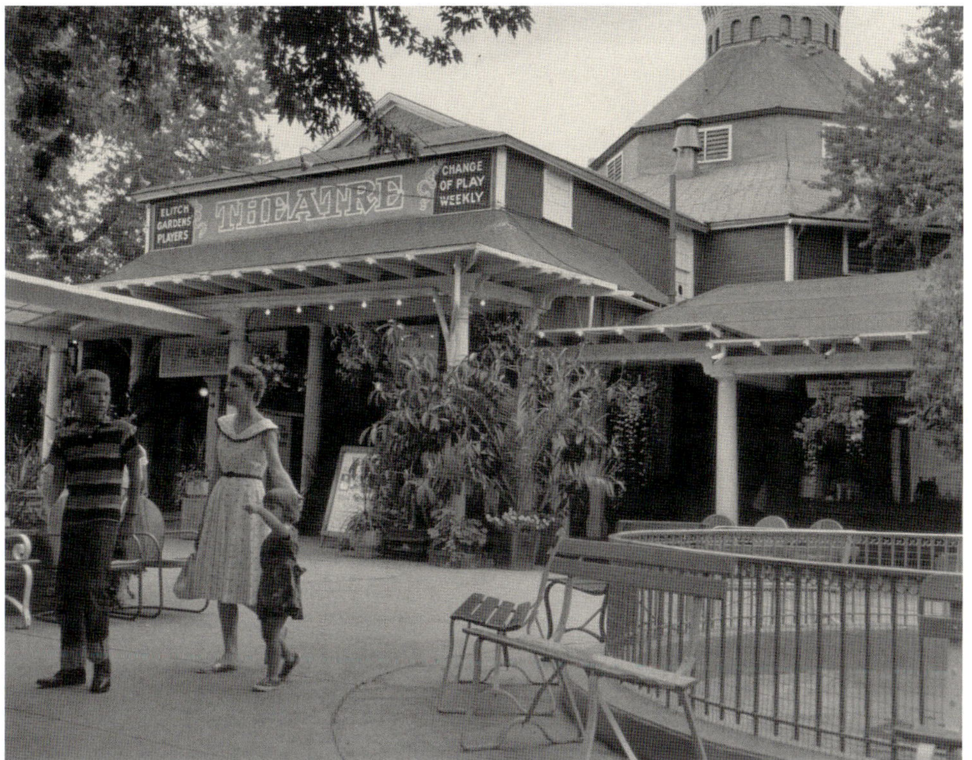

In 1891, Mary Elitch opened Elitch Theatre to honor the memory of her husband, John Elitch, who had died the previous winter. In 1897, she established a summer stock company that lasted decades; productions continued until 1991. Stars who trod the boards here ranged from Sarah Bernhardt to Cloris Leachman and from Douglas Fairbanks to William Shatner. After the park's closure in 1994, the theater remained standing, now situated among residential and commercial buildings. A multiyear renovation has ensued. (DPL, X-24657.)

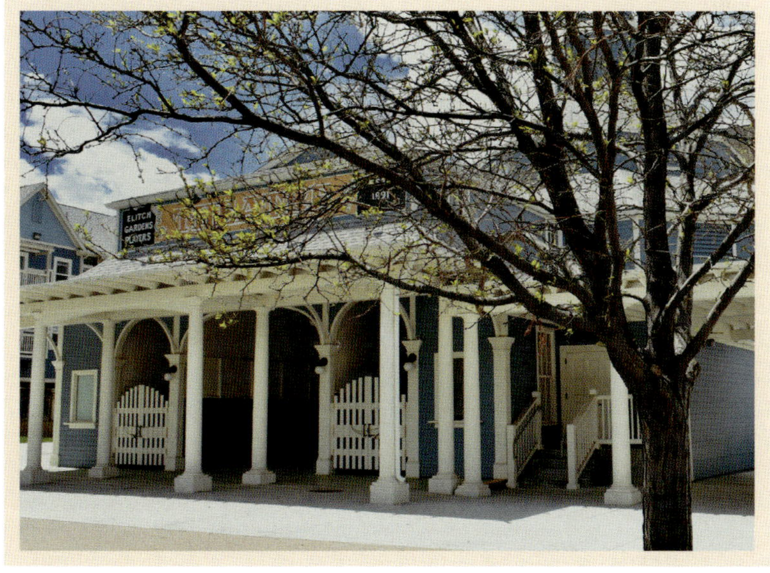

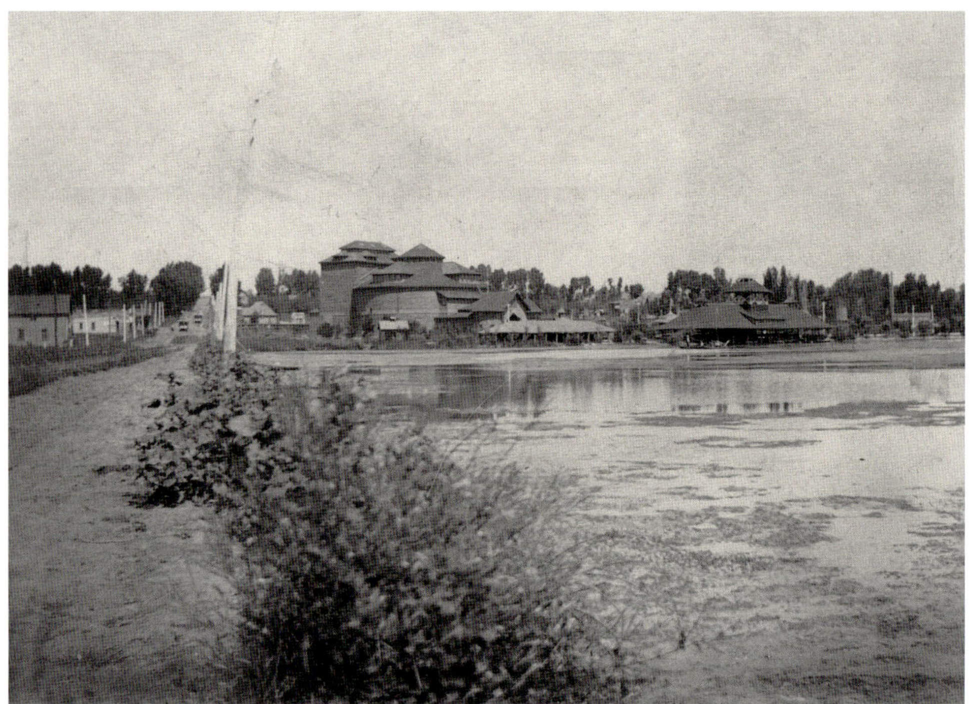

Manhattan Beach, founded in 1890 on the northwestern shore of Sloan's Lake and seen here in 1898, competed with Elitch Gardens and other amusement parks but always struggled, forced to rebuild after multiple fires and to cope with other disasters, including drowning boaters and a rampaging elephant that killed a six-year-old boy. It became Luna Park in 1909 and permanently closed in 1914. Later, the city purchased the land to complete Sloan's Lake Park, Denver's second largest. (DPL, X-27724.)

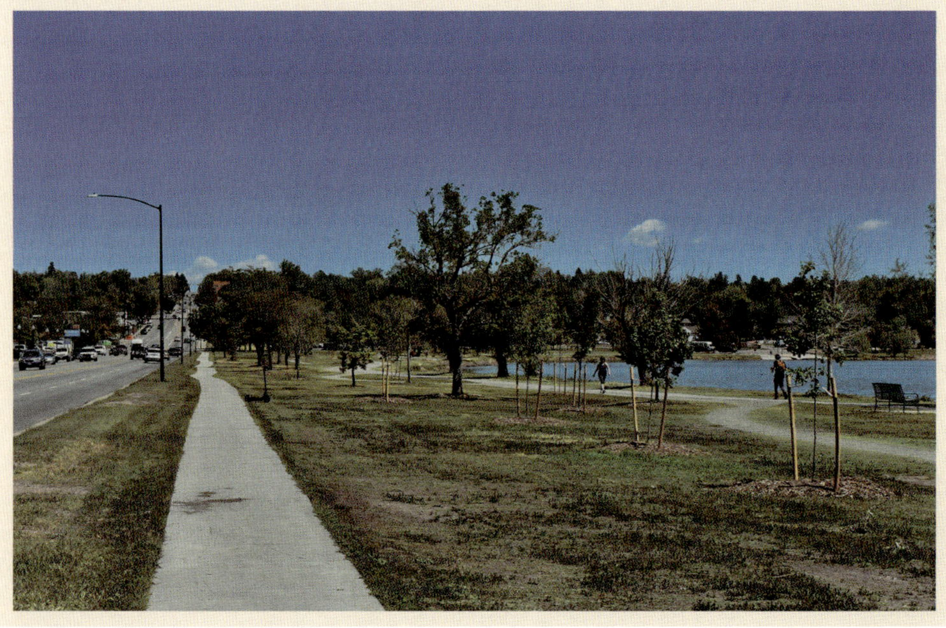

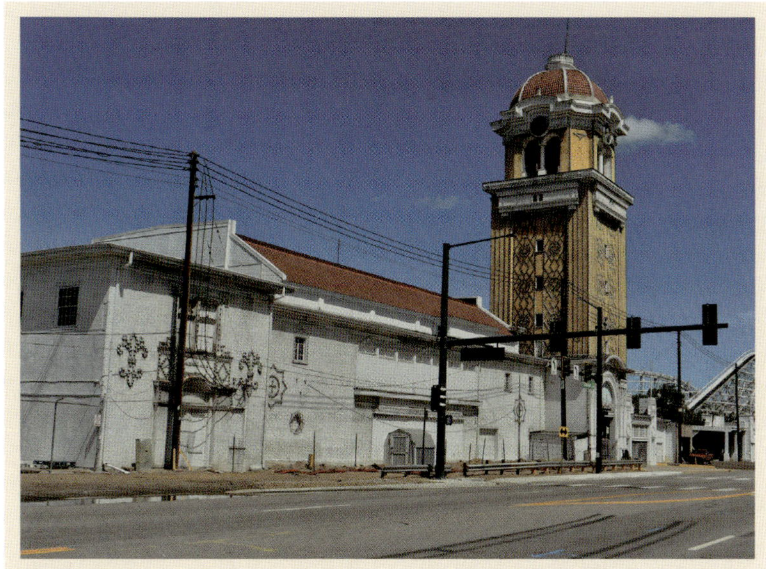

Still operating in the 21st century, Lakeside opened in 1908 as "Lakeside, the White City," its architect Edwin H. Moorman taking the 1893 Chicago World's Fair for inspiration. The landmark Tower of Jewels, with its thousands of white bulbs, could be seen for miles, including from nearby Elitch Gardens' roller coasters. Builder Philip Zang was also a brewer, so Lakeside served alcohol, unlike dry Elitch Gardens and Manhattan Beach. The Krasner family has owned Lakeside since 1933. (DPL, MCC-889.)

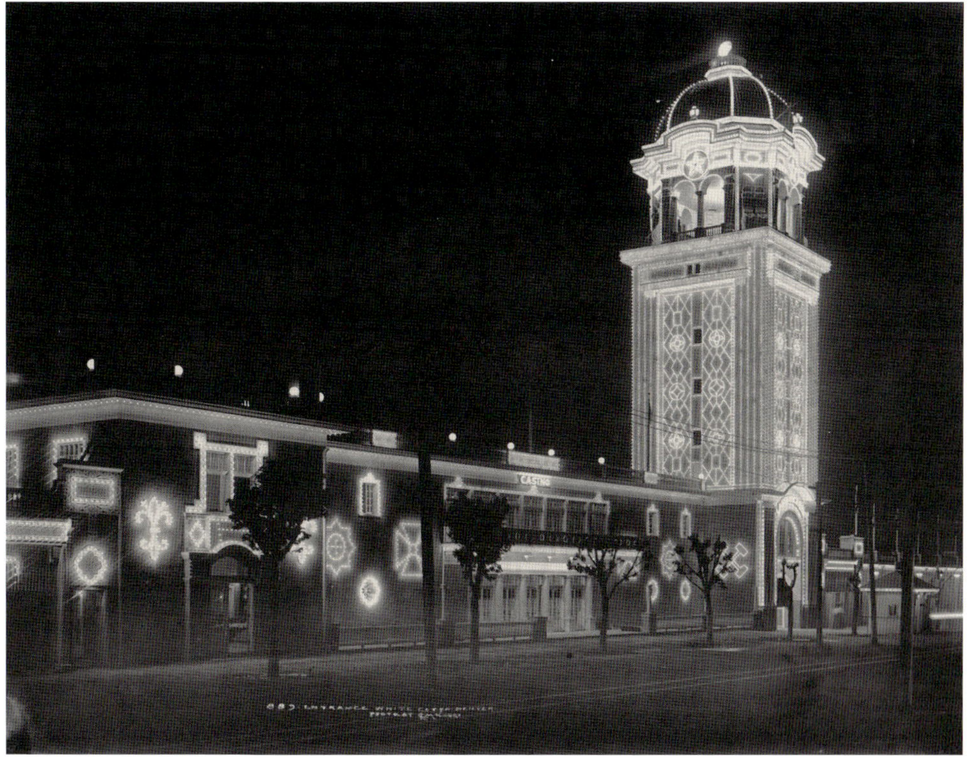

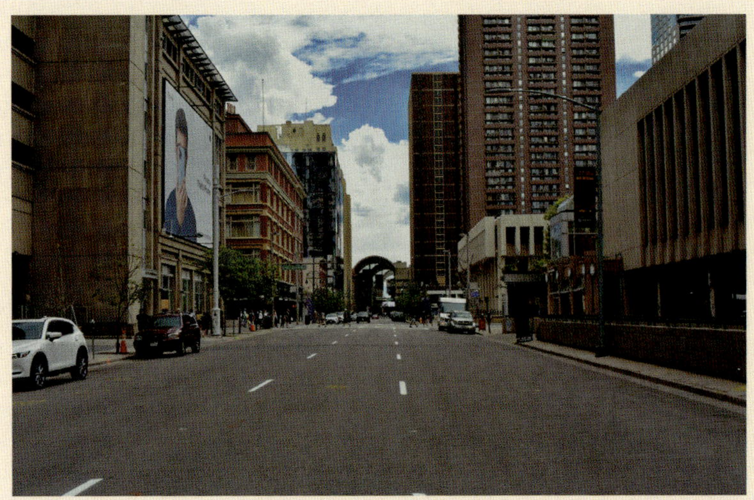

In 1926, Harry Mellon Rhoads snapped this dusk view of Curtis Street looking toward Sixteenth Street from Seventeenth Street when it was Denver's primary entertainment district. Theaters competed to have the most wondrous electric-lit facade; thousands of white bulbs made night into day. The former Tabor Grand Opera House was now the Colorado Theater (right) but would later regain the Tabor name. Today, the Joslin's and Baur's buildings remain, the others having disappeared. (DPL, Rh-77.)

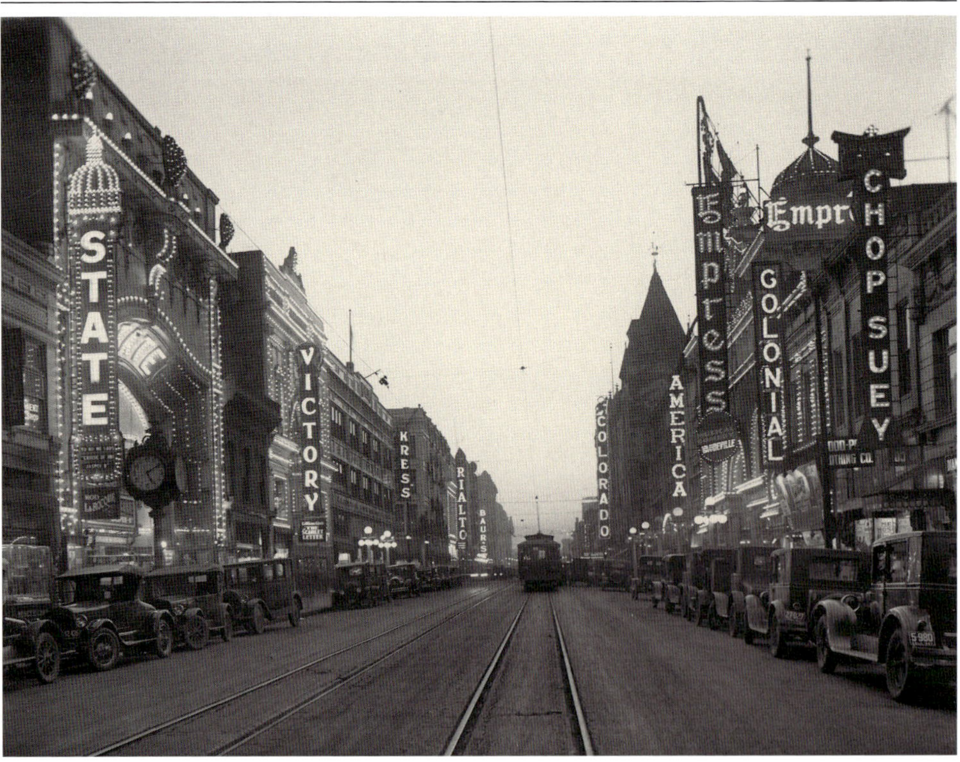

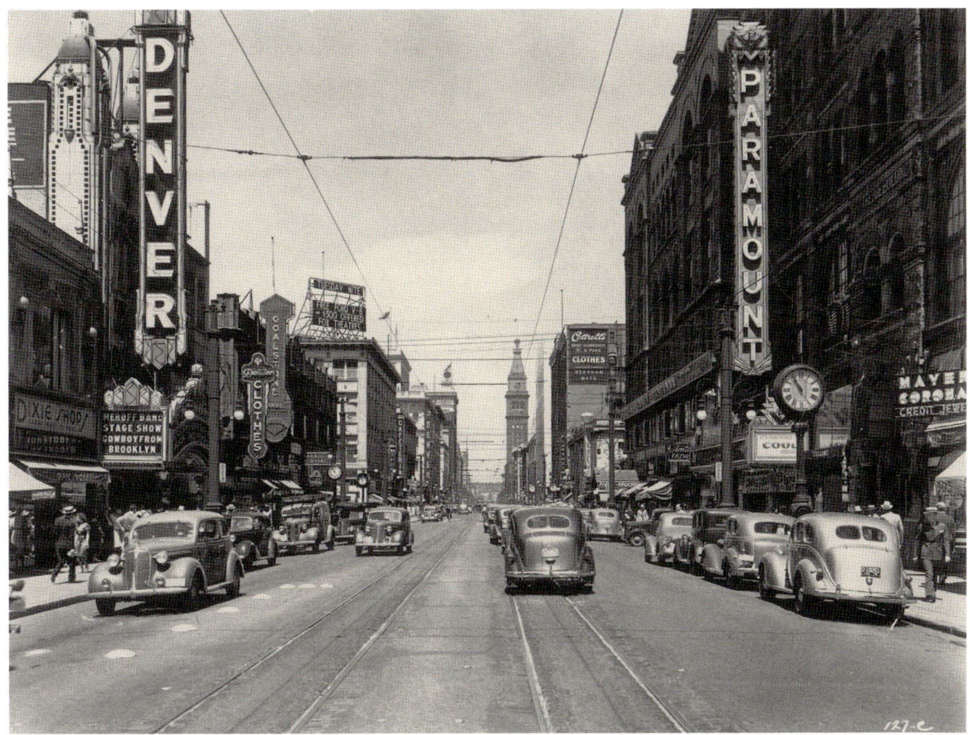

With the advent of "talkies," the Curtis Street theater district began to fade, and new, more palatial movie palaces opened in upper downtown. Facing each other across Sixteenth Street at Glenarm Place were the French Renaissance–style Denver Theater, opened in 1927 (left), and the Art Deco, Temple Hoyne Buell–designed Paramount, with its lobby occupying part of the Kittredge Building (right) following in 1930. This 1938 Otto Roach photograph shows them in competition for Depression-era audiences. (DPL, X-23375.)

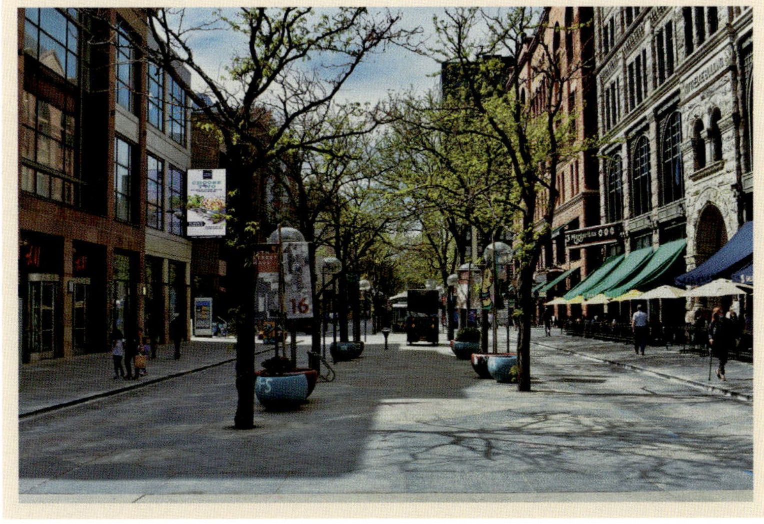

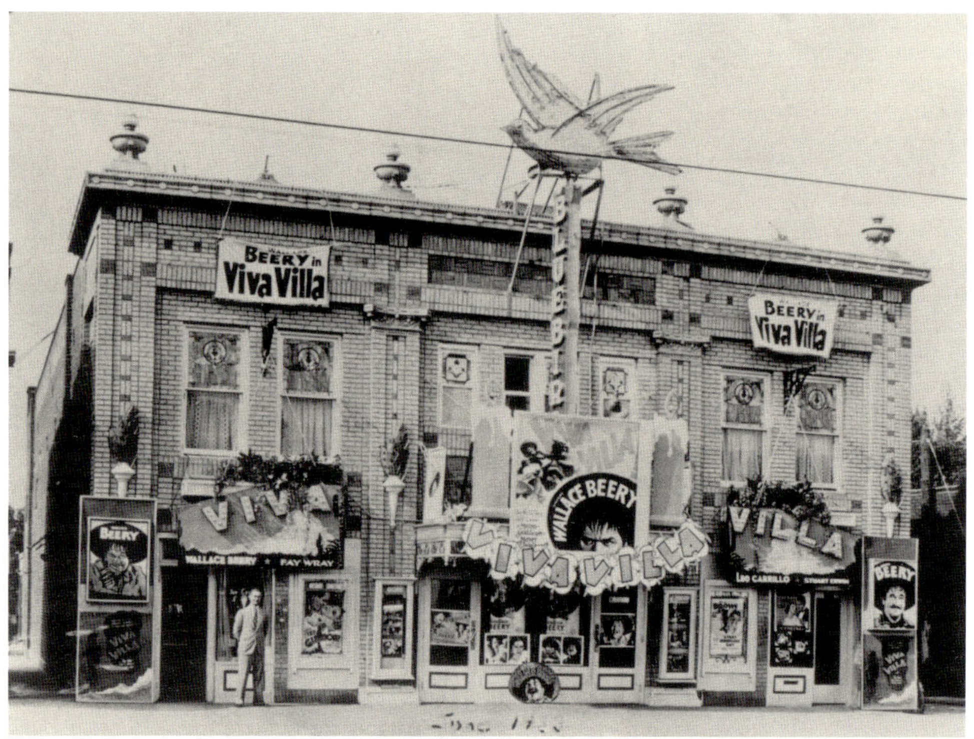

Not everyone went downtown for fun; neighborhood theaters filled the bill for many. The Bluebird on East Colfax Avenue, seen here in 1934, was designed by Harry W.J. Edbrooke and opened in 1912 as the Thompson, named for grocer John Thompson. During the Depression, operators Harry Huffman and Frank Ricketson promoted "bank nights" and "grocery nights," with cash and groceries given away, to drive attendance. After years screening pornography, it reopened as a music performance venue in 1994. (DPL, X-24805.)

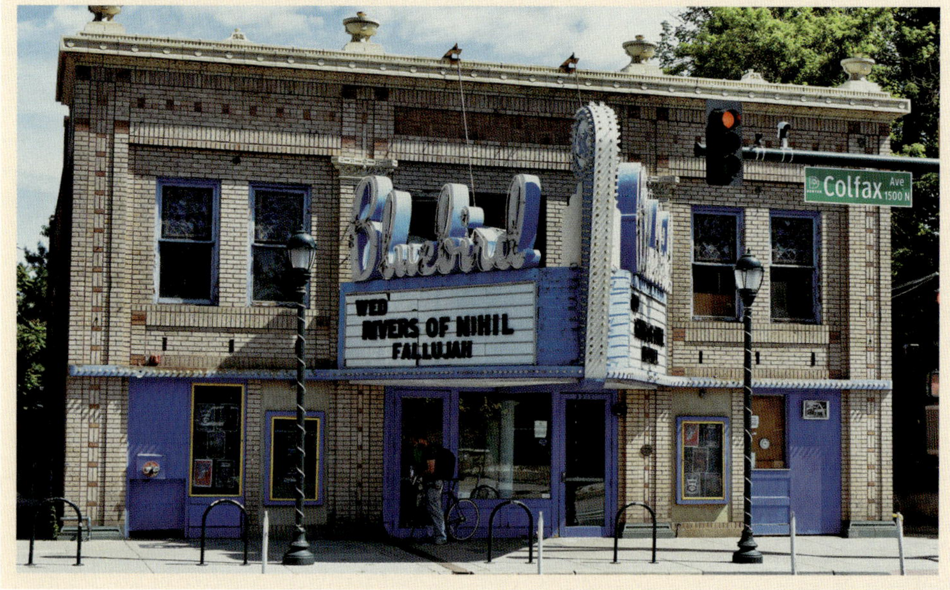

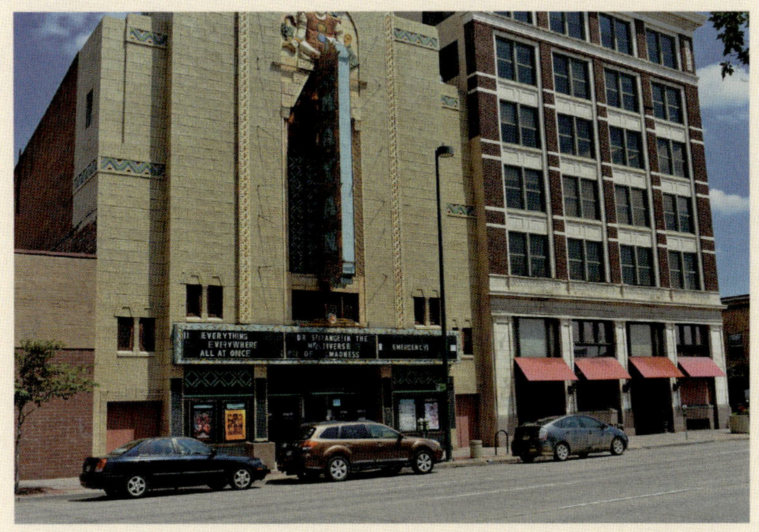

In Denver, there is no more beautiful neighborhood theater than the Mayan, designed by Montana S. Fallis in the Mayan deco style, with Julius Ambrusch contributing his terra-cotta artistry. The theater opened in 1930 at 110 Broadway. Denver almost lost the Mayan in 1984. Denver Broncos owner Pat Bowlen and Mayor Federico Peña jumped in to aid the Friends of the Mayan to save it, and today, it continues to show films, following a $2 million renovation. (DPL, X-24681.)

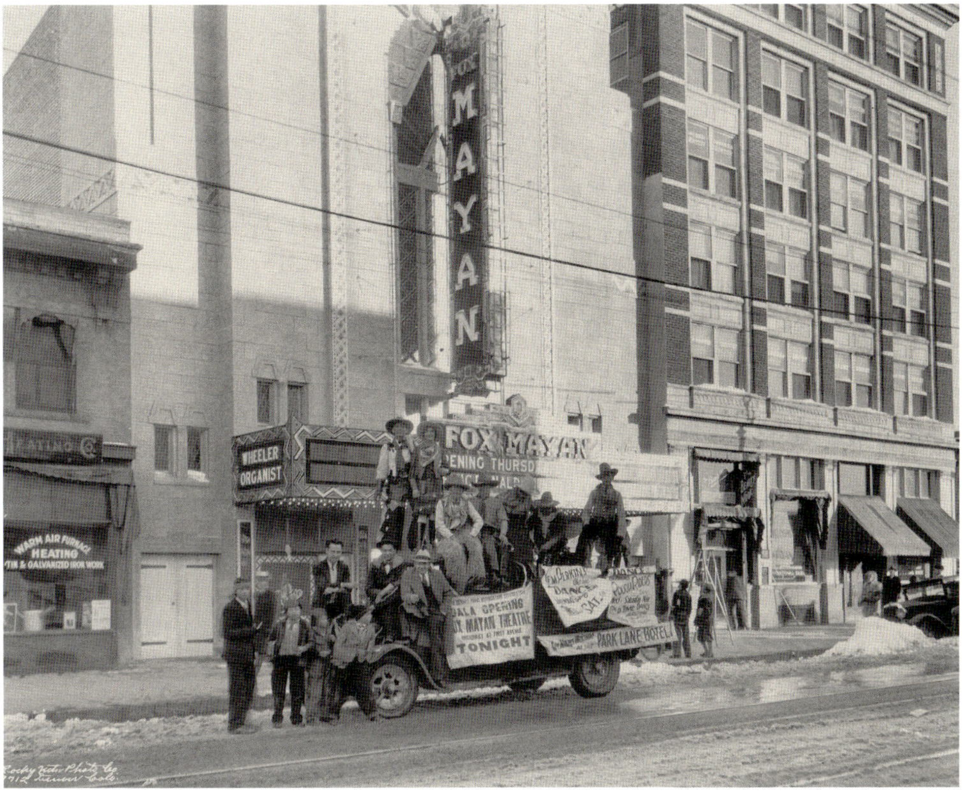

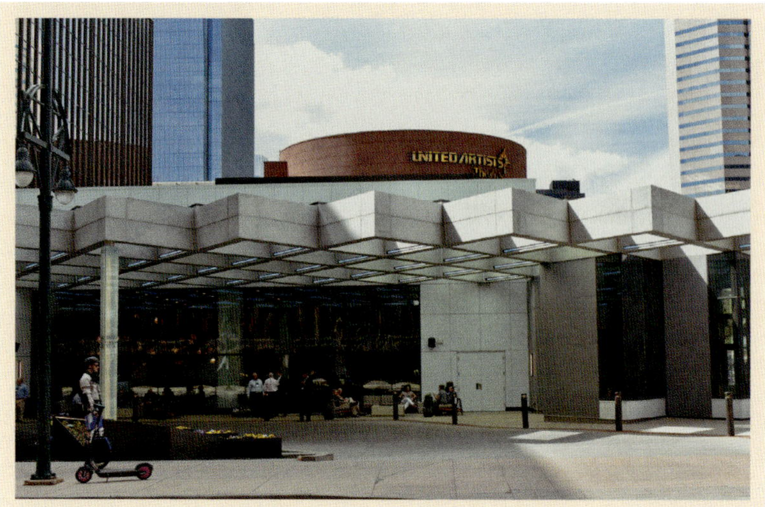

New York developer William Zeckendorf promised a "second Radio City" in his Courthouse Square, nearly two city blocks at Sixteenth Street's upper end. With a Hilton hotel, May-D&F department store, and sunken plaza that became an ice rink in winter, he created one of the most urbane complexes ever built in Denver. Architect I.M. Pei's glass-walled hyperbolic paraboloid disappeared along with the plaza in 1996, but the store building, converted to hotel rooms, survives (left). (Author's collection.)

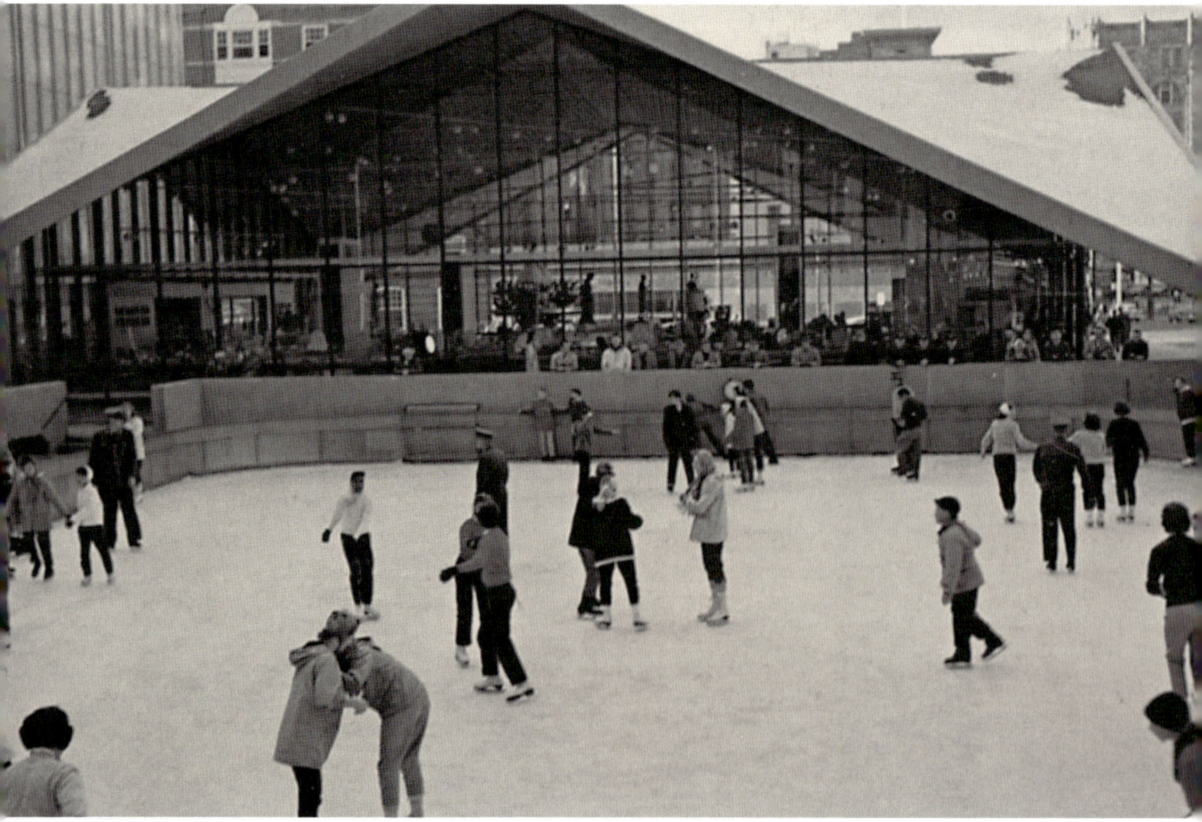

CHAPTER 4

Public Life

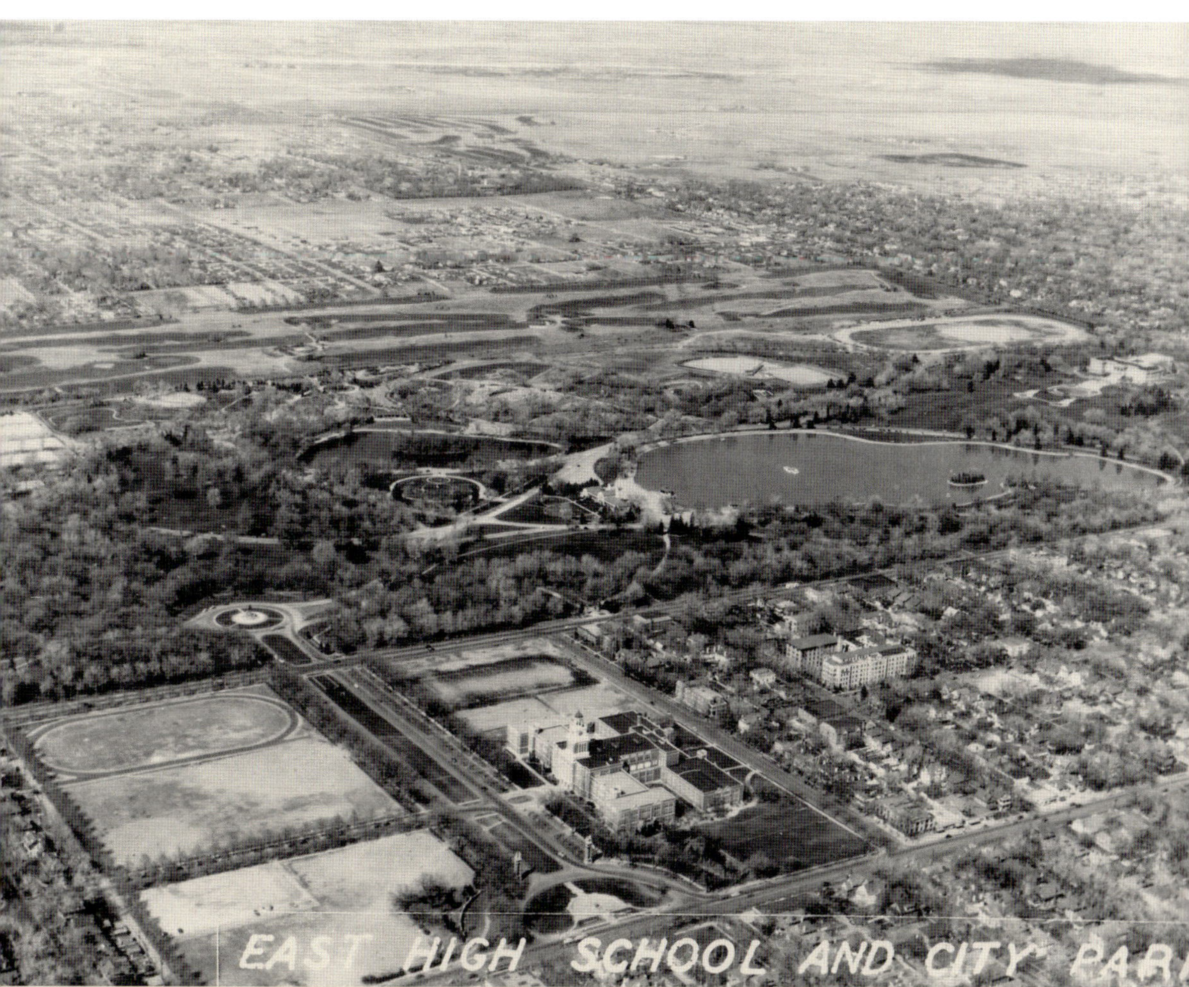

City Park, with its Denver Zoo (left) and the (then called) Denver Museum of Natural History (right) fills the central portion of this c. 1948 aerial photograph. East High School, built in 1924 and modeled after Philadelphia's city hall by architect George Hebard Williamson, fronts the City Park Esplanade, connecting the park to Colfax Avenue at the Sullivan Gateway (bottom). (Author's collection.)

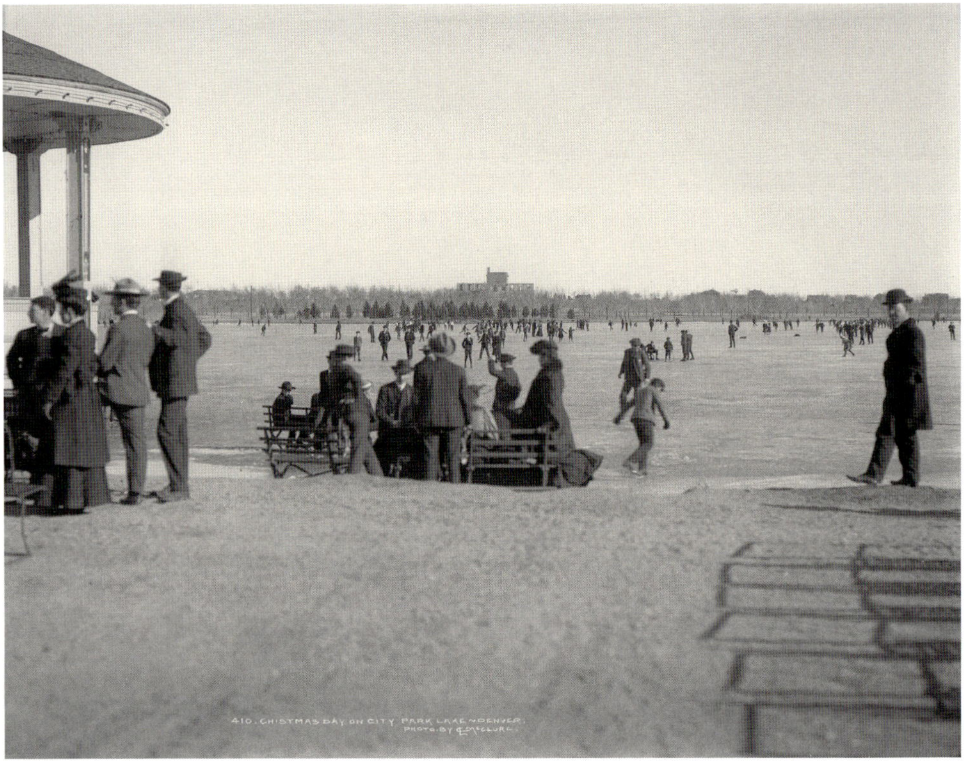

Aiming to replicate New York's Central Park, city fathers obtained land east of York Street and hired Harry Meryweather and Walter Graves to design City Park in 1882. Landscape architect Reinhard Schuetze improved their design beginning in 1893, creating Big Lake in 1896, complete with floating bandstand. Big Lake is now Ferril Lake, named after Colorado poet laureate William Hornsby Ferril. The Colorado Museum of Natural History is under construction in the distance in this Louis Charles McClure photograph of Christmas Day skaters around 1902. (DPL, MCC-410.)

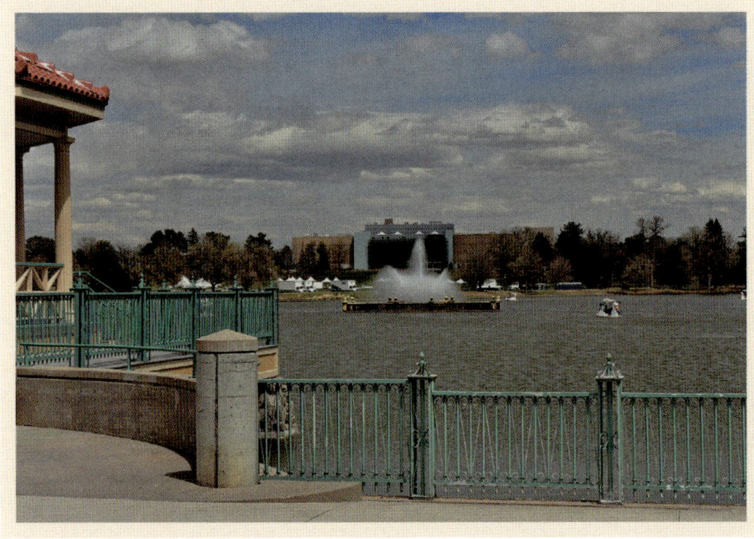

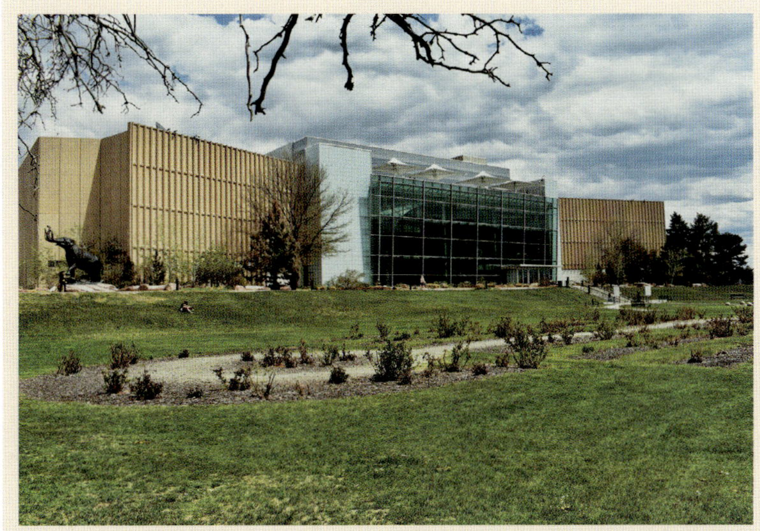

On City Park's eastern edge and highest point, the Colorado Museum of Natural History (Denver Museum of Nature and Science since 2000) opened in 1908 in this Neoclassical building photographed by Louis Charles McClure. Its genesis dates to 1868, when Edwin Carter, from a Breckenridge cabin, began collecting Colorado bird and mammal specimens. Today's museum, with planetarium, IMAX theater, vast collections, and international scientific reputation, occupies much more square footage, with additions over a century-plus completely enclosing the original structure. (DPL, MCC-1932.)

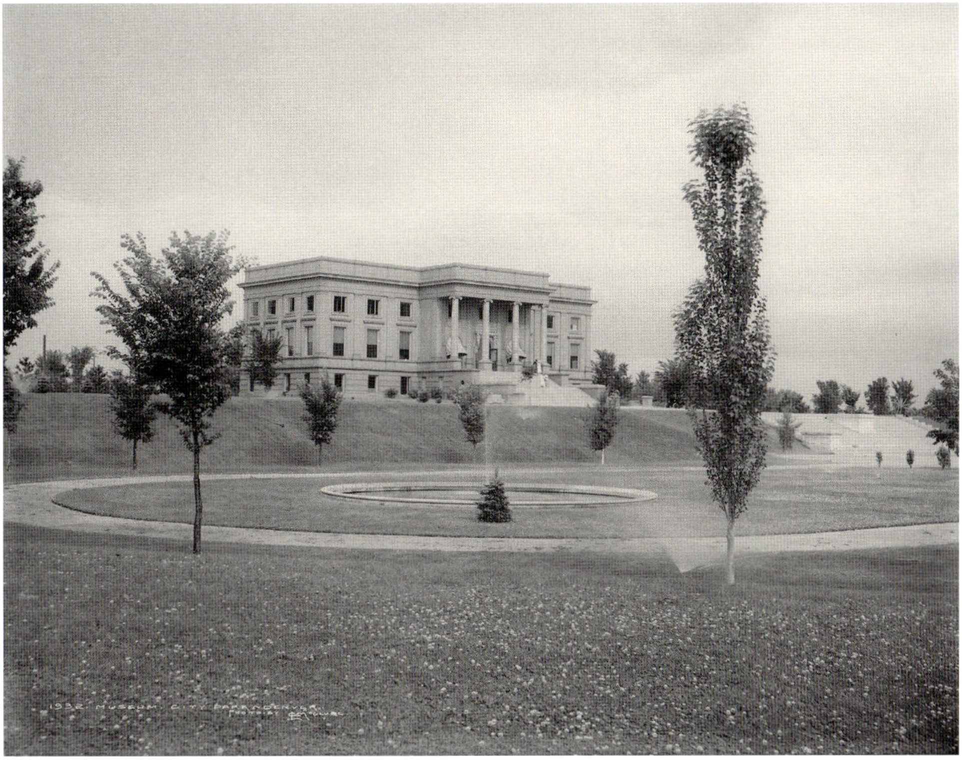

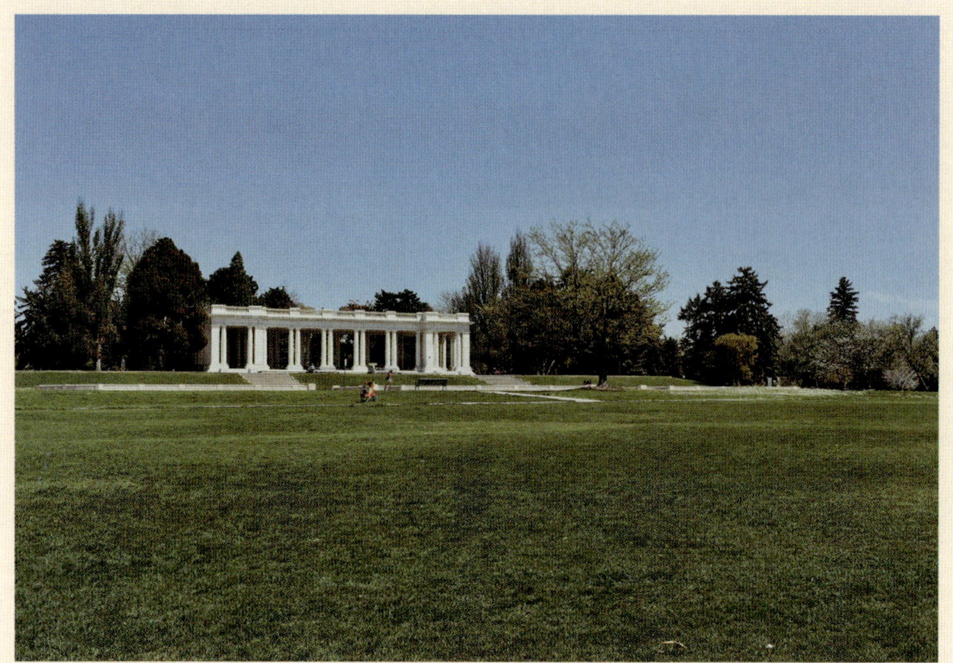

Harry Mellon Rhoads captured this image of crowds watching an aviation demonstration with a Curtiss Jenny in Cheesman Park in 1916. Reinhard Schuetze also designed this park, occupying former Protestant cemetery land, in 1898. He recommended a Neoclassical pavilion on its highest point, which came to fruition in 1910 when Alice Cheesman and her daughter Gladys Cheesman Evans donated $100,000 for a white marble structure to honor their late husband and father, 1861 Denver pioneer Walter Scott Cheesman. (DPL, Rh-702.)

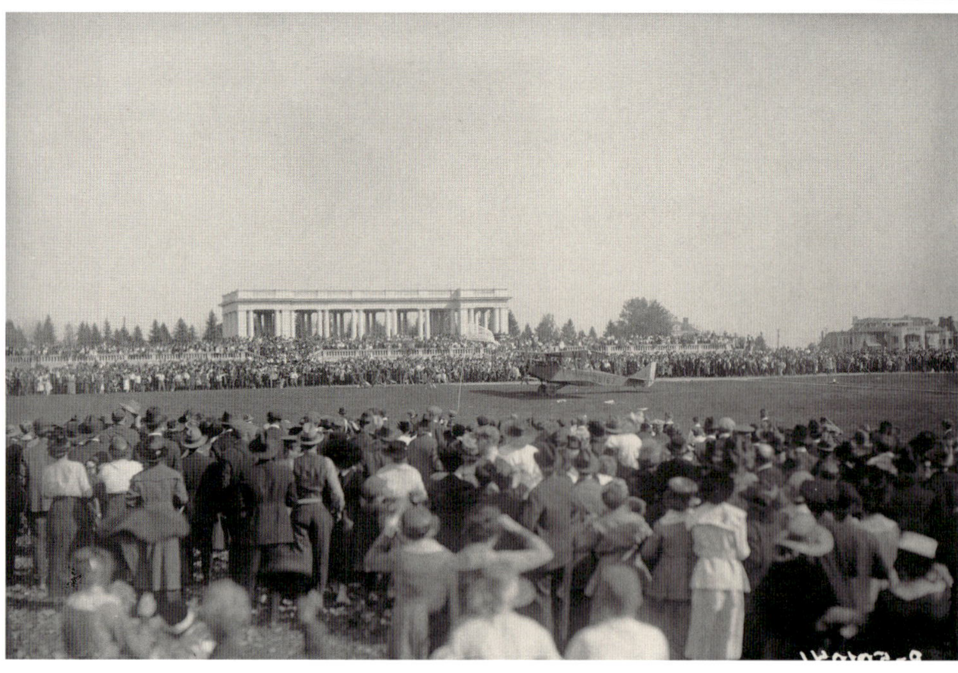

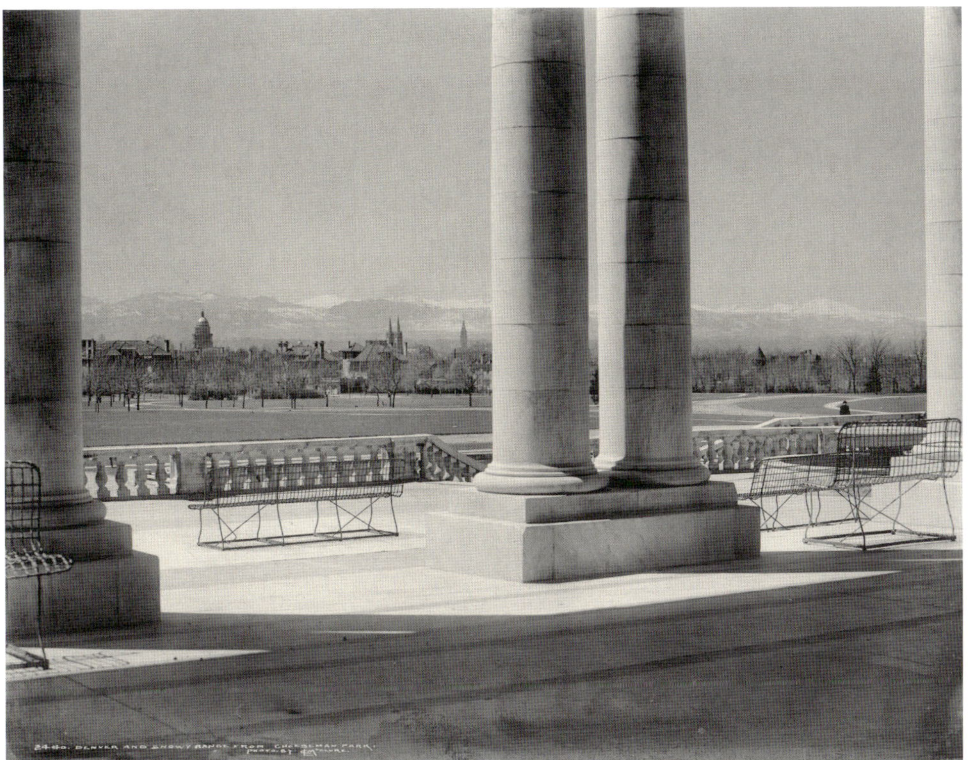

The Cheesman Pavilion's architects were Willis A. Marean and Albert J. Norton, who utilized Colorado Yule marble, the same used on the Lincoln Memorial and US Supreme Court in Washington, DC, as the structure's primary material. Around 1915, photographer Louis Charles McClure took a series of images featuring the amazing views then obtained from the pavilion, including this one showing the Colorado Capitol, Cathedral (now Basilica) of the Immaculate Conception, and Daniels and Fisher Tower. (DPL, MCC-2440.)

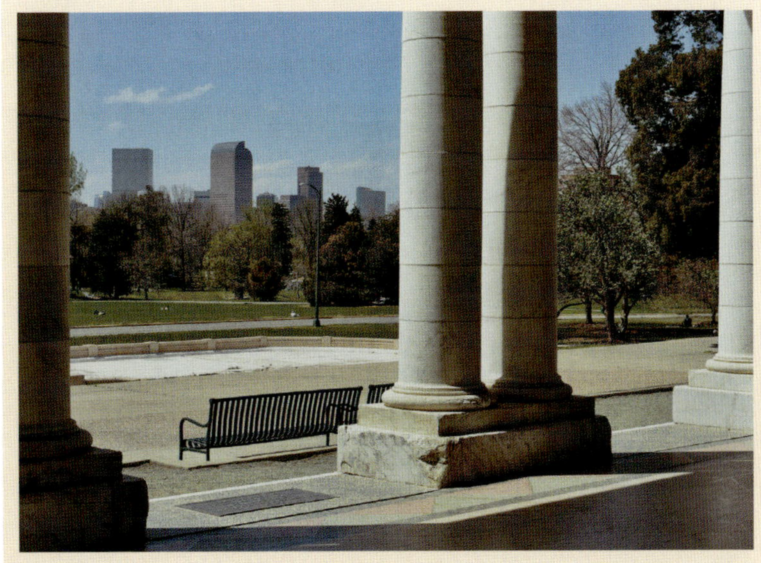

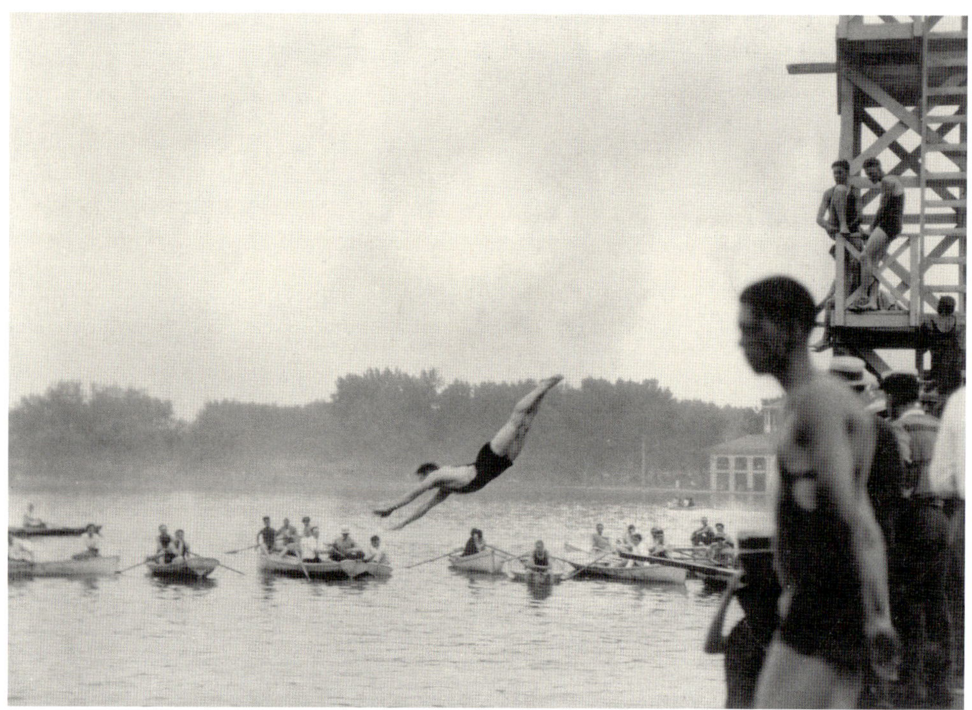

Washington Park, also by Reinhard Schuetze with contributions by Saco DeBoer, features two large lakes. On Smith Lake's northwest shore, a bathhouse arose in 1912 fronting a beach. The city built piers in 1914, and in the 1930s, the Works Progress Administration added high diving towers, seen here. The park superintendent, a Ku Klux Klan member, forbade non-whites. In 1932, Black people attempted to swim; a disturbance ensued. The lake closed to swimming in 1957. (DPL, X-27796.)

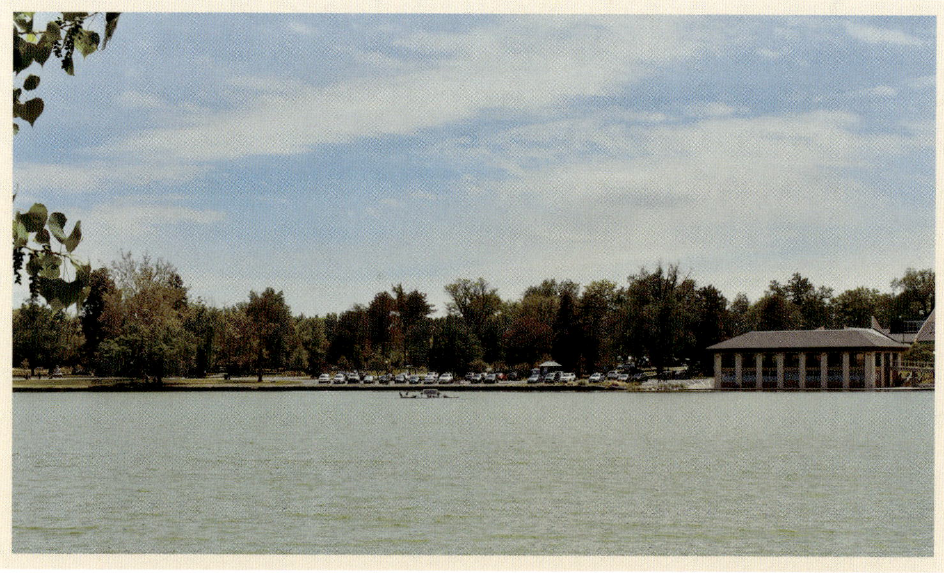

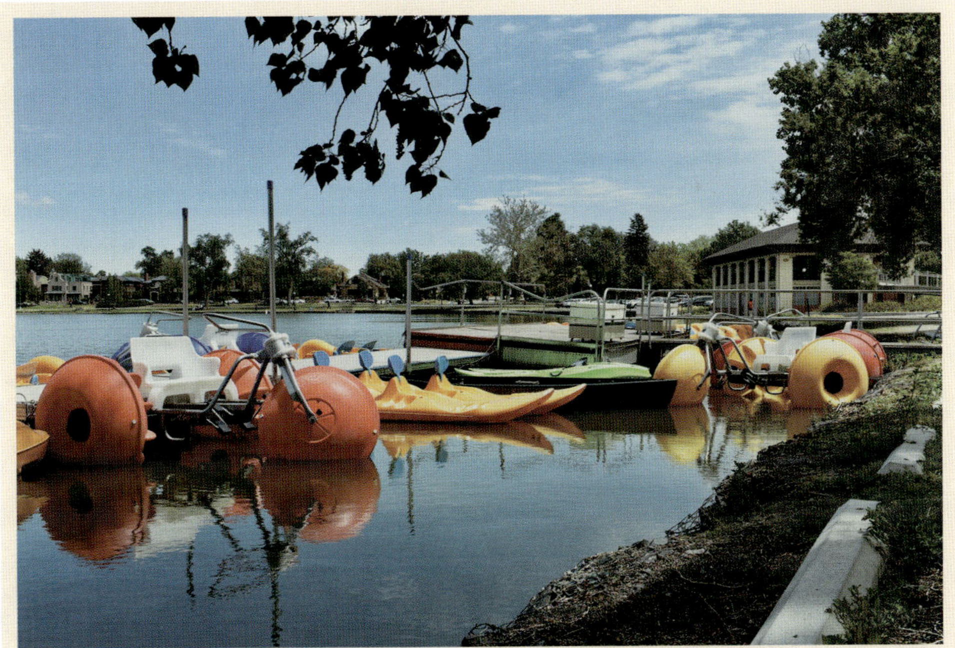

South Denver residents skated on Smith Lake when it froze, as seen in this c. 1913 image. Jules Jacques Benoit Benedict designed Washington Park's signature structure, the Washington Park Boathouse (right), in 1913. During summer, parkgoers could rent boats on its lower level or enjoy a picnic on its open-air upper level. In winter, skaters used it as a warming house and partook of hot chocolate and other treats. Ice skating ceased in 1982. (DPL, X-27789.)

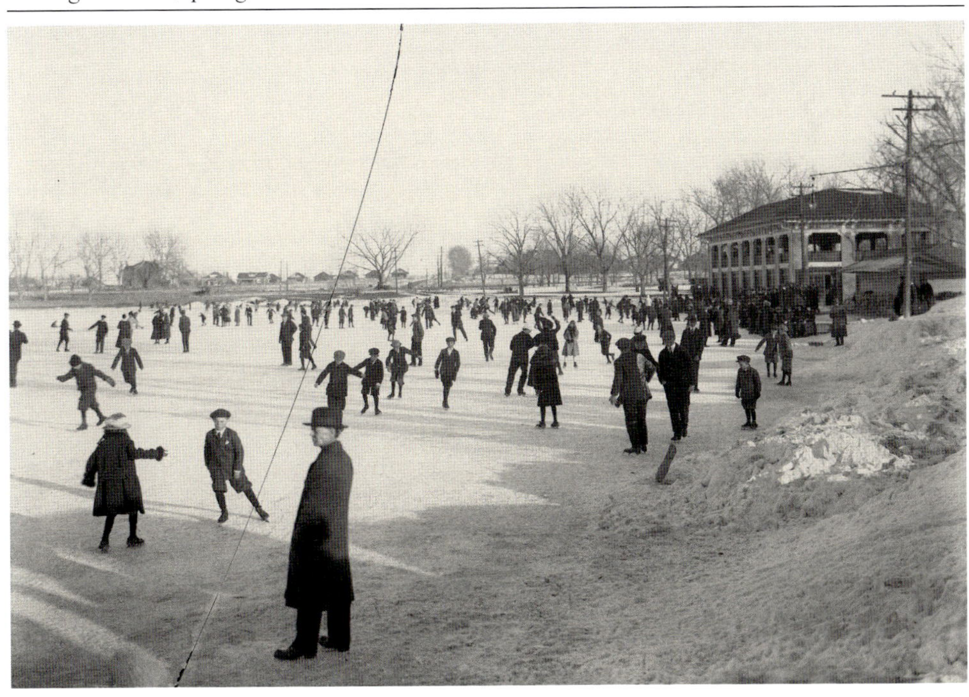

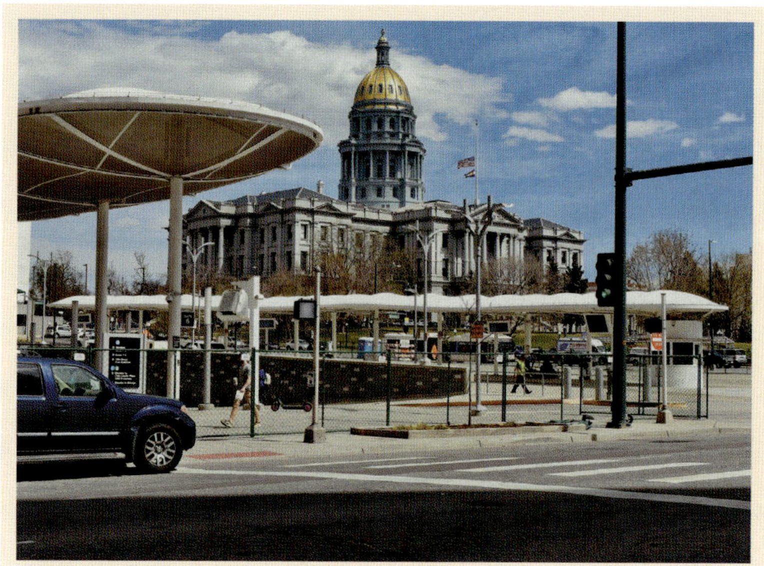

Colorado's capitol, designed by Elijah E. Myers and Frank Edbrooke, was open but not fully complete in this October 1897 photograph of the Chaffee Light Artillery participating in the Festival of Mountain and Plain. This event ran for several years, promoting the idea that Colorado had survived the Panic of 1893 and would thrive again. In 1908, the dome was plated in 200 ounces of gold, a process repeated several times subsequently, most recently in 2014. (HC, 10049228.)

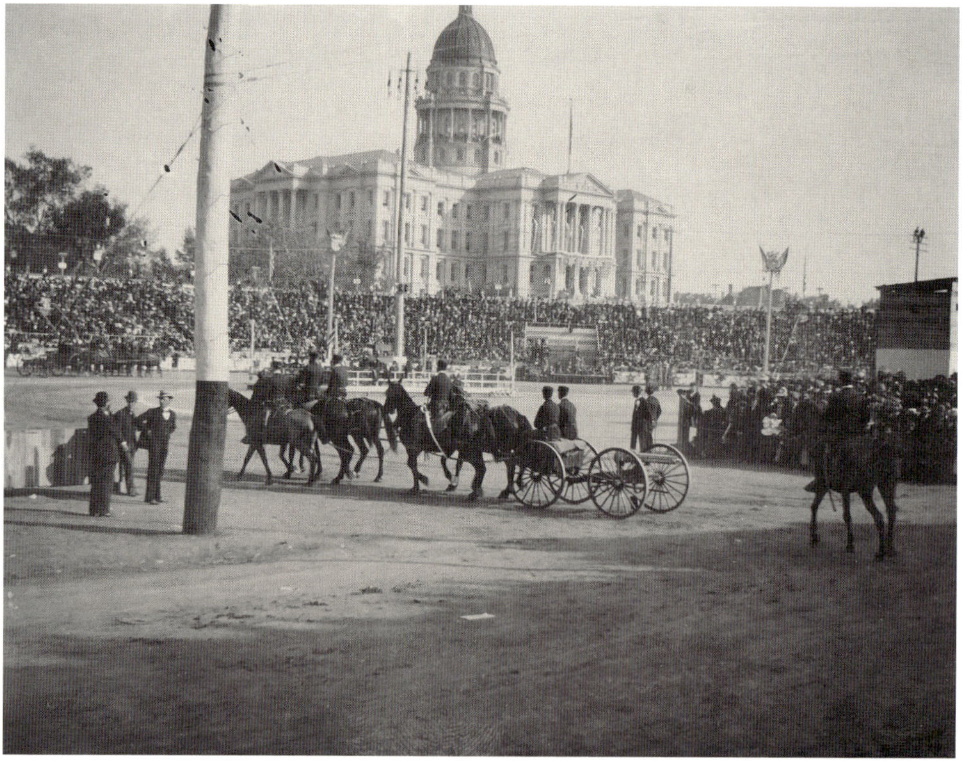

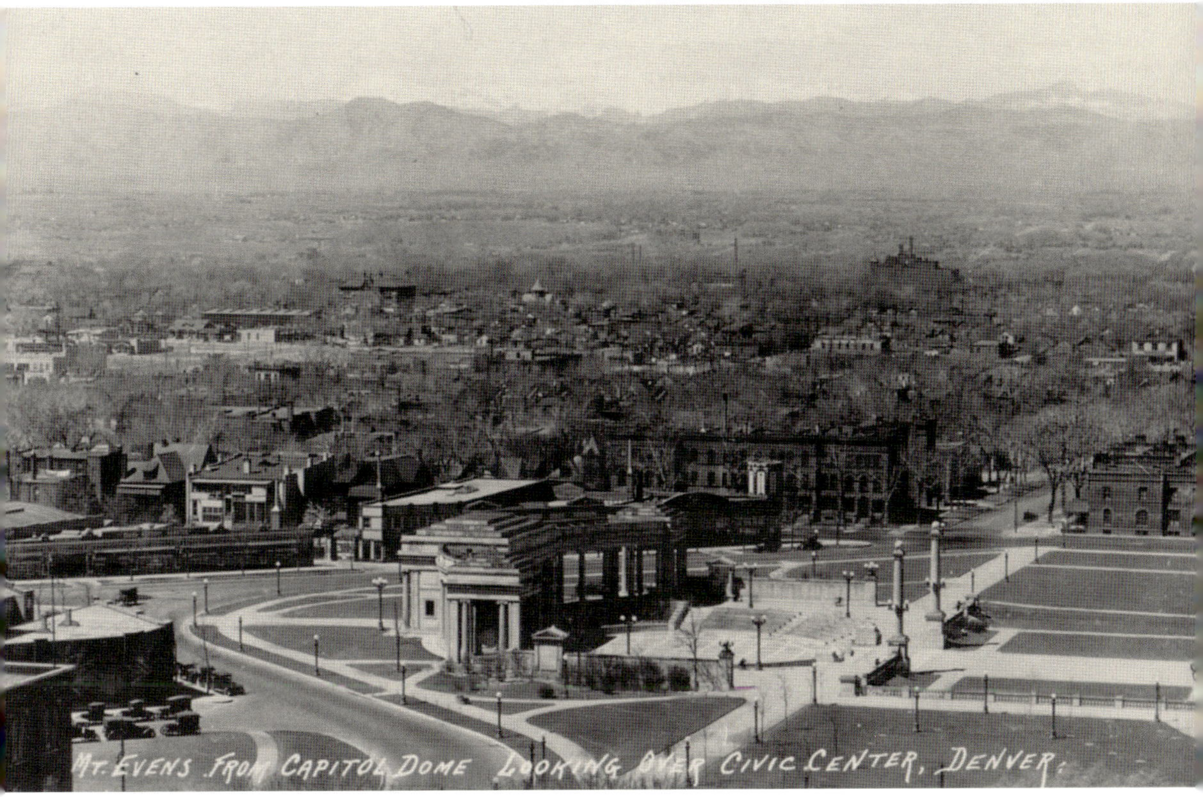

Photographers have documented views from the capitol's dome for more than a century. Mayor Robert Speer's vision for Civic Center, first proposed in 1906 and subsequently developed by a succession of artists and architects, began coming together in the late 1910s. The 1919 Greek Theatre and Colonnade of Civic Benefactors, by Willis Marean and Albert Norton, has hosted countless events, from plays to protests. Gio Ponti's and James Sudler's Denver Art Museum (1971, left) towers over it today. (Author's collection.)

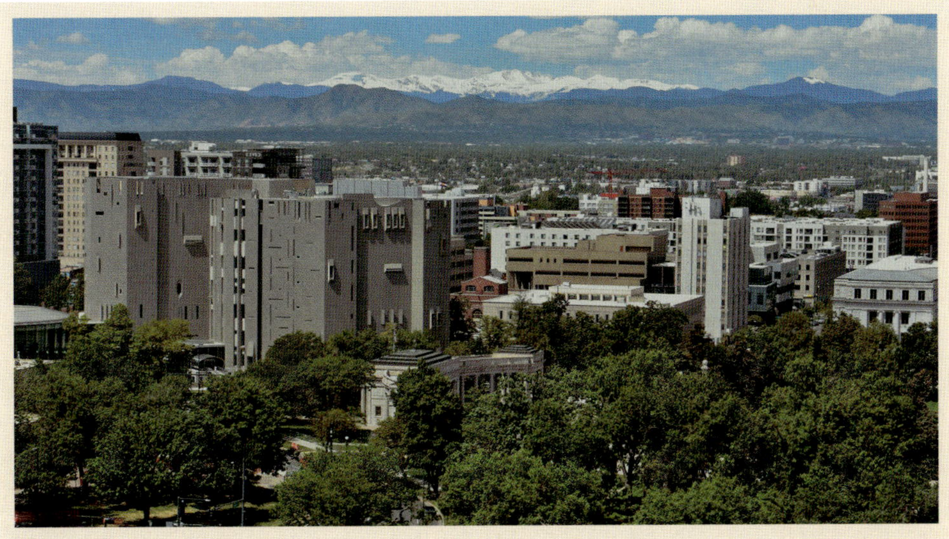

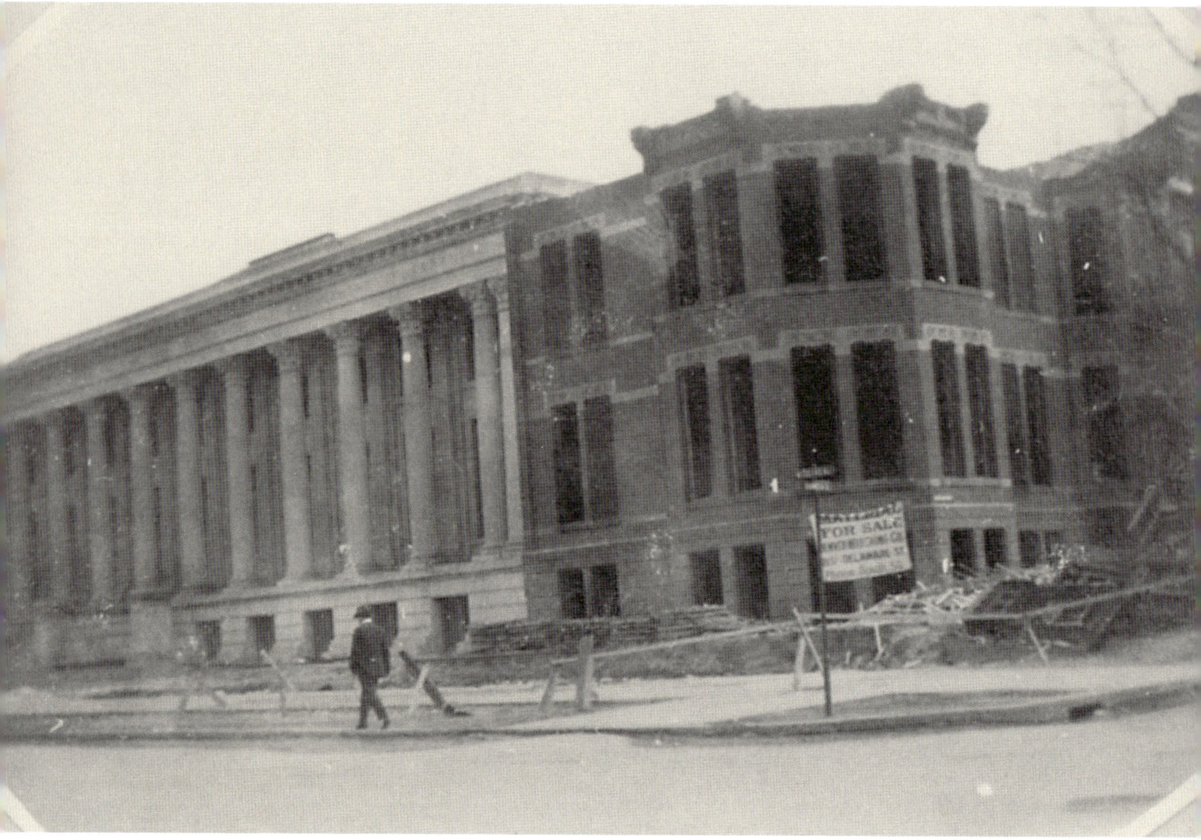

La Veta Place (right), Denver's first upscale apartment building, was undergoing demolition in 1909 or 1910 as the new Denver Public Library (left), a Neoclassical temple designed by Albert Randolph Ross, began welcoming patrons. The 1880 La Veta Place housed 14 luxurious apartments but had become less chic by 1902, when the library bought it. Andrew Carnegie partly funded the library, which featured librarian John Cotton Dana's first-in-the-nation open shelving system. Today, it is a city-operated events venue. (DPL, X-28089.)

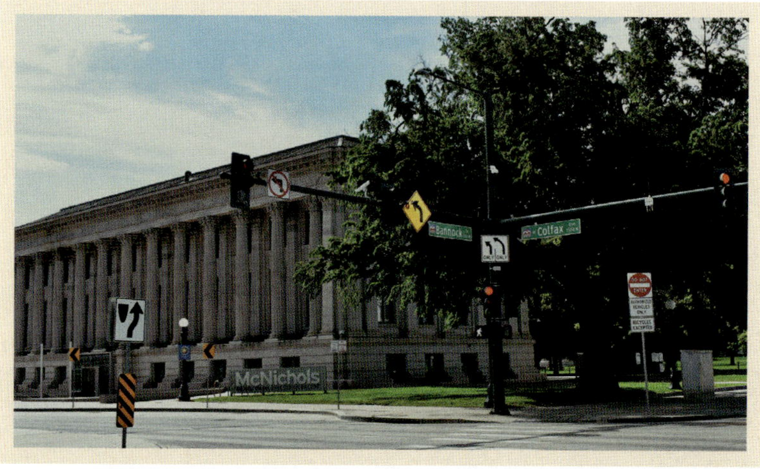

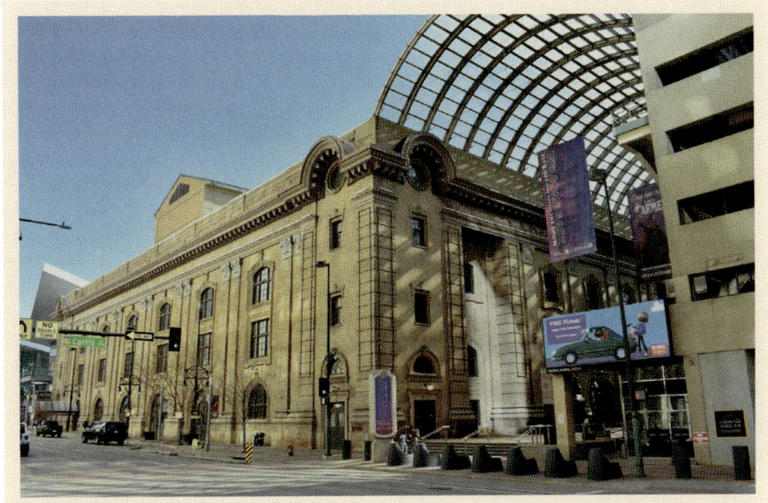

Although not conceived by Mayor Robert W. Speer, completing the Robert Willison–designed Denver Municipal Auditorium climaxed his first term. After an Independence Day public opening concert, the Democratic party occupied it for several days, nominating William Jennings Bryan for the presidency at its 1908 convention. With a removable proscenium, it served double duty as a 3,300-seat performance venue or 12,000-person convention hall. In 2005, after a complete interior rebuild, it reopened as the Ellie Caulkins Opera House. (DPL, MCC-1027.)

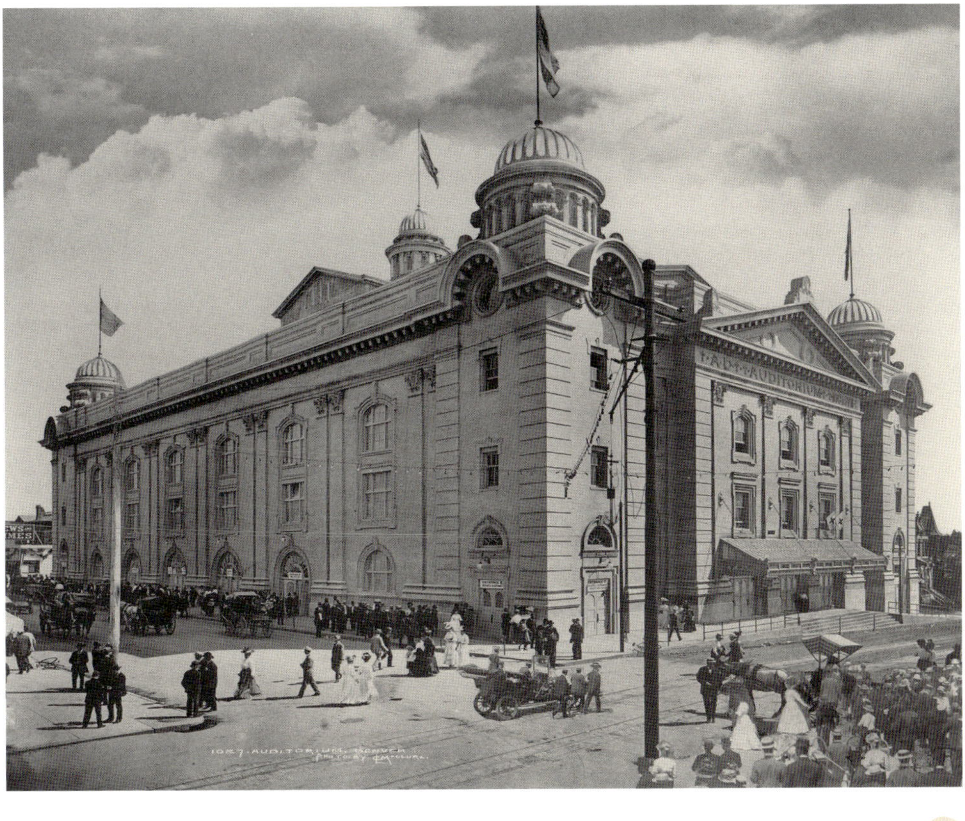

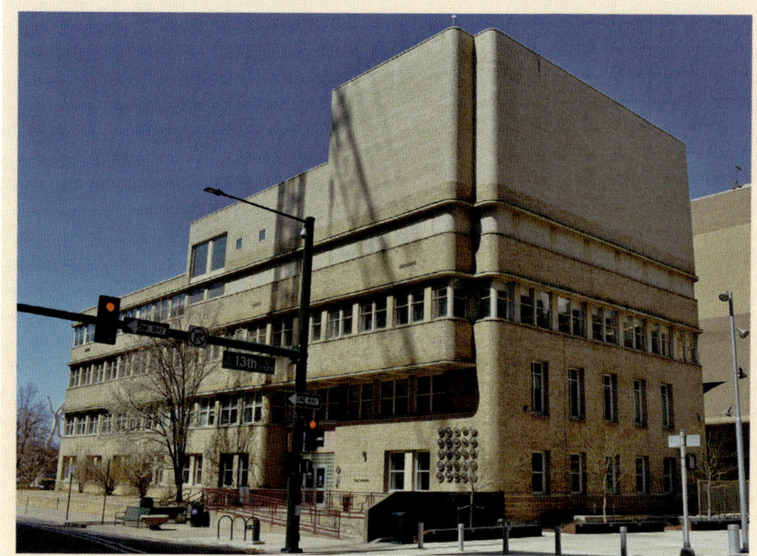

For decades, Denver's police department was headquartered at city hall at Fourteenth and Larimer Streets. In 1940, it relocated to this Art Moderne structure at 1245 Champa Street designed by George Meredith Musick, Earl Chester Morris, and Charles Francis Pillsbury and built by the New Deal's Public Works Administration; the fourth floor served as a jail. The Denver Police Department relocated in 1977, about the same time that the Denver Performing Arts Complex arose nearby. Today, it serves as Colorado Symphony Orchestra's headquarters. (DPL, X-29683.)

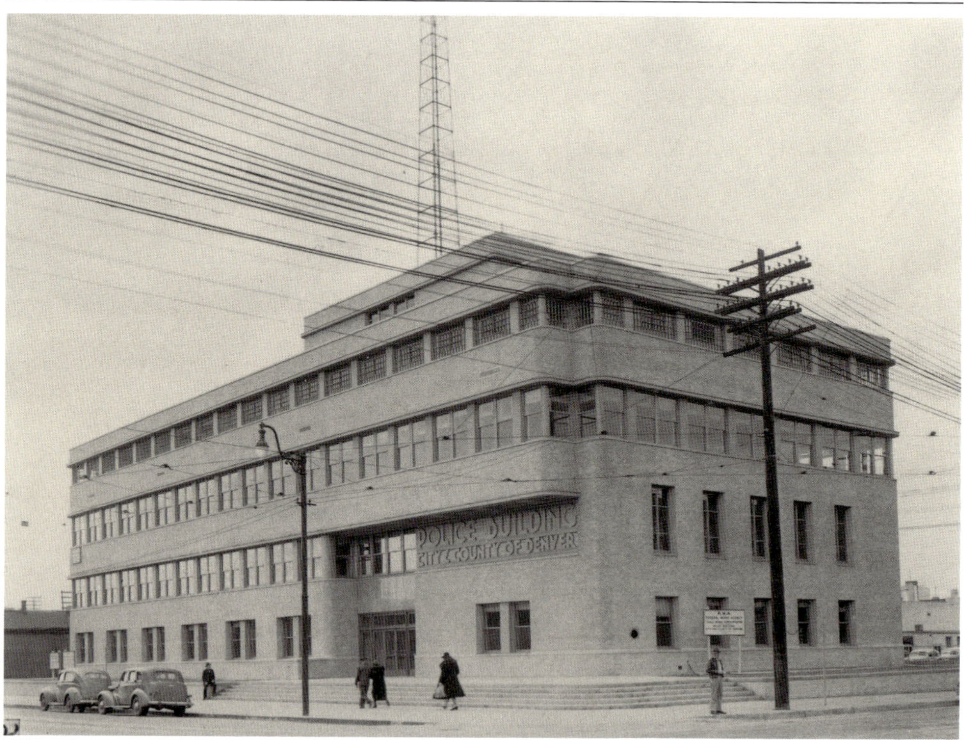

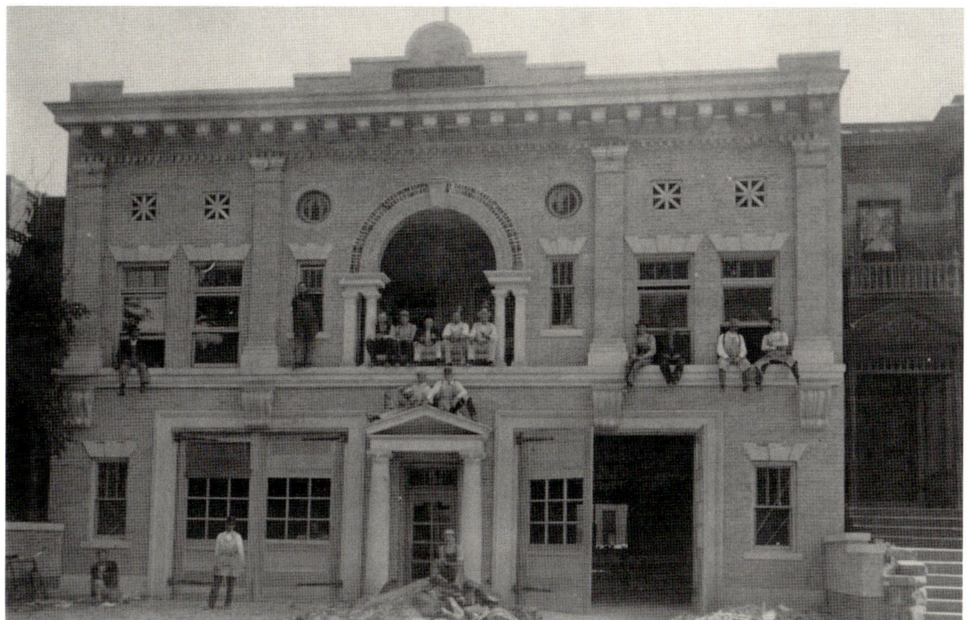

Replacing an earlier firehouse at Colfax Avenue and Broadway (demolished for the Pioneer Fountain), the Glen Huntington–designed Denver Fire Department Station One at 1326 Tremont Place opened in 1909 and served for 66 years. In early years, the lower floor housed horse stalls, but operations were motorized in the 1920s. In 1975, the station was replaced by a new facility nearby, and in 1980, the Denver Firefighters Museum opened in the old building. (HC, 10049257.)

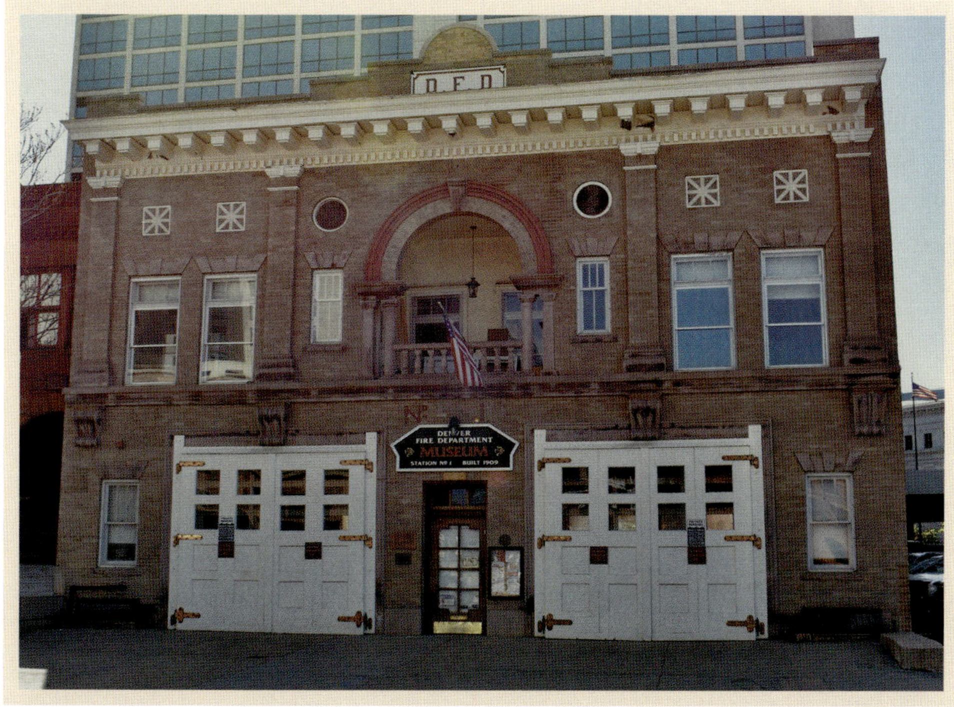

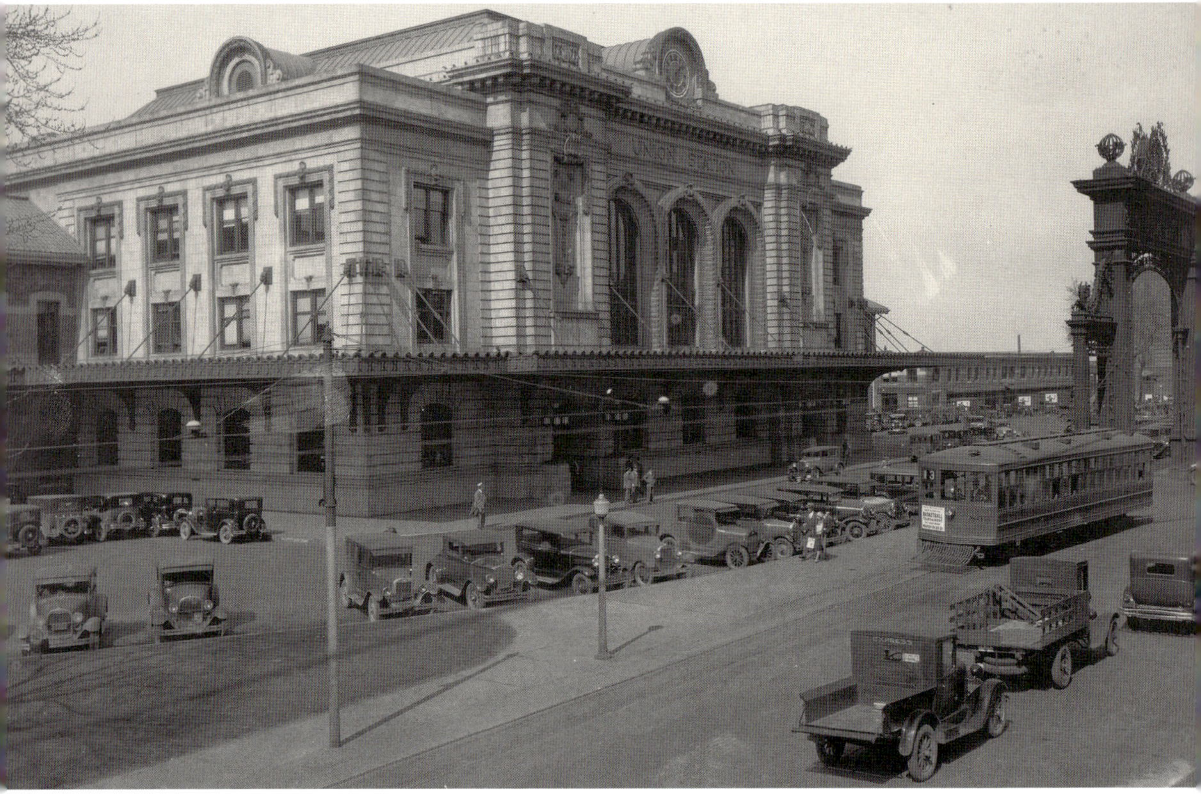

Trains first arrived in Denver in 1870, but it took until 1881 for a consortium of railroads to build Union Station, consolidating several scattered depots. An 1894 fire devastated the structure, which was soon rebuilt, but increasing passenger volume necessitated a larger waiting room. Designed by Aaron Gove and Thomas Walsh, the granite Beaux-Arts central section opened in 1912. In 2014, after a two-year renovation, it reopened as Regional Transportation District's express bus and rail hub, also serving Amtrak. (Author's collection.)

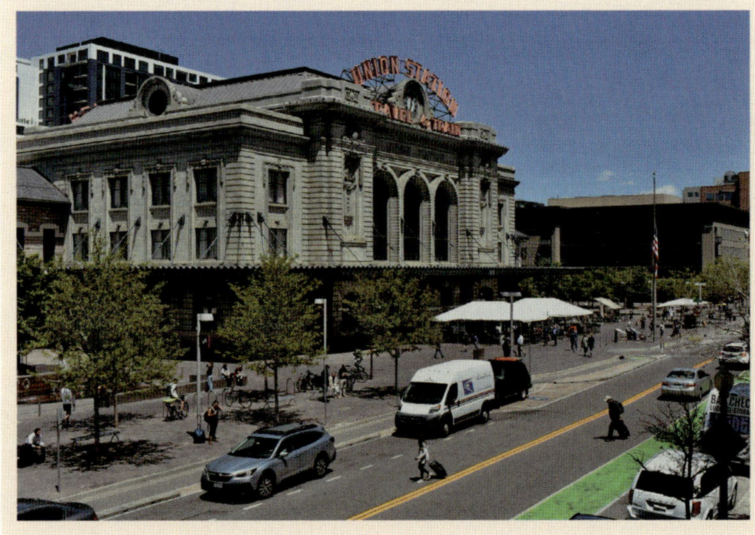

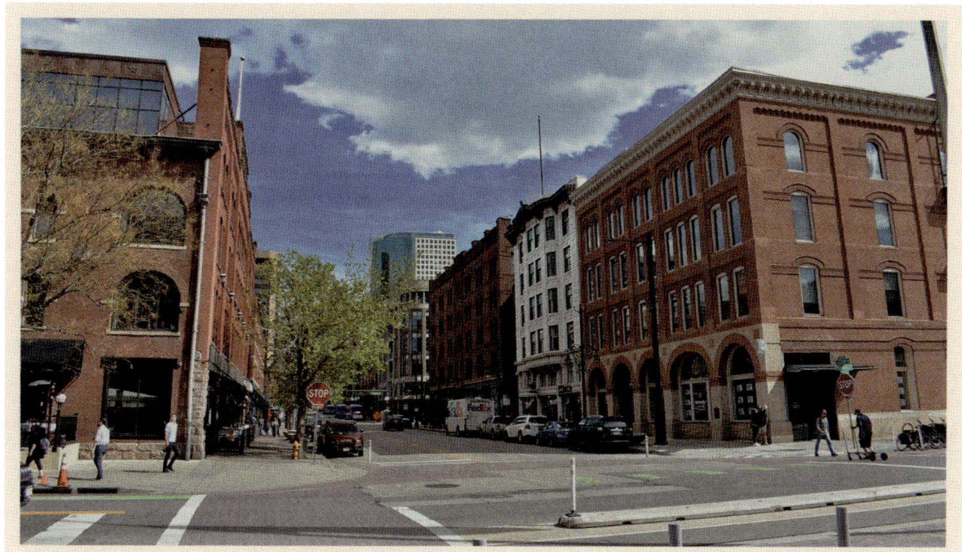

A pet project of Mayor Robert Speer, the Welcome Arch stood in front of Union Station from 1906 until 1931, when Mayor George Begole ordered its removal as a maintenance problem and traffic hazard. East High School student Mary Woodsen designed it to include 1,600 light bulbs. In 1908, "Welcome" on the Seventeenth Street–facing side was replaced with "Mizpah," in reference to the Biblical story of Jacob and Laban, Genesis 31:49: "The Lord watch between me and thee, when we are absent from one another." (Author's collection.)

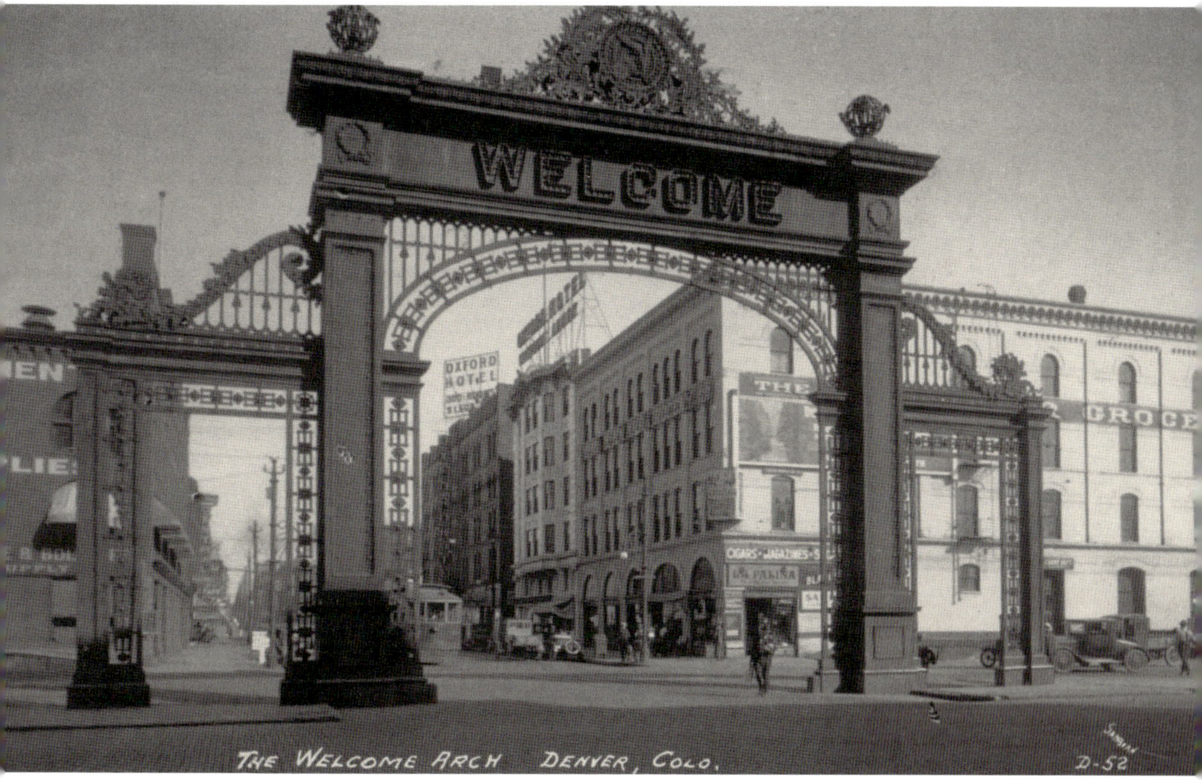

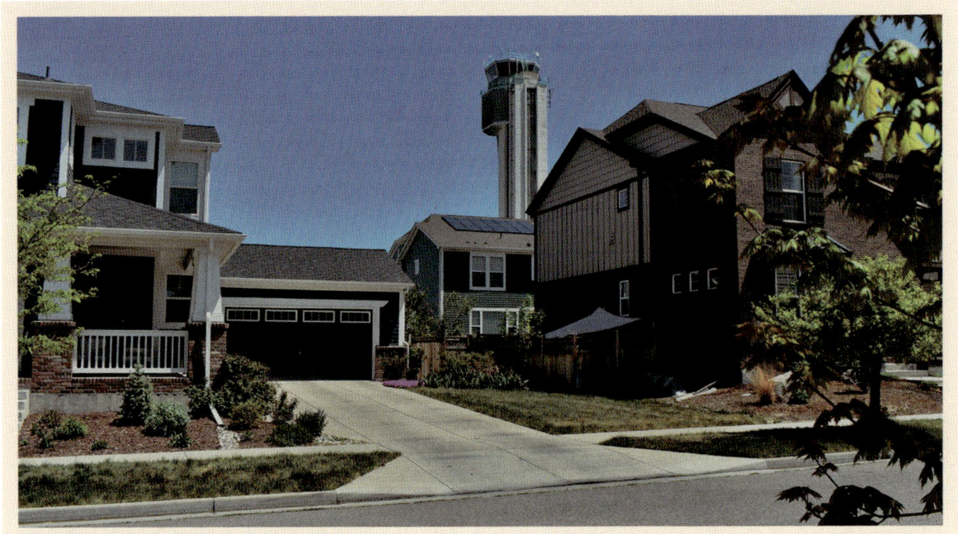

In this c. 1964 postcard view, Stapleton Airfield is in the midst of expansion, having completed, in 1962, the 170-foot-tall control tower. The early-1950s clock tower (left), a legacy of the Quigg Newton mayoralty, would soon give way to a massive new terminal building. After Stapleton International Airport closed in 1995, every part of it was demolished except the control tower, retained as a landmark for Central Park, the neighborhood built on the former airport land. (Author's collection.)

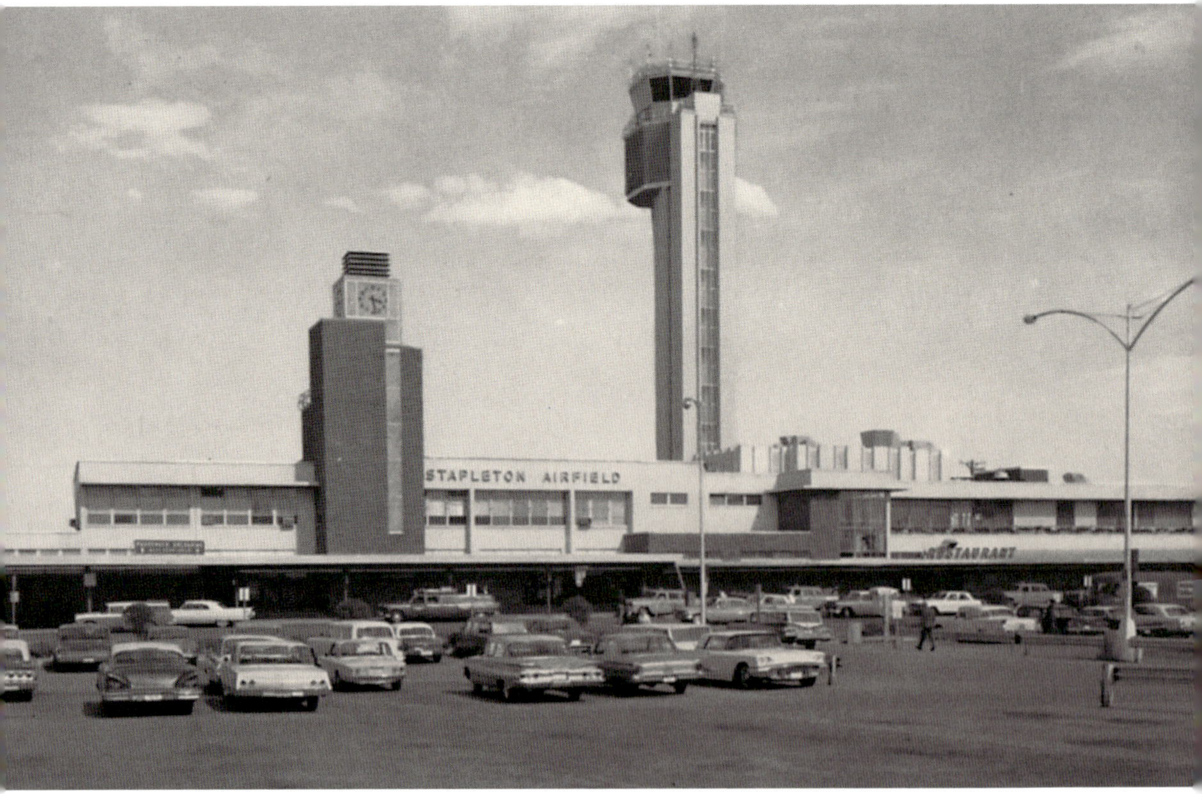

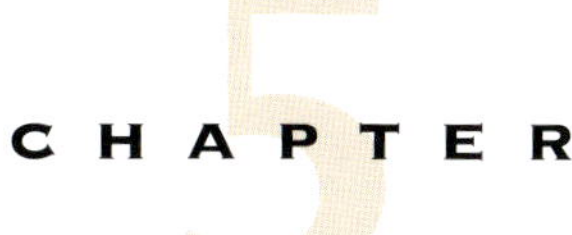

INSTITUTIONS

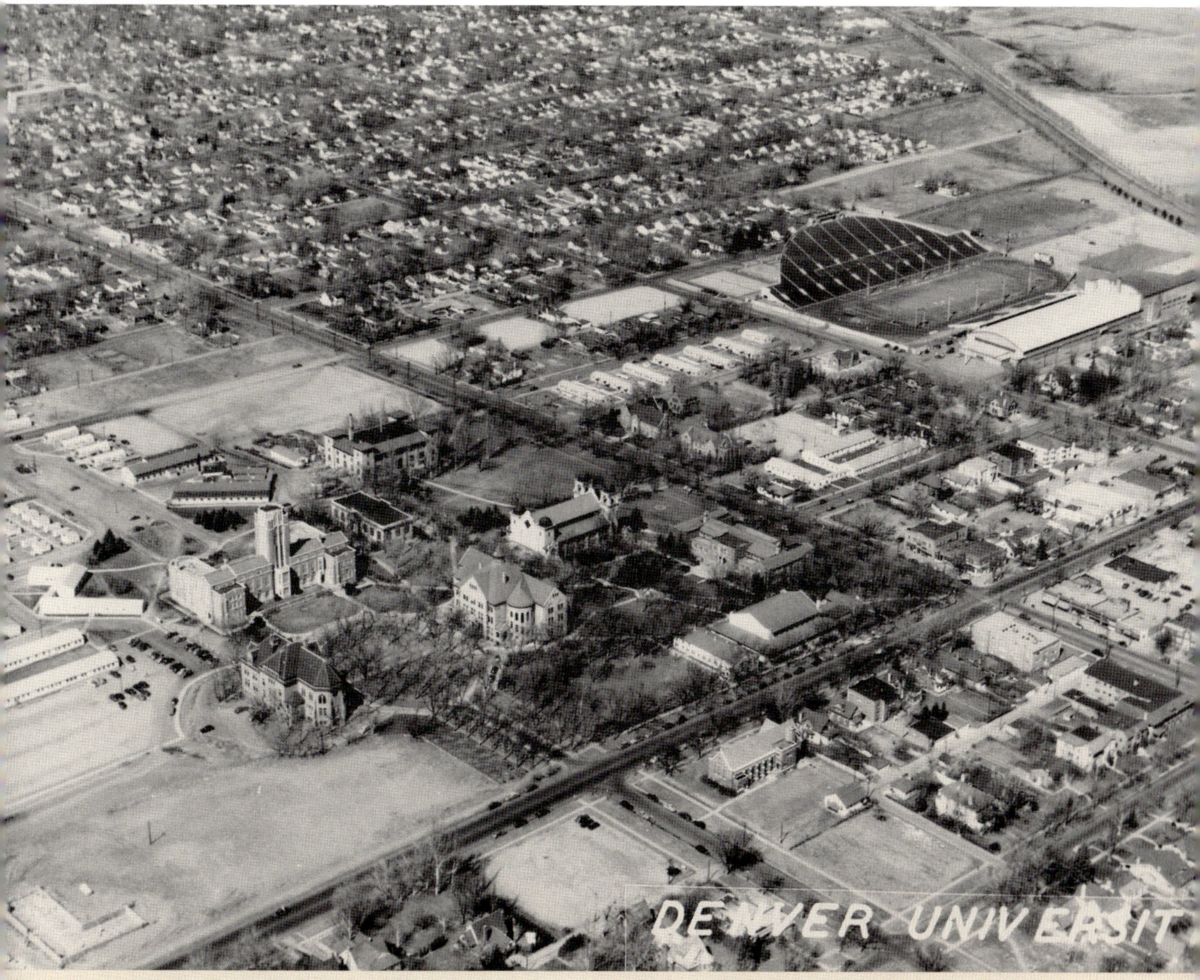

The University of Denver retains most of the historic buildings seen in this c. 1948 aerial photograph, although it lost the Buchtel Memorial Chapel (center) to a fire in 1983. It demolished its distinctive Hilltop Stadium (upper right) in 1971 and Field House (far right) in 1998 for new structures. Today's Interstate 25 runs next to the railroad tracks at upper right. (Author's collection.)

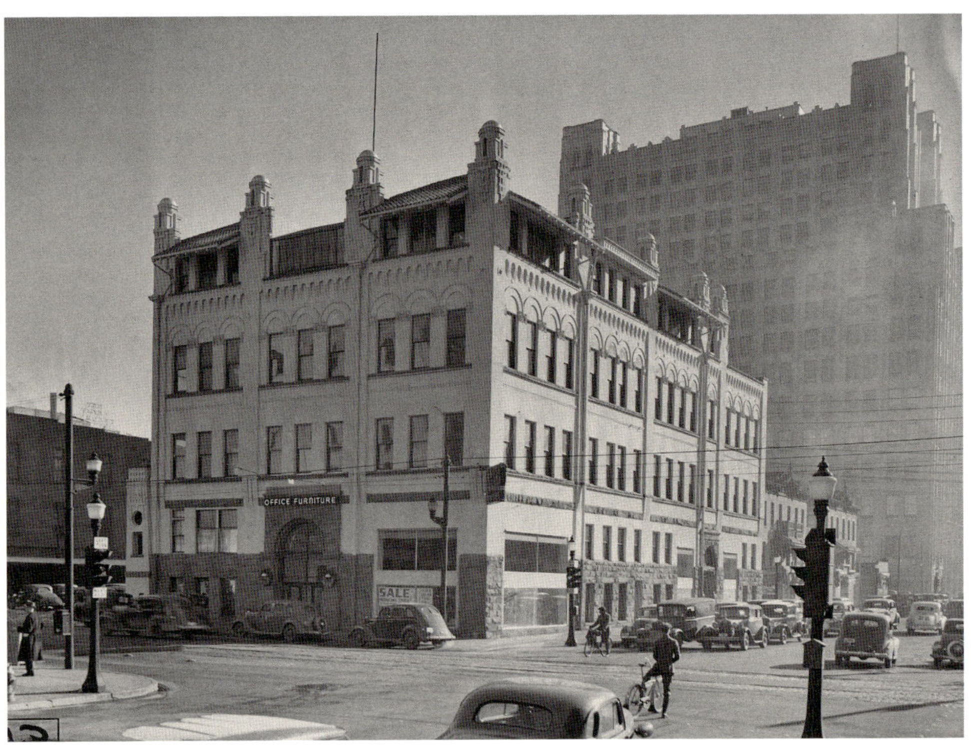

Before the University of Denver constructed its University Park campus, it was located downtown in structures at Fourteenth and Arapahoe Streets, including this one, built in 1888 as the Haish Memorial Training School, funded by barbwire manufacturer Jacob Haish. Later, the university housed other departments in it before selling it to commercial interests, as seen in this 1940s image by Harry Mellon Rhoads with the Mountain States Telephone & Telegraph Building behind it, still standing today. (DPL, Rh-1300.)

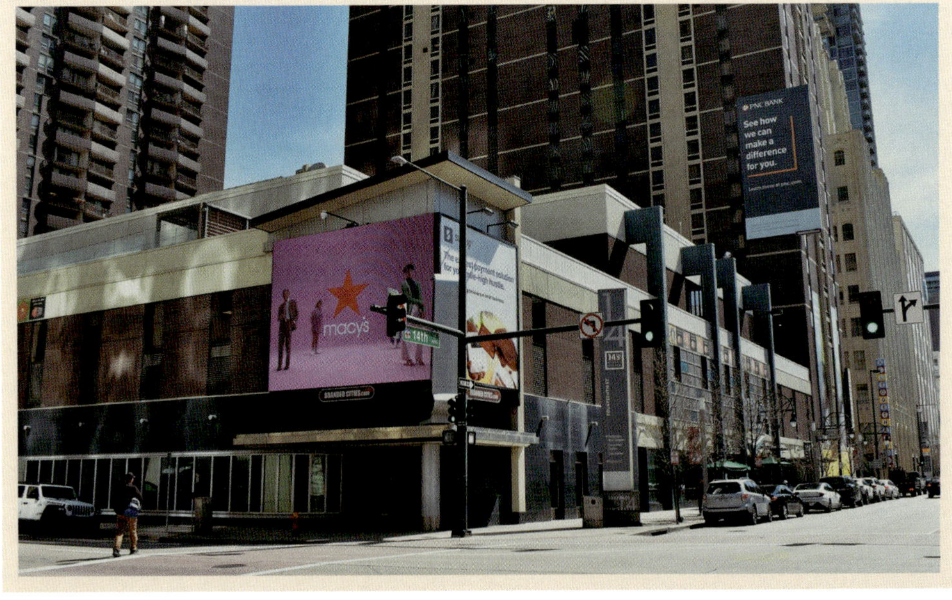

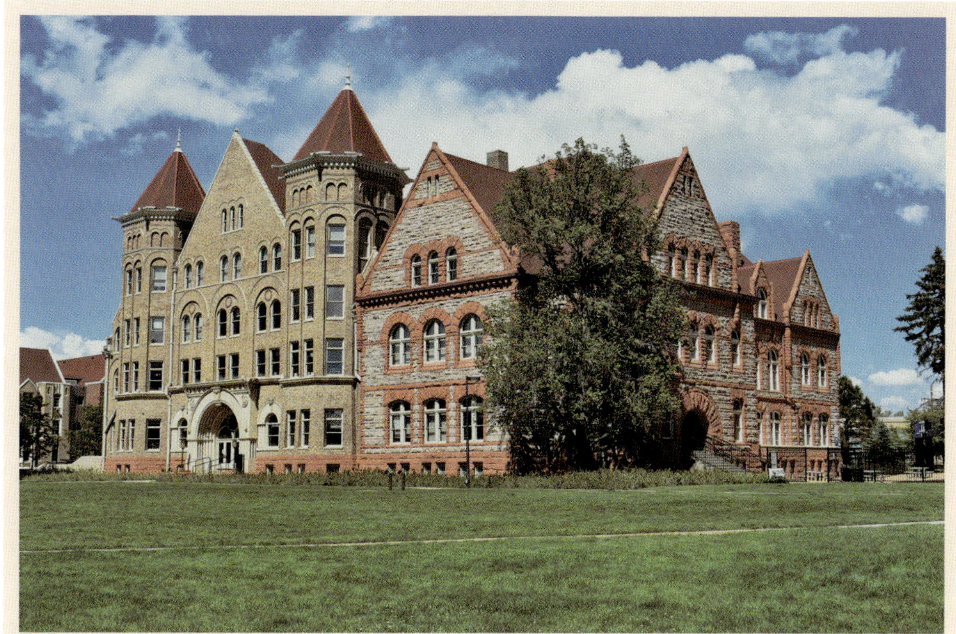

Colorado Women's College in eastern Park Hill had been in operation for just a decade or so, accepting its first students in 1909, when Louis Charles McClure took this photograph of Treat Hall, named for the institution's first president, Jay Porter Treat, and designed in the Richardsonian Romanesque style by Frank Jackson. After the institution closed, the University of Denver bought it in 1982, operating various programs until 2004, when Johnson & Wales University took over, operating until 2021. (DPL, MCC-3591.)

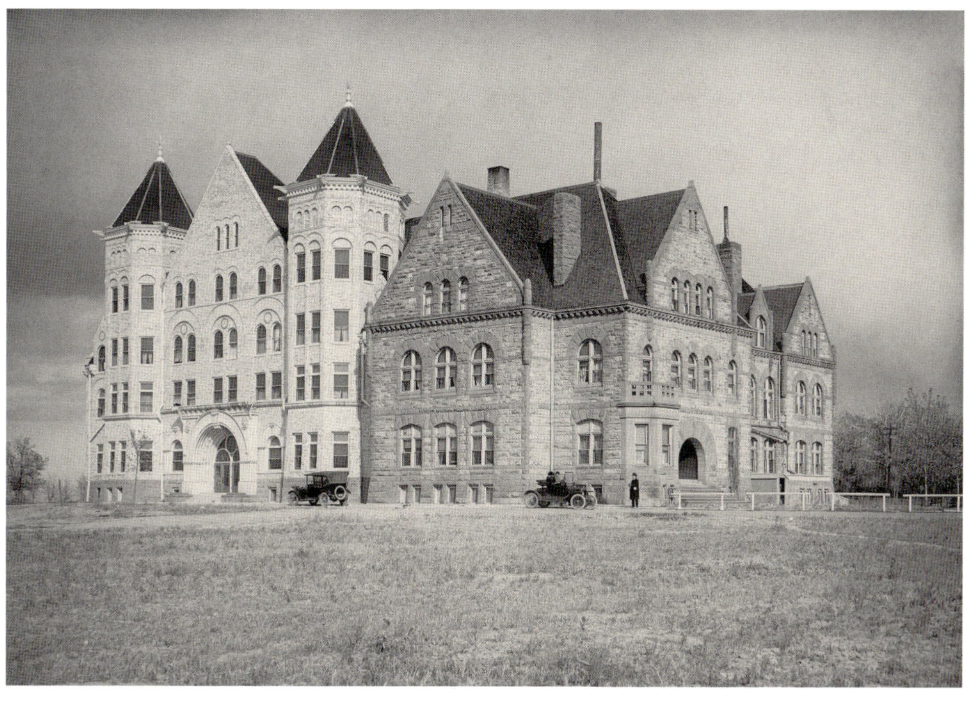

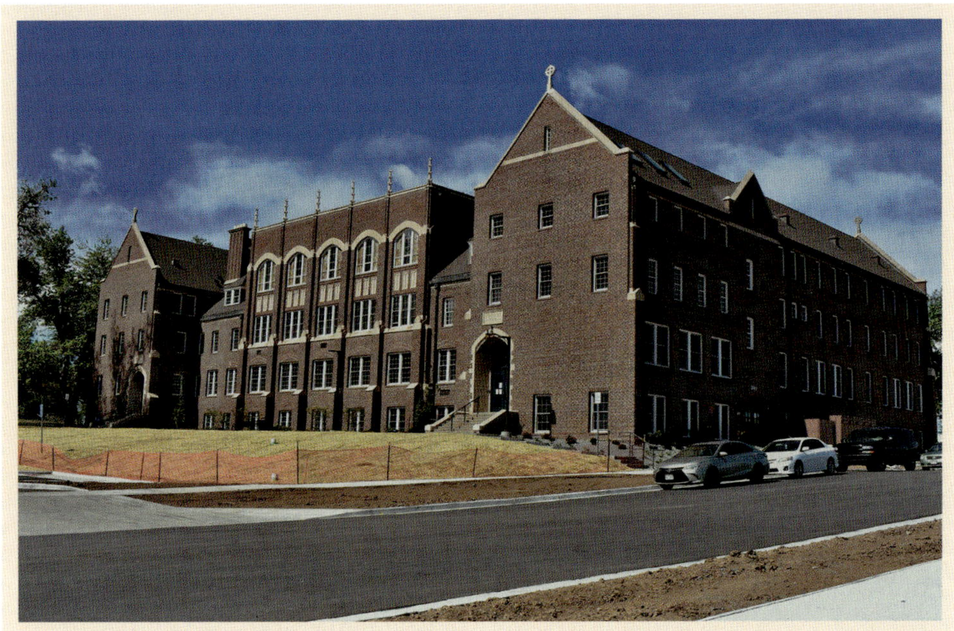

Founded by Mother Pancratia Bonfils in 1888 and operating a Frank Edbrooke–designed six-story combination school and dormitory since 1891, Loretto Heights Academy had grown enough by the 1920s to require more dormitory space. The solution was the Harry W.J. Edbrooke–designed Pancratia Hall, in Collegiate Gothic style, seen here shortly after its 1930 completion. With academic operations having ceased, the hall, one of several repurposed campus buildings, is now home to 72 income-qualified apartments for families. (DPL, Rh-131.)

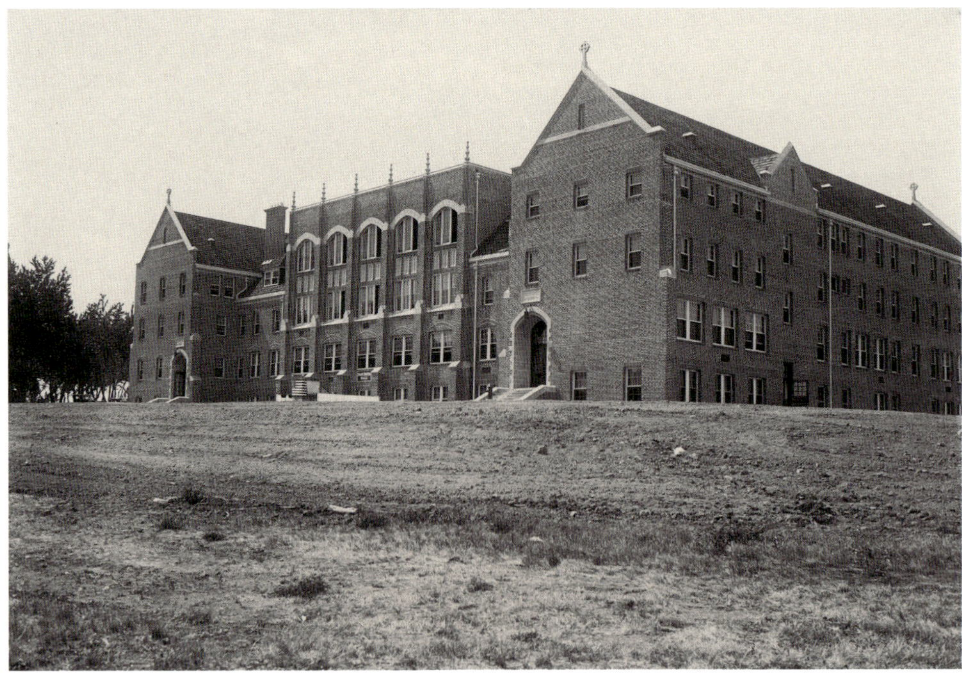

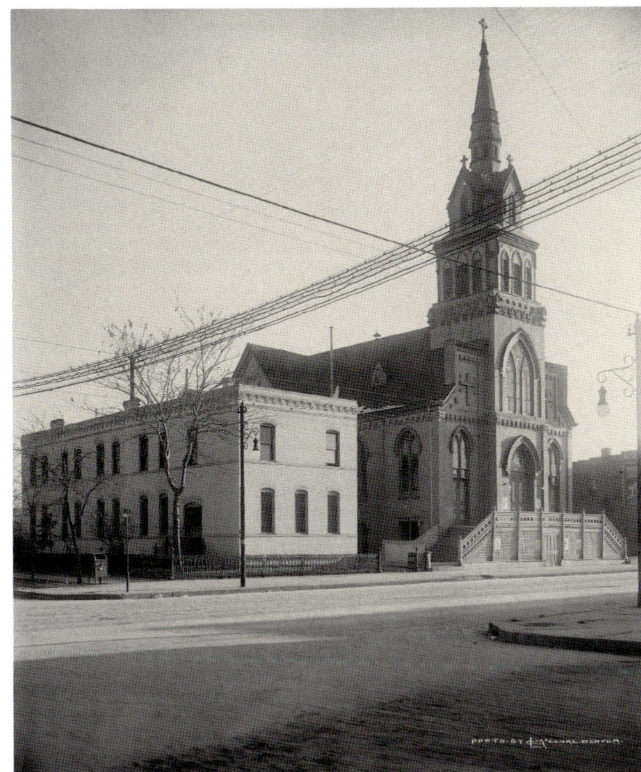

The oldest Denver church still in its original building, Sacred Heart, designed by Emmett Anthony in the Carpenter Gothic style, was Denver's third Roman Catholic church. Completed in 1880 near Larimer and Twenty-Eighth Streets, its original parishioners were Irish and Italian immigrants; today, its congregation is largely Hispanic/Latino. Former Black slave Julia Greeley, baptized here in 1880, became known as Denver's "Angel of Charity" for her philanthropy and as of this book's publication is under Vatican investigation for canonization. (DPL, MCC-4253.)

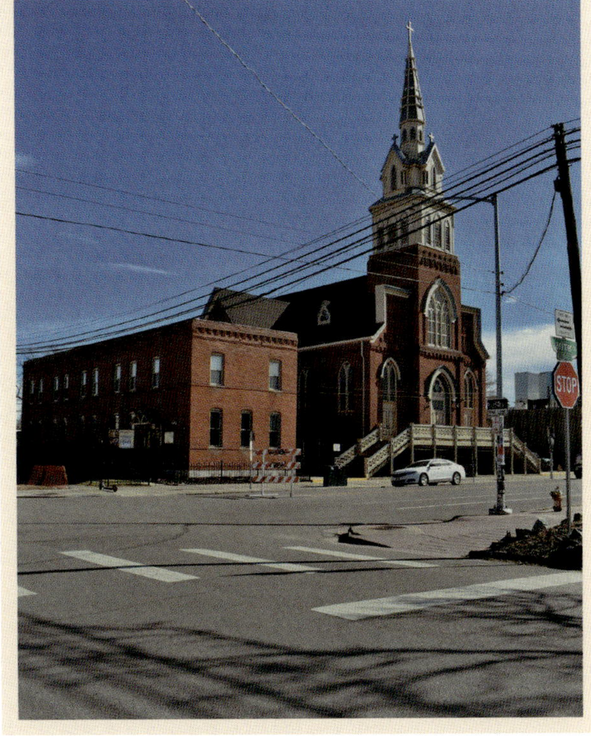

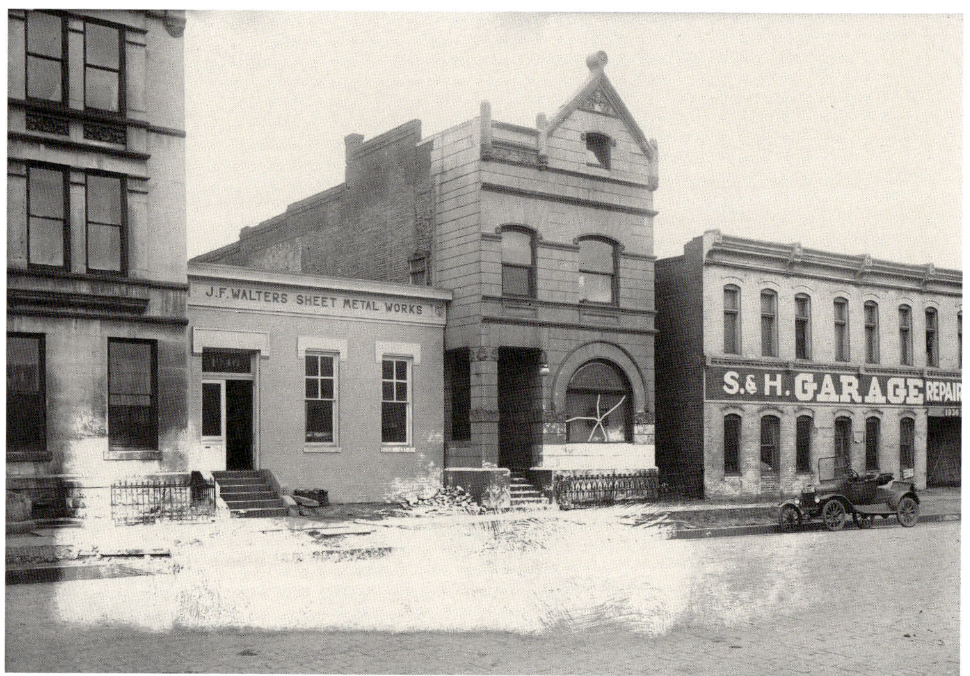

Although remembered today for its original incarnation as a brothel, Jennie Rogers's House of Mirrors (later owned by Mattie Silks), this 1889 building designed by William Quayle became an early home of Denver's first Buddhist congregation. Founded in 1916 with about 250 Japanese and Japanese American members, Tri-State Denver Buddhist Temple, as it known now, occupied the building from 1919, when it was bought for $10,000, until 1947, when it constructed a new temple at 1947 Lawrence Street. (HC, X7755.)

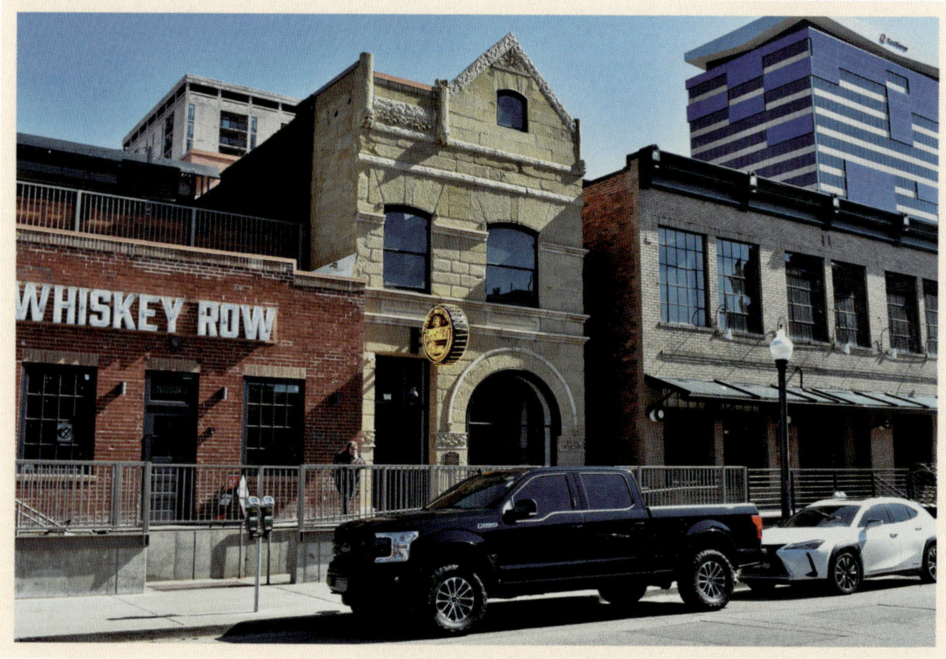

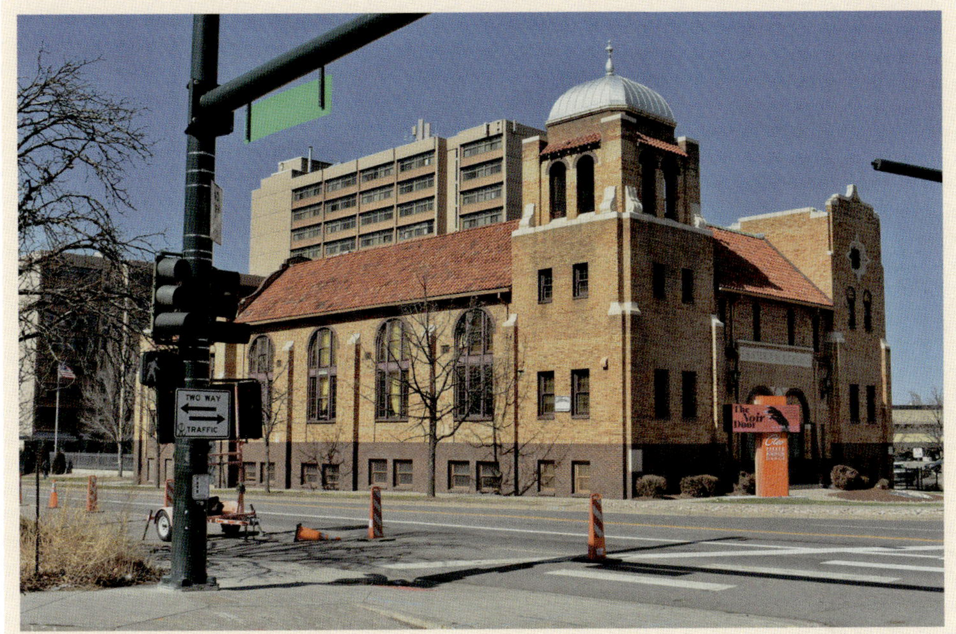

Organized in 1868, Shorter AME Church was first named St. John, changing its name to honor Bishop James Shorter in 1880. In 1889, the church consecrated a new building at Park and Twentieth Avenues and Washington Street. That church burned in 1925, a fire possibly set by the Ku Klux Klan. A new Shorter, designed by the architectural firm Ireland and Parr, opened in its place in 1926. After Shorter relocated, Cleo Parker Robinson Dance took over the structure. (DPL, Rh-4575.)

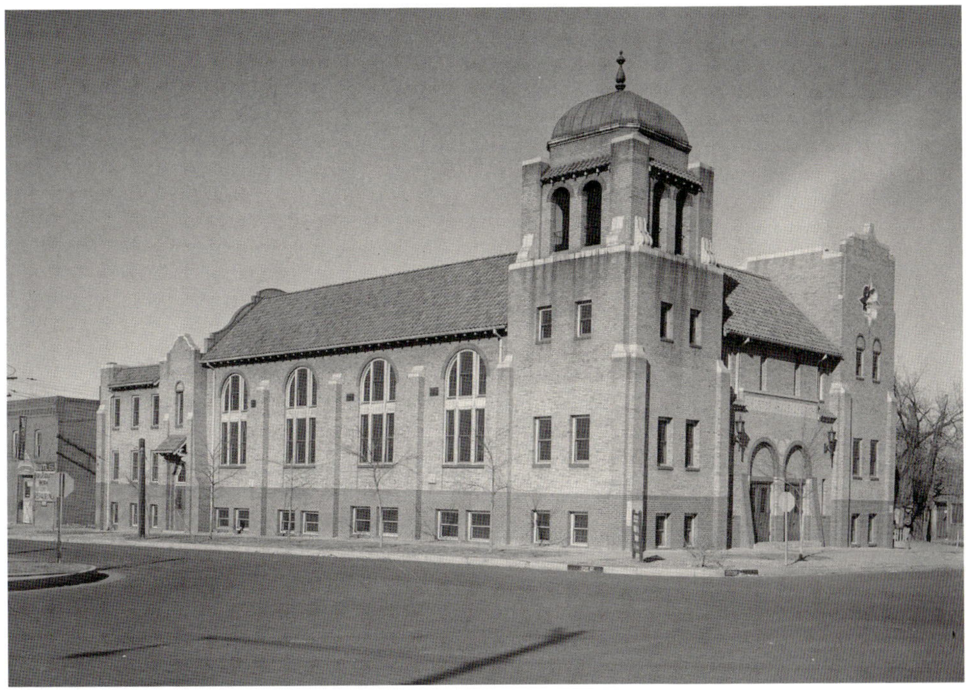

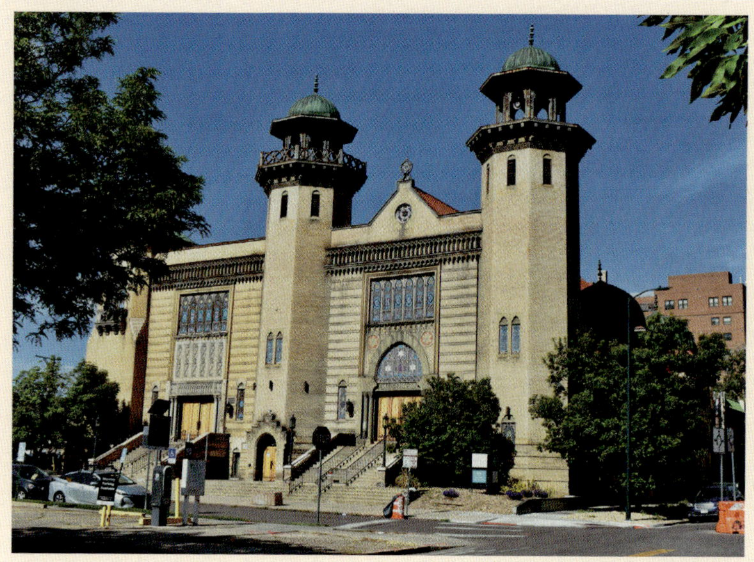

John Humphreys utilized Moorish Islamic influences in designing Temple Emanuel at Sixteenth Avenue and Pearl Street for Denver's oldest (1873) Jewish congregation but died shortly before its 1898 completion. The temple built a matching addition (left) in 1924 and relocated in 1957. The building has since housed Baptists, Pentecostals, and other religious groups and a nonreligious event center. Temple Emanuel member Francis Wisebart Jacobs helped organize, with Rabbi William Friedman, Denver Community Chest, the forerunner of United Way. (DPL, Rh-1204.)

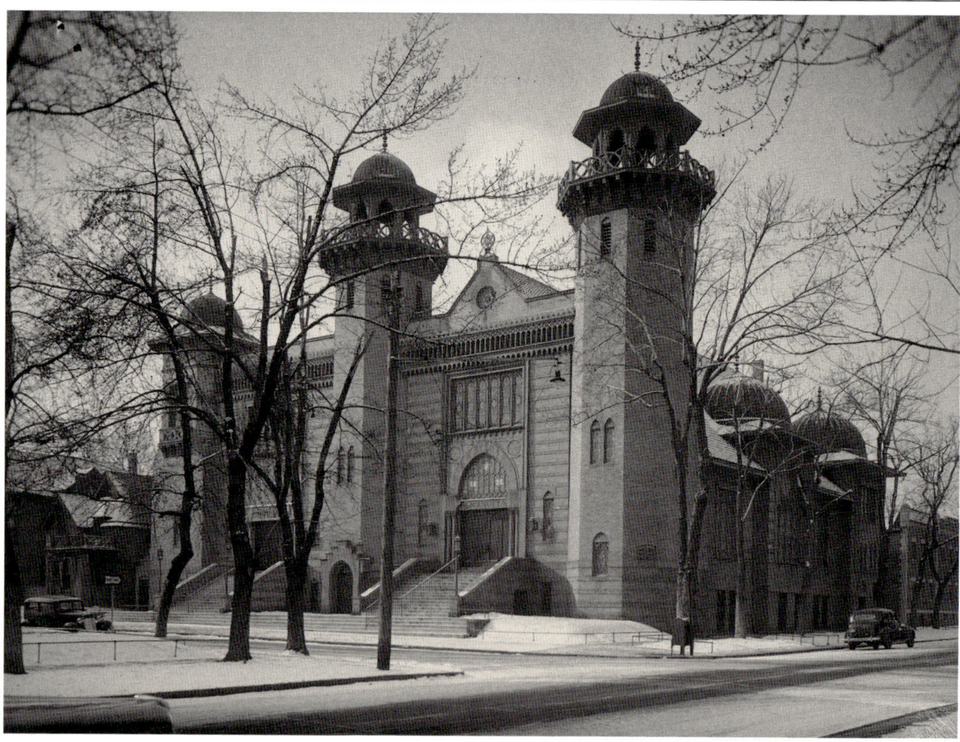

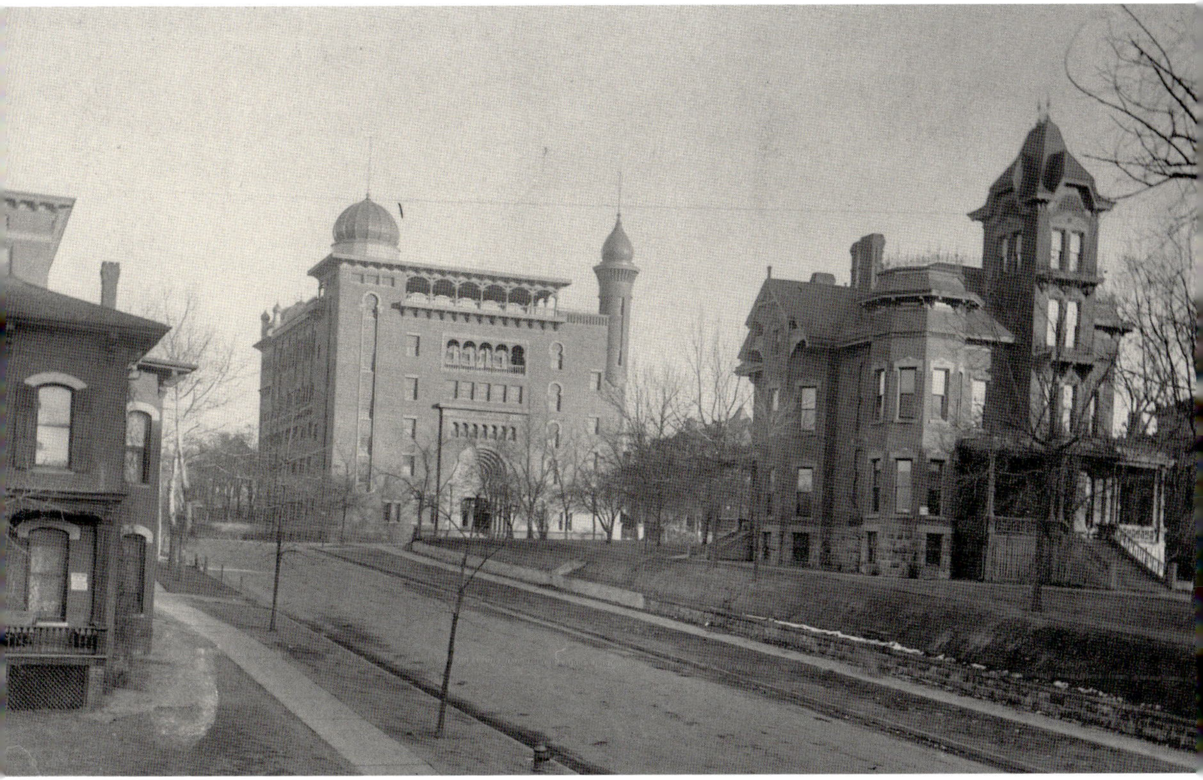

El Jebel Temple, designed by Viggio and Harold Baerresen and dedicated in 1907, remains one of Denver's most eclectic buildings, even as nearby mansions have succumbed to skyscrapers or parking lots. With domes, Moorish arches, and Venetian arcades, the temple once housed Denver's Shriners, who relocated to northwest Denver in 1924. It later housed Rocky Mountain Consistory No. 2, another Masonic group, and Eulipions, a Black theatrical company. Historic Denver Inc. owns an easement, protecting it from demolition. (DPL, X-23095.)

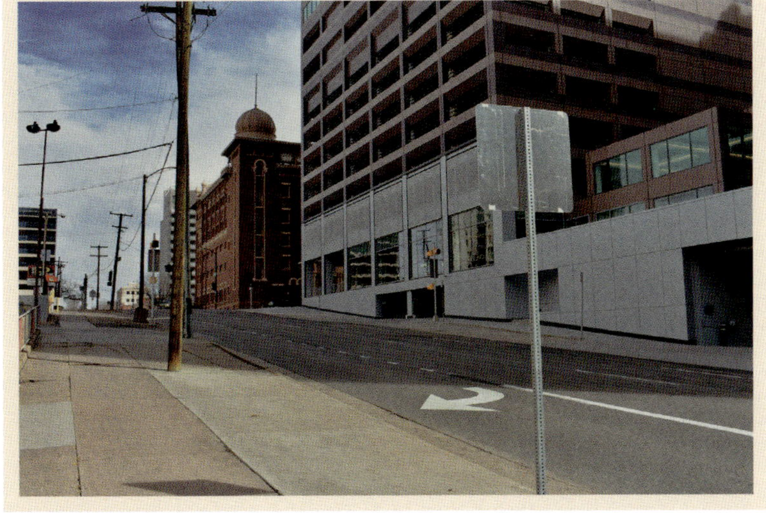

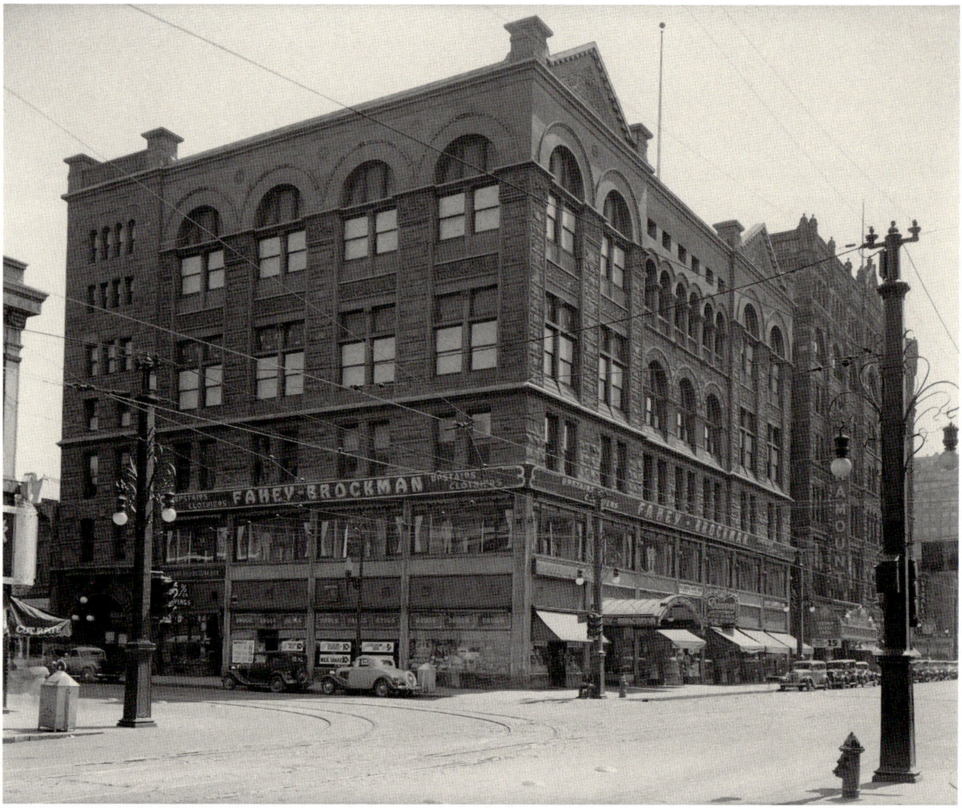

Today, a casual observer would never guess that the Masonic Building at Sixteenth and Welton Streets, seen here in the late 1930s, barely survived a four-alarm 1984 fire. Designed by 33rd-degree Mason Frank E. Edbrooke, the temple opened in 1890. Its cross-alley neighbor, the A. Morris Stuckert–designed Kittredge Building, opened a year later, constructed by Charles Marble Kittredge. Both survive today as renovated jewels on the Sixteenth Street Mall, the Masons continuing to meet in their building. (DPL, X-24873.)

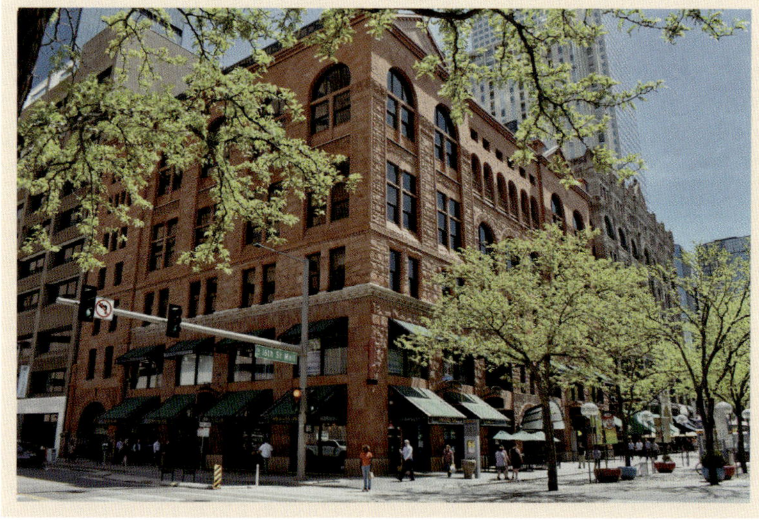

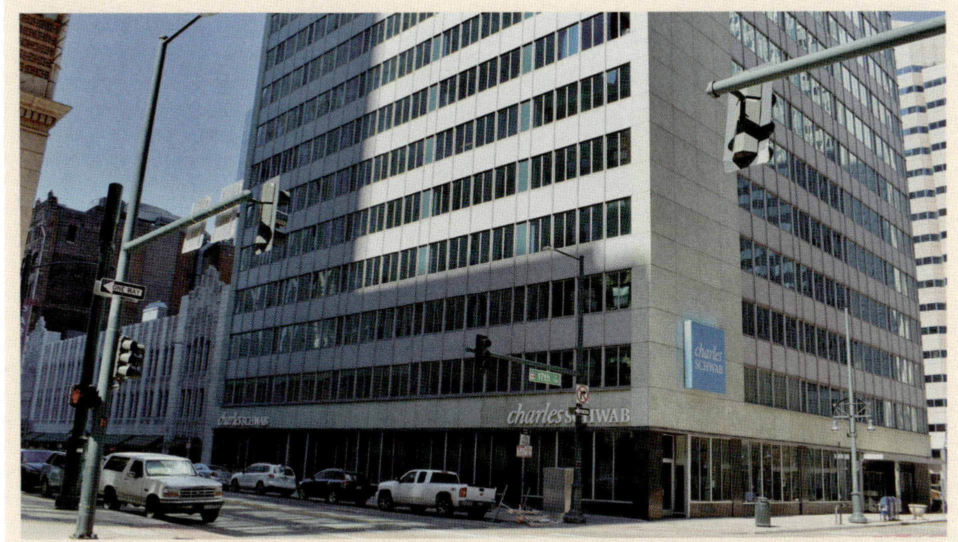

The Denver Club, founded in 1880, still occupies the corner of Seventeenth Street and Glenarm Place, even if its original clubhouse, an 1889 Richardsonian design by Ernest Varian and Frederick Sterner, has been gone since 1953, replaced by Raymond Harry Ervin's International-style skyscraper. Neighboring First Congregational Church was still surrounded by vestiges of the block's original residential character, although the Kittredge Building blocked the southwesterly view. The Temple Buell–designed Paramount Theatre replaced the church in 1930. (DPL, H-256.)

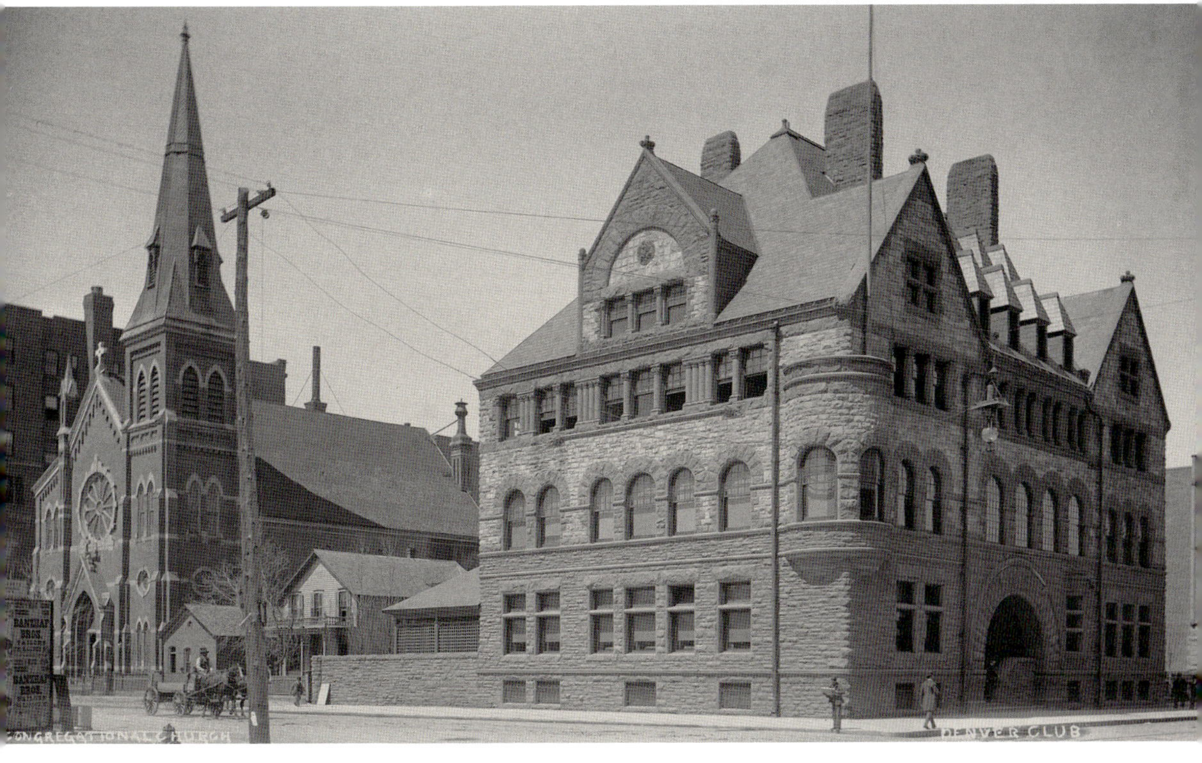

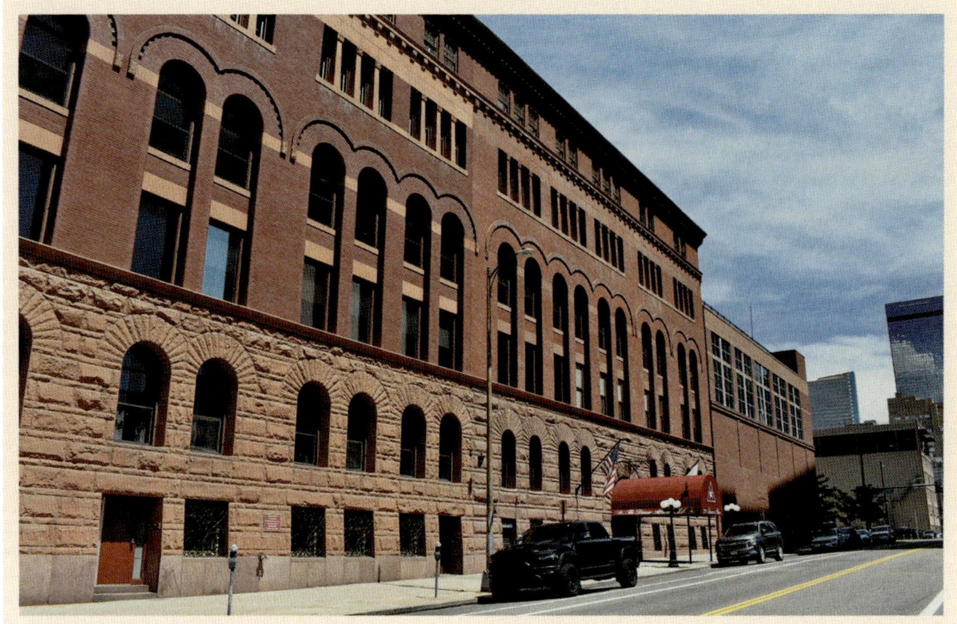

Farther down Glenarm Place, at 1325, another Richardsonian design by Varian and Sterner houses the Denver Athletic Club, one of America's oldest downtown athletic clubs. Founded in 1884, the club's building opened in 1890 and was added onto in 1892, 1973, 1984, and 1996. Also in 1890, the Denver Athletic Club sponsored Denver's first organized football game, pitting the University of Colorado team, not yet the Buffaloes, against club members, who proved to be the better athletes. (HC, 20100027.)

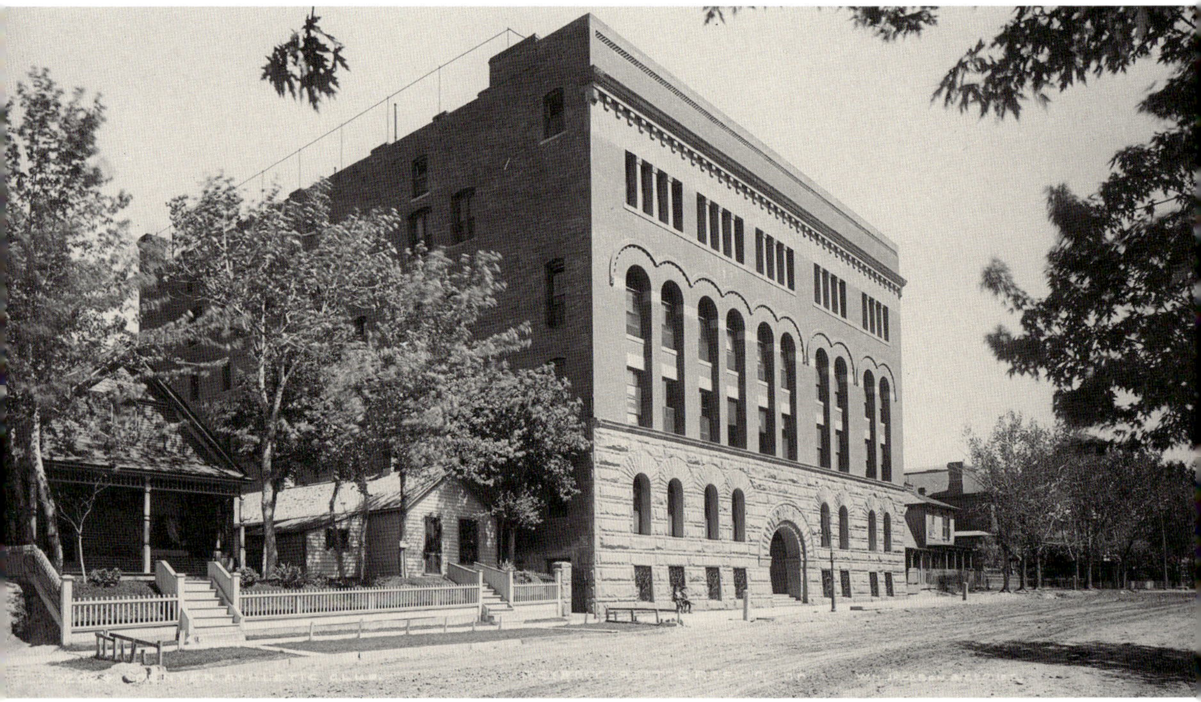

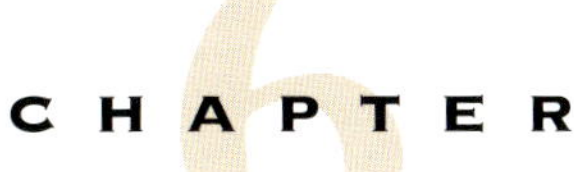

Residences

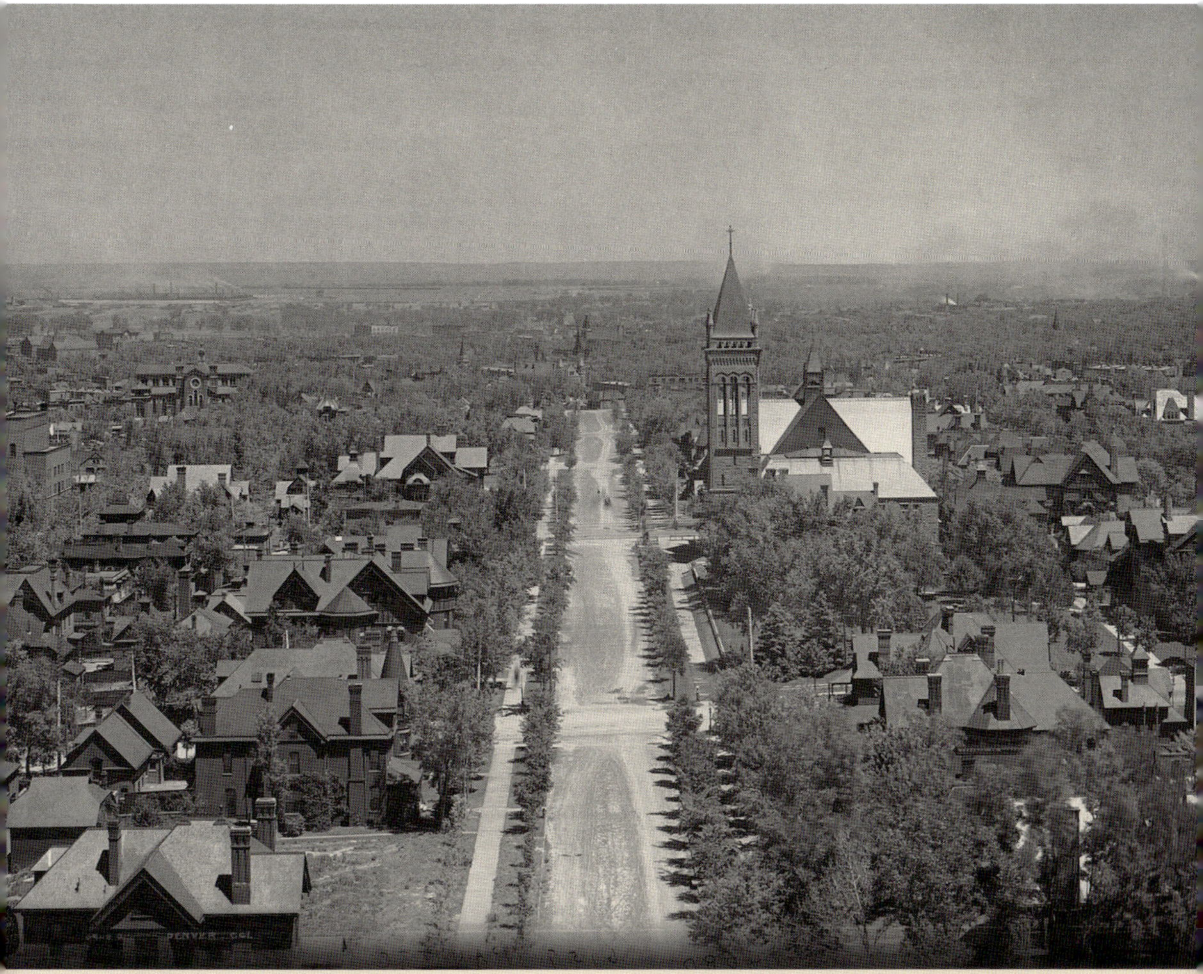

Central Presbyterian Church is the tallest element in this c. 1890 William Henry Jackson photograph of Sherman Street looking north from the capitol dome. One of Capitol Hill's prestigious thoroughfares, Sherman Street was lined on both sides from Colfax Avenue to Twentieth Avenue by millionaires' mansions, including those of Simon Guggenheim, Peter Gottesleben, Erastus Hallack, and Benjamin Woodward. (HC, 10025123.)

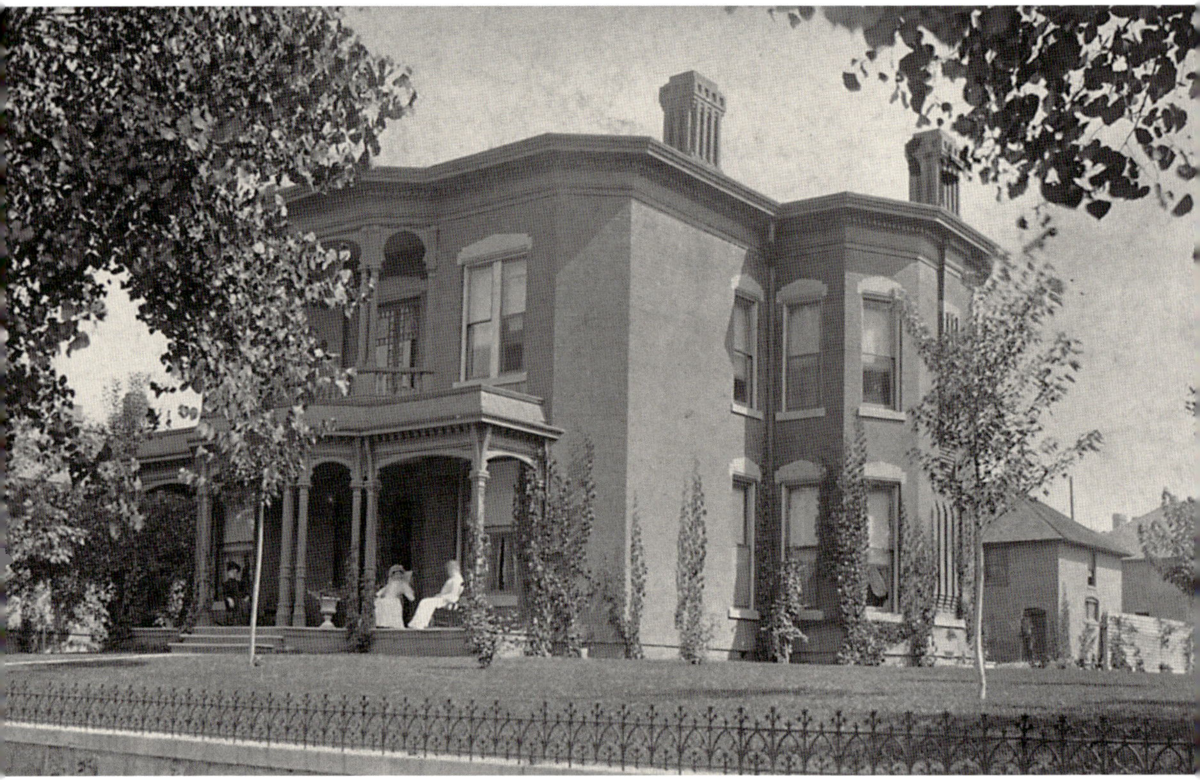

Surrounded now by art museums, the Byers-Evans House was once one of many fine homes south of downtown in today's Golden Triangle neighborhood. William Newton Byers and his wife, Elizabeth, built it in 1883, selling it in 1889 to William Gray Evans, son of second territorial governor John Evans, and his wife, Cornelia, who named the house Victoria. The Evans family built additions and lived in the home until 1981; it has been a museum since 1990. (DPL, X-26104.)

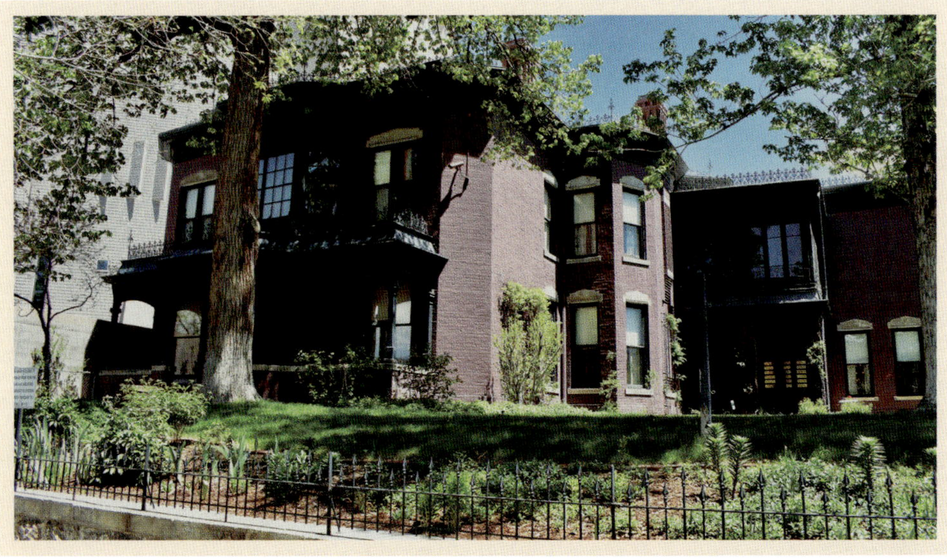

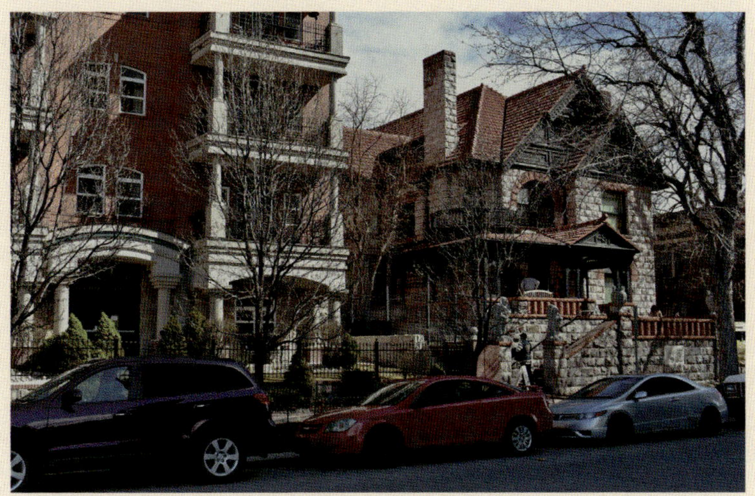

During their eight-year partnership, William Lang and Marshall Pugh were Denver's foremost residential architects, specializing in eclectic Queen Anne/Richardsonian Romanesque designs. On Pennsylvania Street, they designed the house at 1344 (left) for mining and cattle magnate Joshua Monti; it was later demolished by a Baptist organization. The house at 1340 (right) was built for Isaac Large, who sold it to mining engineer J.J. Brown and his wife, Margaret Tobin Brown. Today, it is the Molly Brown House Museum. (DPL, WHJ-10352.)

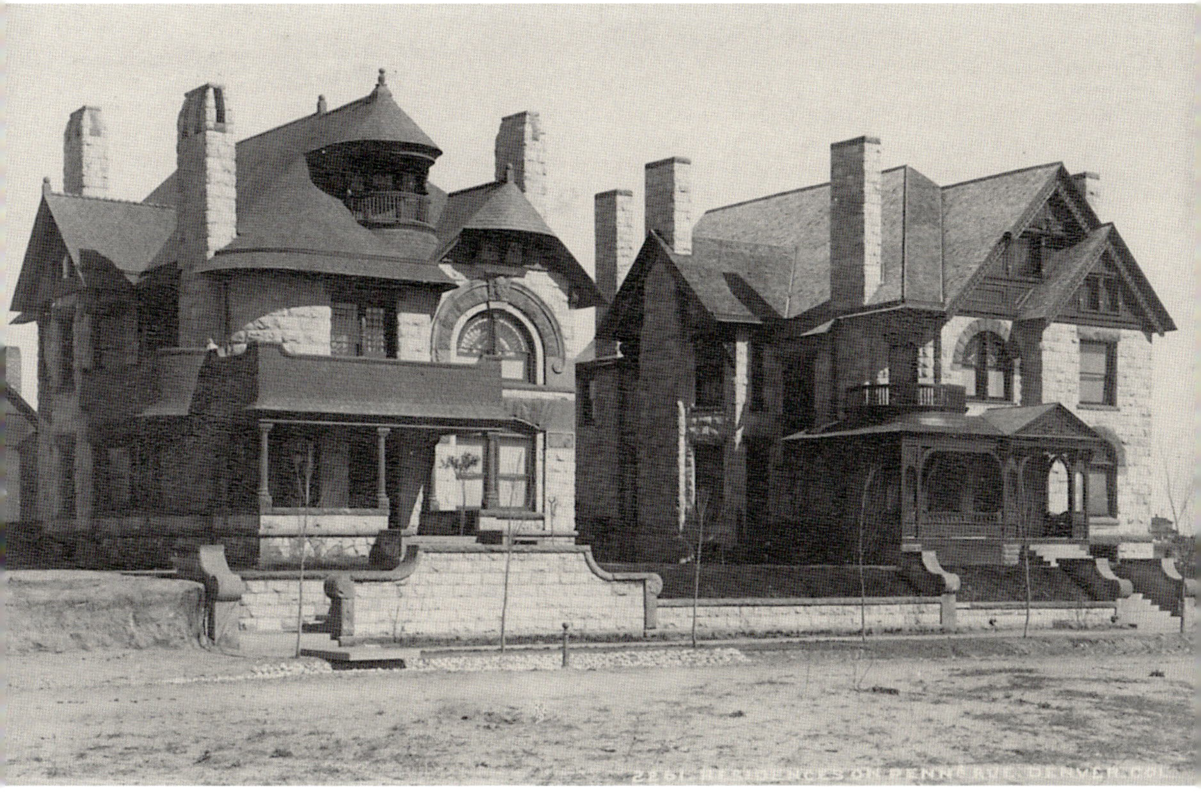

The identity of the Black man on the porch at 1415 Vine Street is unknown, but the home's first owner, banker Samuel Rose, is well documented. This was part of a grouping of four homes along Vine Street (one now demolished) designed by William Lang and Marshall Pugh. Sadly, after the Panic of 1893, the brilliant Lang lost his practice and, quite possibly, his mind; he died, aged 51, after being struck by a train in Illinois in 1897. (DPL, X-19076.)

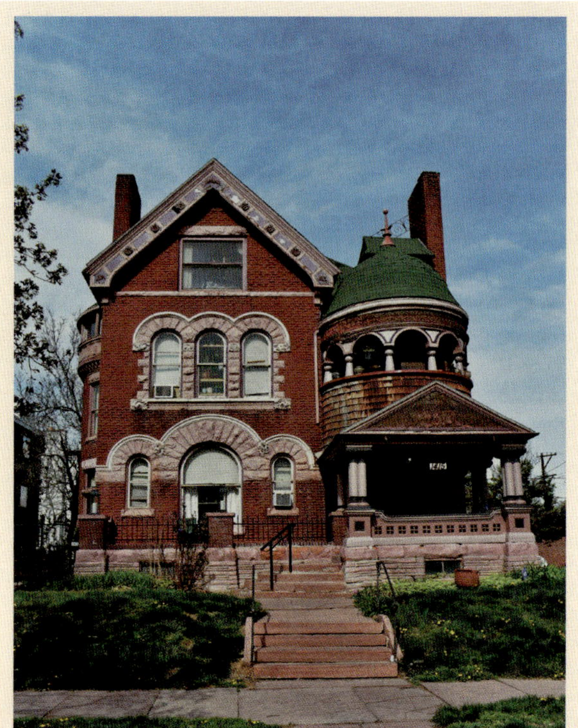

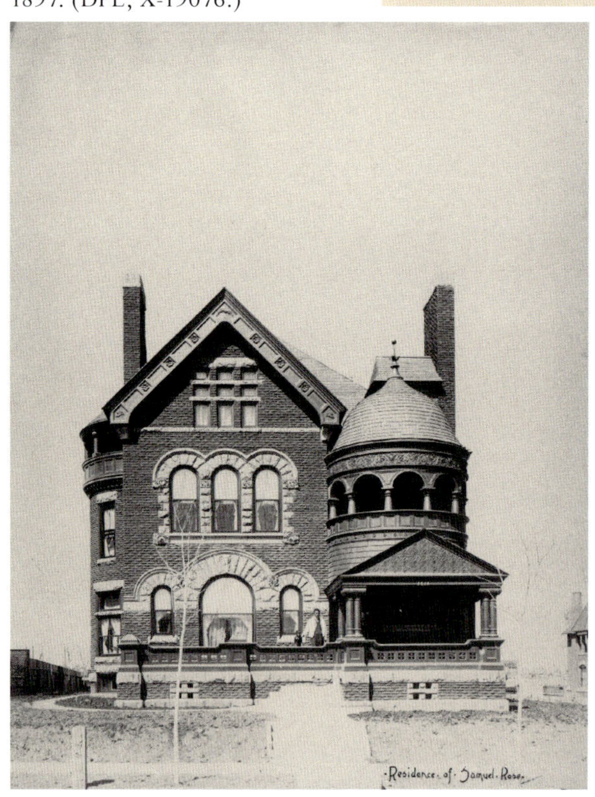

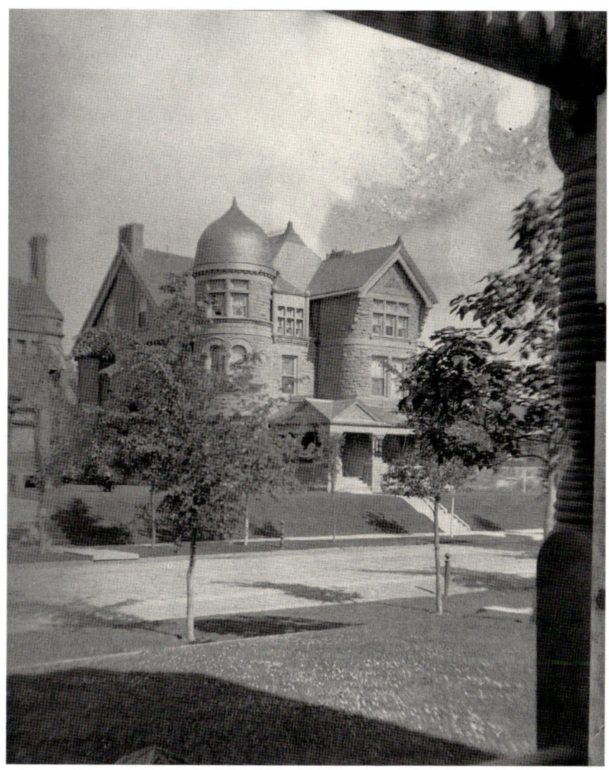

In today's Swallow Hill Historic District, Lang and Pugh designed a Longmont sandstone masterpiece, 1600 Ogden Street, for real estate speculator George W. Bailey. His family lived here until the Panic of 1893 decimated his fortune. Wholesale grocer Frederick W. Struby then bought it. Jean and Paul Shank, "Architects of Appetites," operated gourmet restaurant the Tiffin Inn in the house during the 1940s and 1950s; today, the Bailey Mansion houses a law office. (DPL, X-27087.)

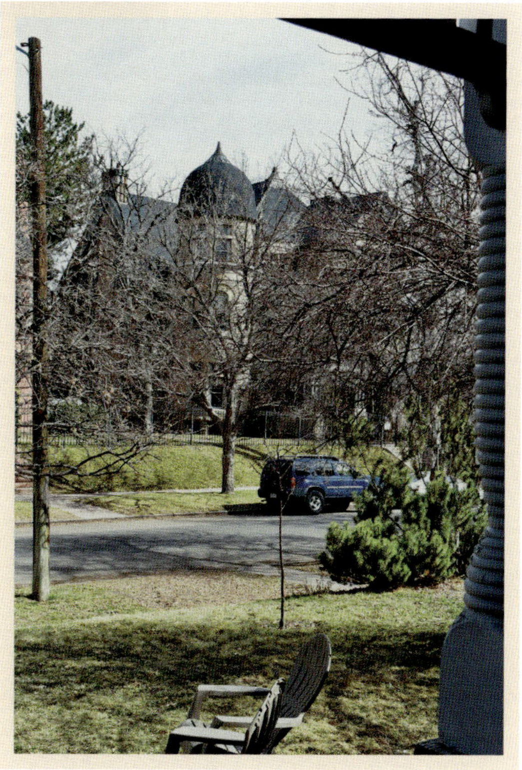

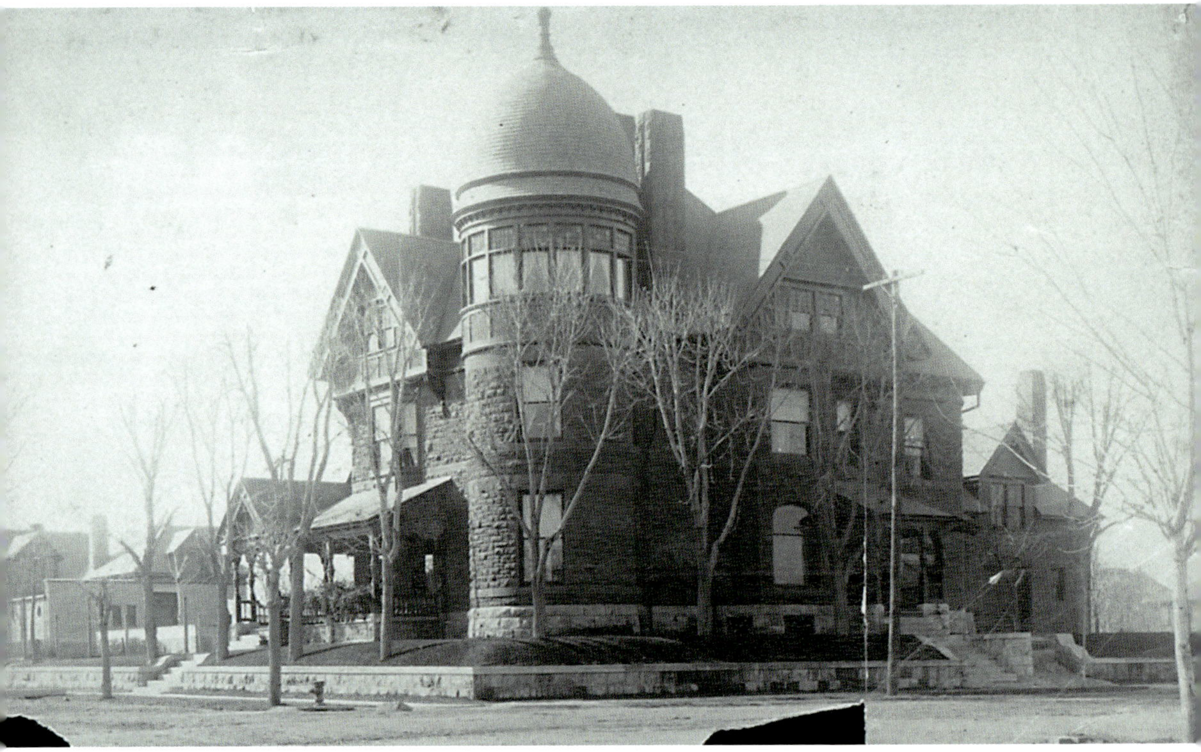

The lone survivor of a once robust district of millionaires' mansions, the George C. Schleier residence at 1665 Grant Street looks as good in the 21st century as it did in the 19th thanks to decades of careful stewardship. Schleier, originally from Baden, Germany, was an 1858 pioneer who made his fortune in real estate and other ventures. He built the Frank Edbrooke–designed mansion, with its onion-domed corner tower, for his second wife around 1889. (DPL, WHJ-10350.)

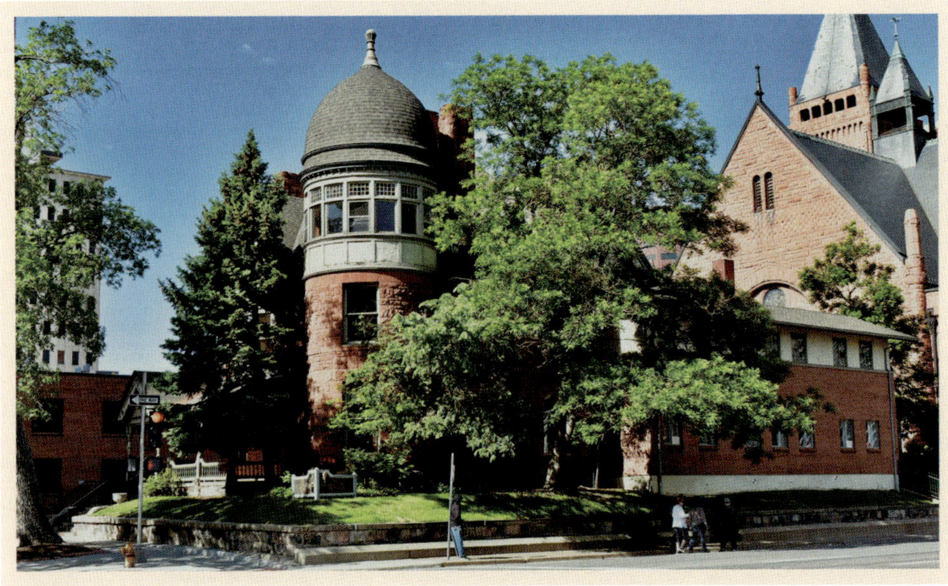

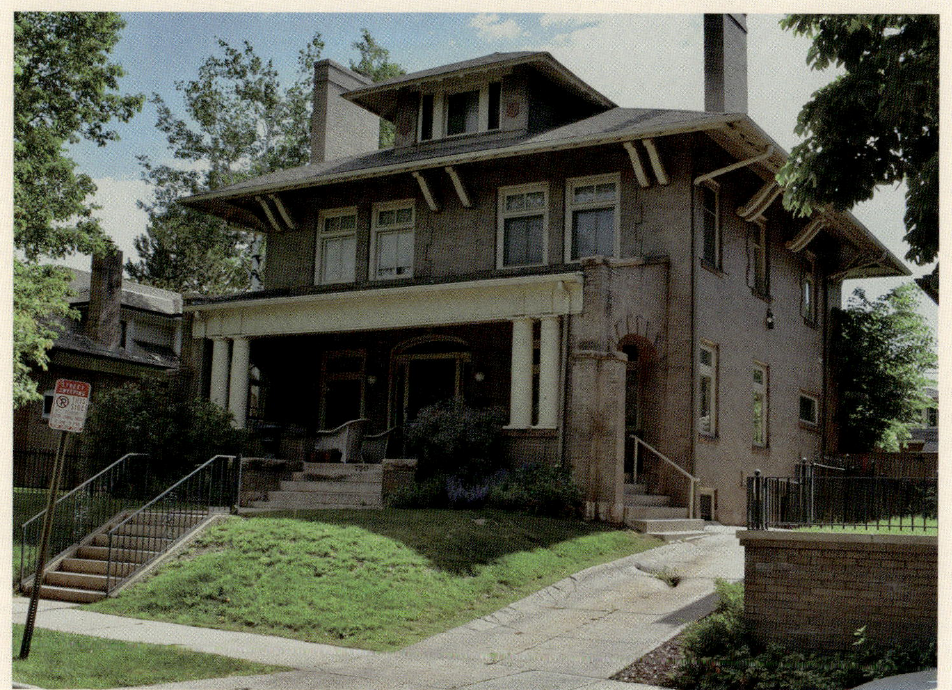

This National Register of Historic Places property and Denver Landmark at 750 Lafayette Street was the childhood home of Mamie Doud, who married a handsome young Army officer, Dwight David Eisenhower, in the living room (or at nearby Corona Presbyterian Church; accounts differ) in 1916. They visited her parents, John and Elivera Doud, more than once during his presidency, the Secret Service stationed in front. Edwin Moorman designed the capacious 1905 home. (DPL, C-516.)

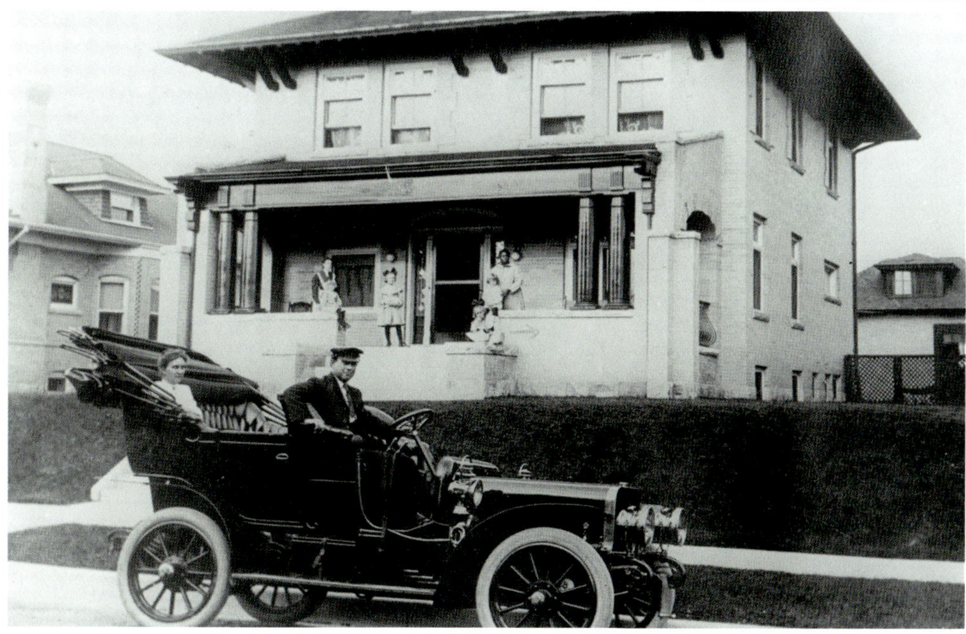

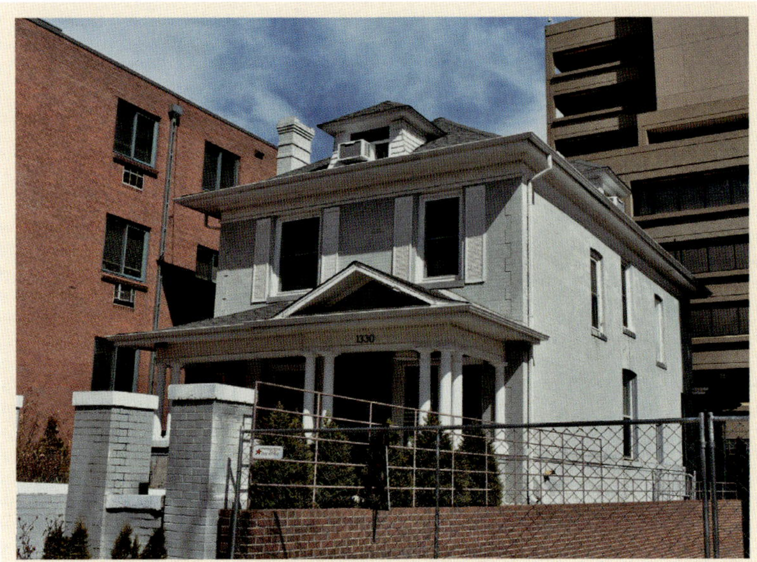

Hardware dealer Harry Fisher Rhoads and his wife, Addie, bought this dignified foursquare at 1330 Logan Street in 1898, moving in with four children, including Harry Mellon Rhoads, then 17. The younger Rhoads, handy with a camera, began working as a photographer for the *Denver Republican* in 1900. The *Rocky Mountain News* bought that paper in 1913; Rhoads continued documenting Denver for the *Rocky* until retiring in 1969, the longest career of any American newspaper photographer. (DPL, Rh-1394.)

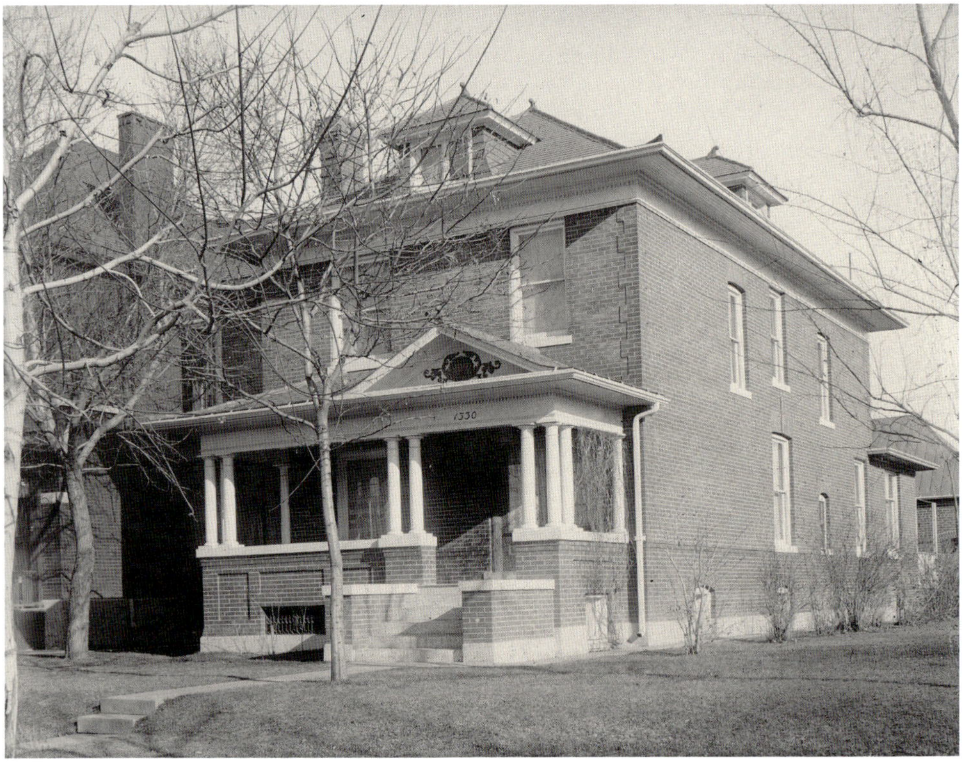

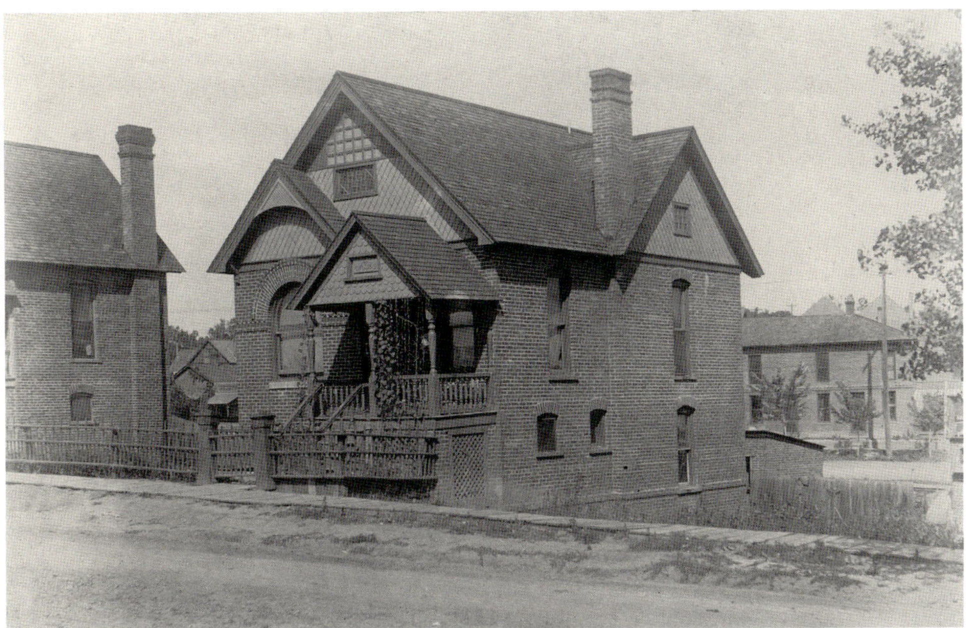

Northwest Denver's Jefferson Park once boasted historic riches, mostly erased by 21st-century developers. Residents of River Drive, worried their street would succumb, successfully worked to establish the River Drive Historic District in 2019. Perched on a bluff overlooking the South Platte River, the area was home to railroad and Zang Brewery workers. A carpenter first occupied this 1889 home at 2613 West River Drive; later, Cuban cigar maker Julian Serrano and his wife, Aurora, lived here. (DPL, X-18150.)

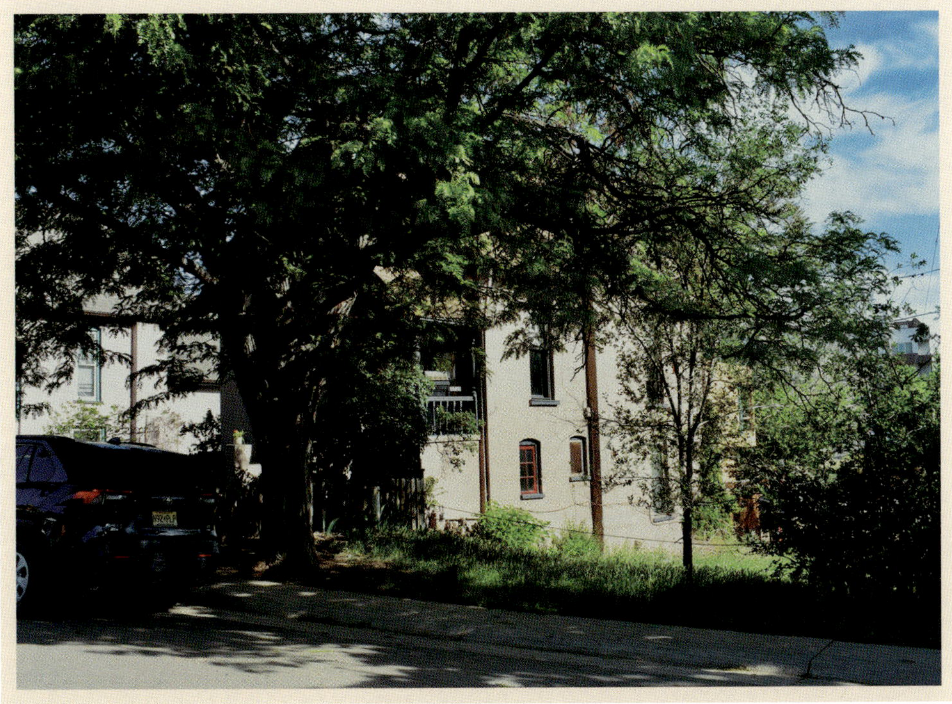

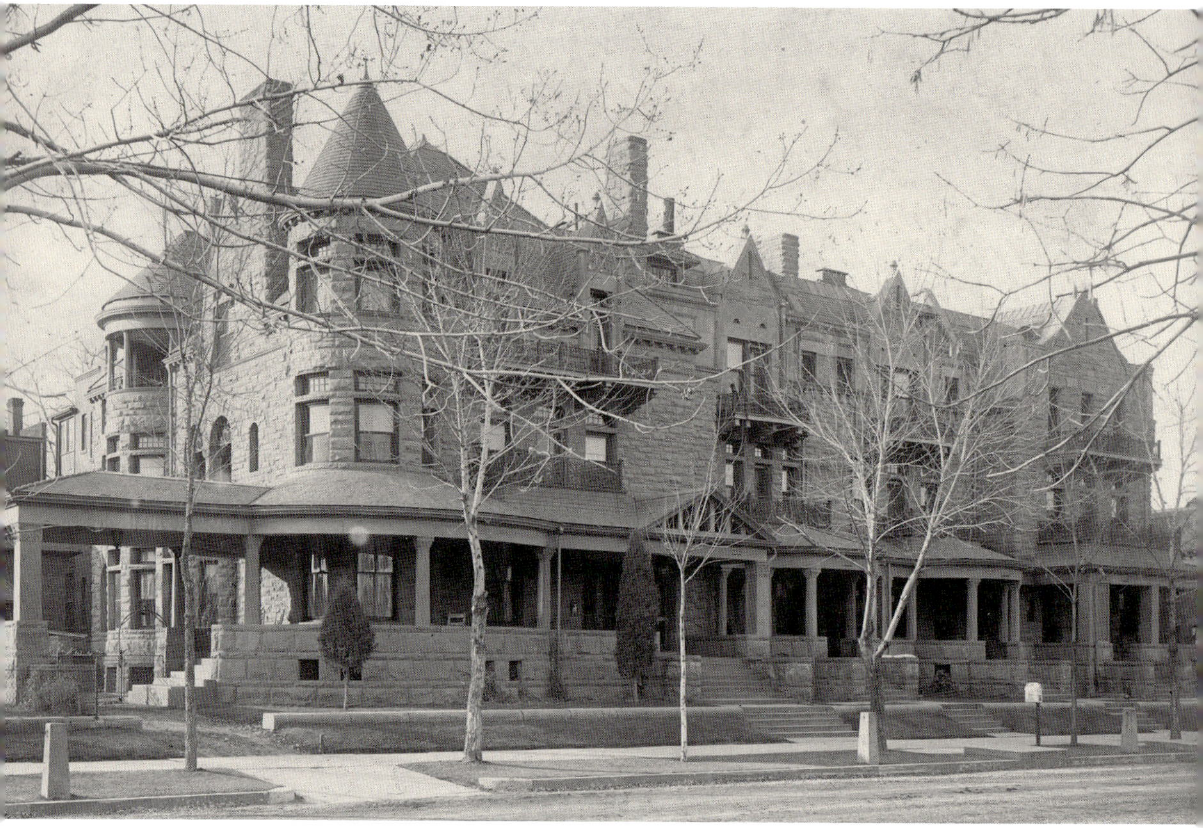

Built of red sandstone, Charline Place, at 1421–1441 Pennsylvania Street, originated as four adjoining townhomes. Erected for Charles H. Smith in 1890 to a Richardsonian/chateauesque design by Ernest Phillip Varian and Frederick Junius Sterner, the building, now a condominium, currently houses 30 units. It nearly faced demolition in the 1970s. Varian and Sterner also designed the Denver Club, Denver Athletic Club, and Colorado Springs' Antlers Hotel. (DPL, X-22365.)

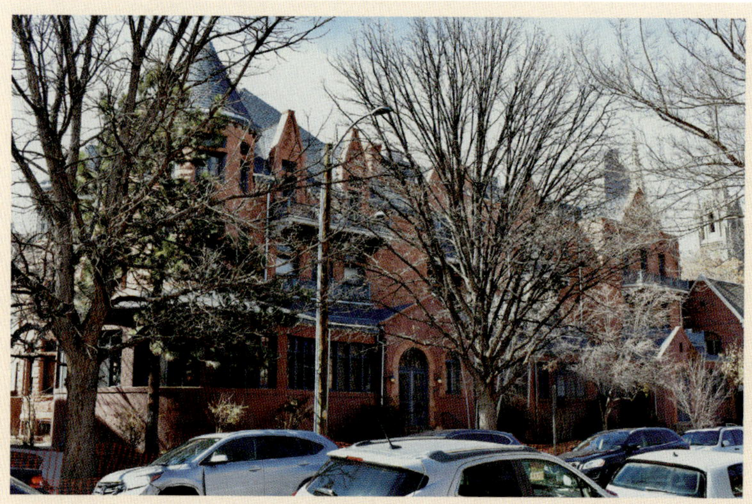

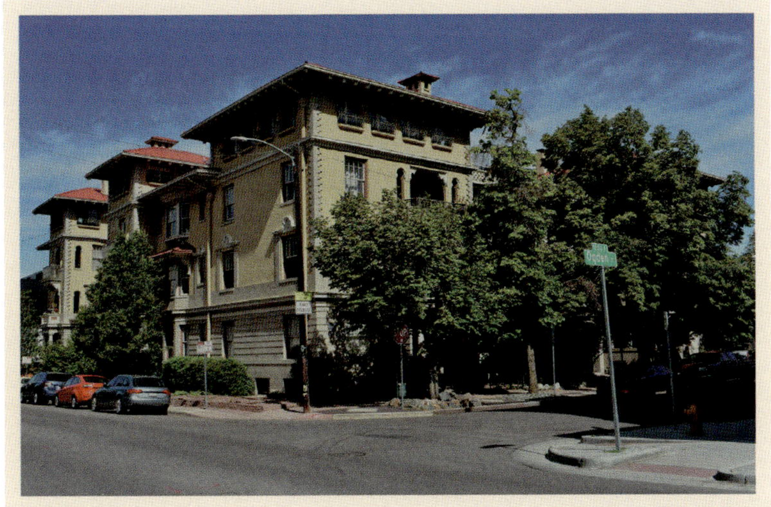

The Cornwall, at 1317 Ogden Street, may be the most spectacular multifamily residence in Capitol Hill. Designed by Walter E. Rice in the Mediterranean Revival style and completed in 1901 for William T. Cornwall, it once boasted a fourth-floor ballroom that hosted suffragist speaker Carrie Chapman Catt on her crusade for women's voting rights. Rice, a developer/architect, created much of the building's terra-cotta ornamentation himself in a basement studio. Originally apartments, it became condominiums in the 1970s. (DPL, MCC-504.)

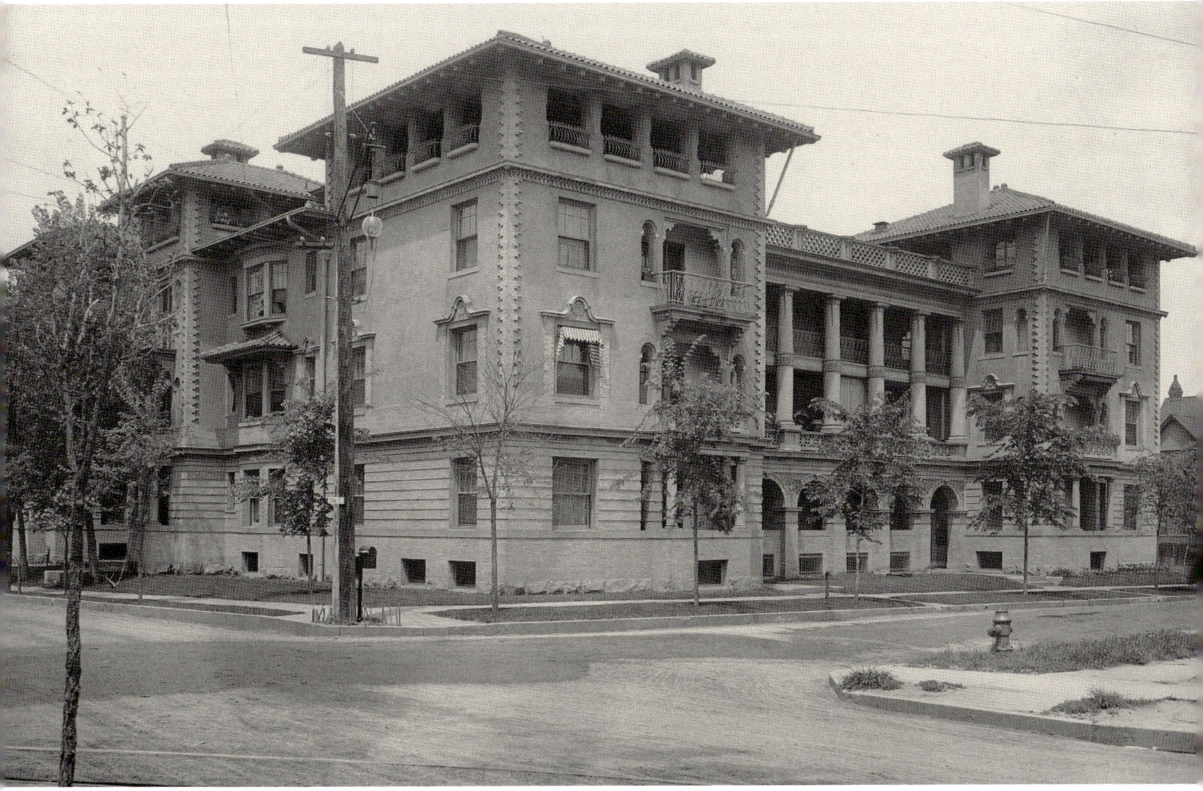

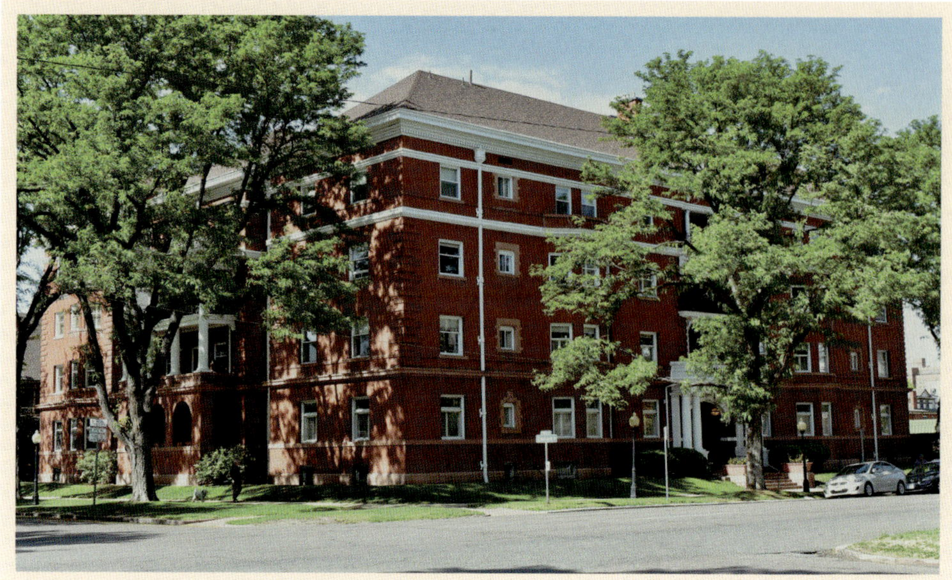

The 20th century saw Denver turn increasingly to apartment living. The most prestigious was the 1901 Perrenoud at East Seventeenth Avenue and Emerson Street. Designed by Denver native Frank Snell for Swiss immigrants Adele, Zelie, and R. Louise Perrenoud, this was the "swellest yet," per contemporaneous accounts. Built for $125,000, it housed 24 apartments, now condominiums, arranged around four light courts. The lobby featured an elaborate skylight, and basement amenities included a billiard room, bowling alley, and ballroom. (DPL, X-25307.)

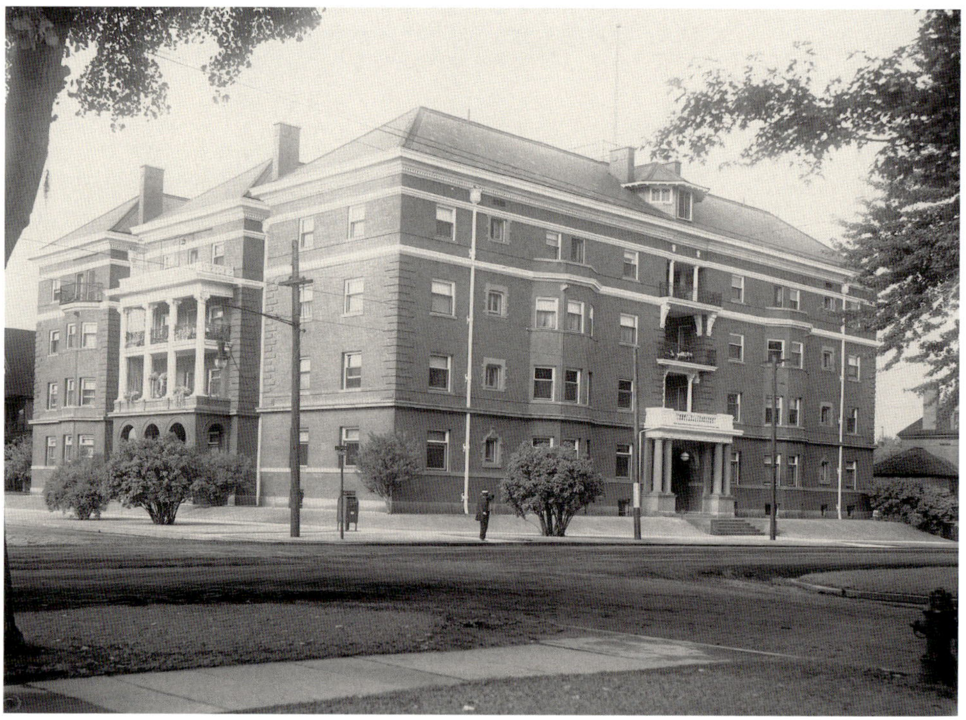

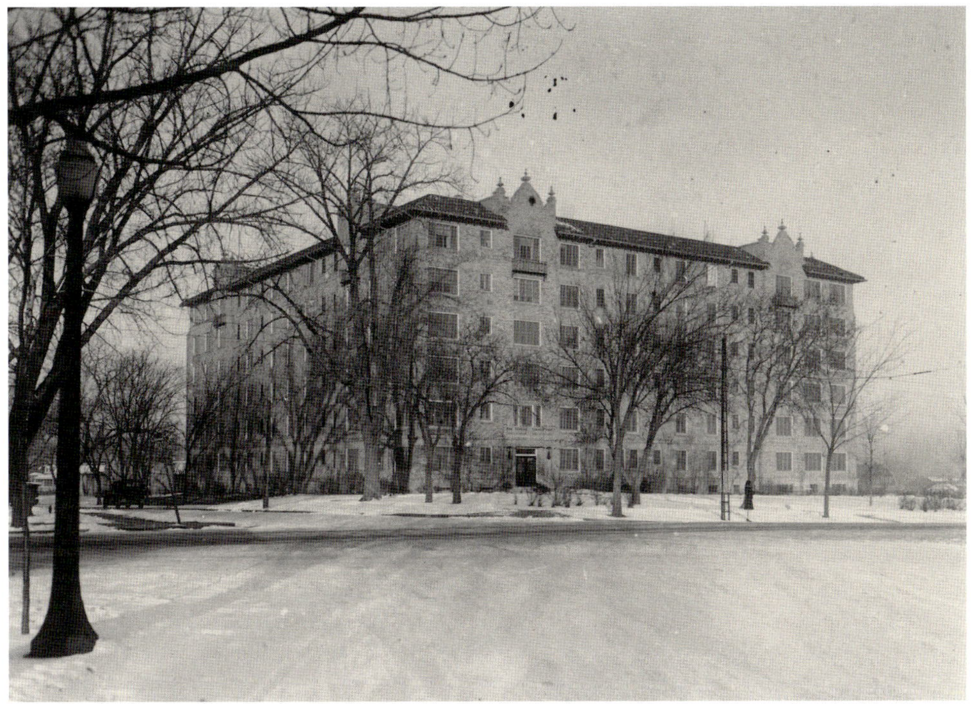

The Norman Apartments, built in 1924 where Marion Street Parkway branches off South Downing Street, remains as a condominium, one of Denver's most prestigious multifamily buildings. Overlooking the Denver Country Club, it bears the middle name of its architect and developer, William Norman Bowman, who chose more conservative Colonial Revival detailing instead of the then ascendant Art Deco style. He also chose to live in it. Luxury amenities included valet parking, laundry service, and maids' quarters. (DPL, X-25303.)

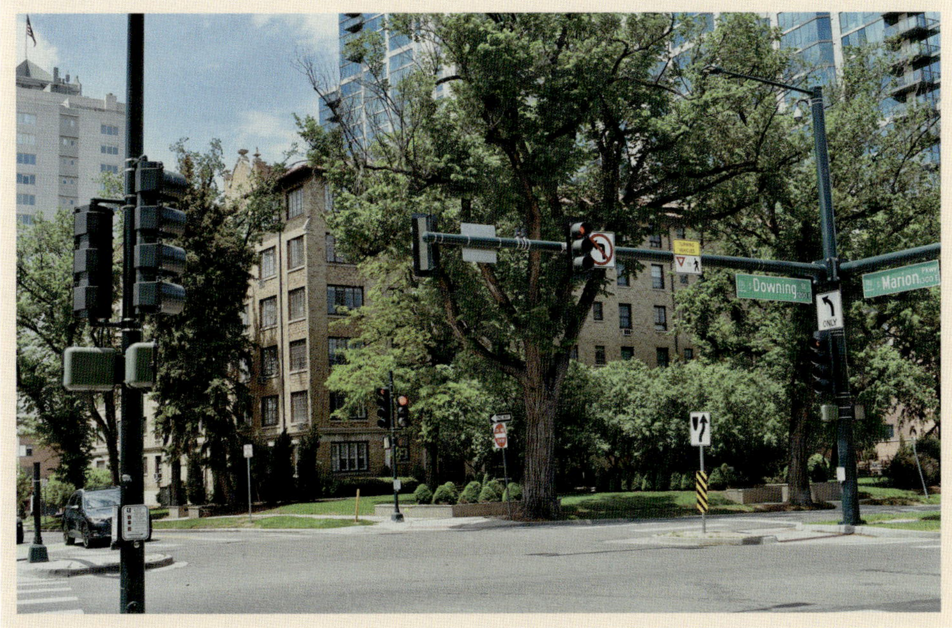

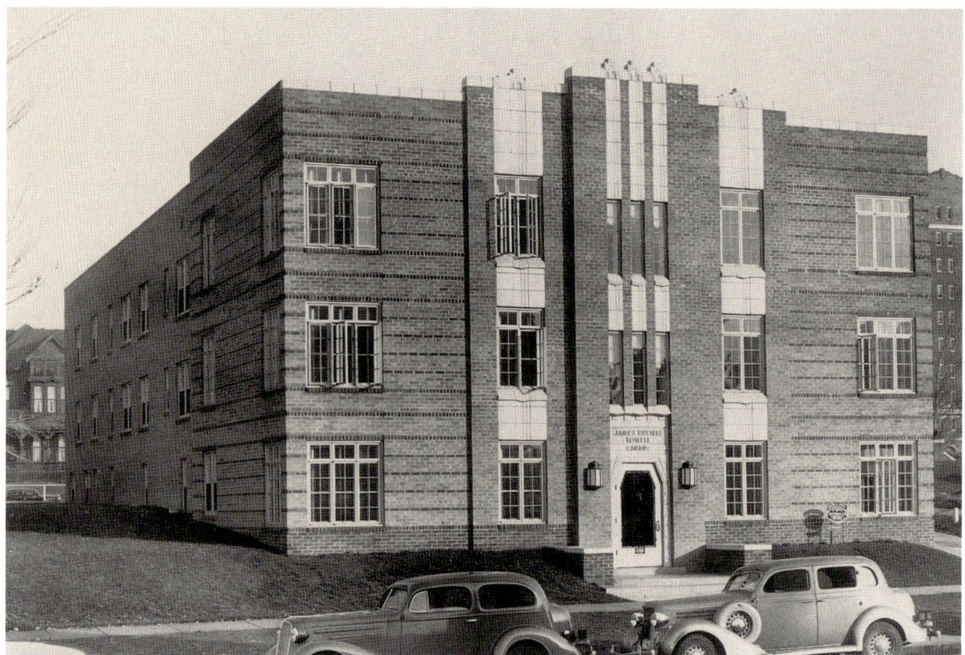

Originally part of the John Iliff estate and the spot where Buffalo Bill Cody presented his Wild West show in 1898, Poet's Row on Sherman Street remains one of Denver's most charming blocks of apartments. Here, the 1936 James Russell Lowell Apartments at 1020 Sherman Street wears an Art Deco look, while others, including the Mark Twain and Eugene Field, boast Art Moderne influences. Other Poet's Row namesakes include Robert Browning, Louisa May Alcott, Thomas Carlyle, and Robert Frost. (DPL, X-25297.)

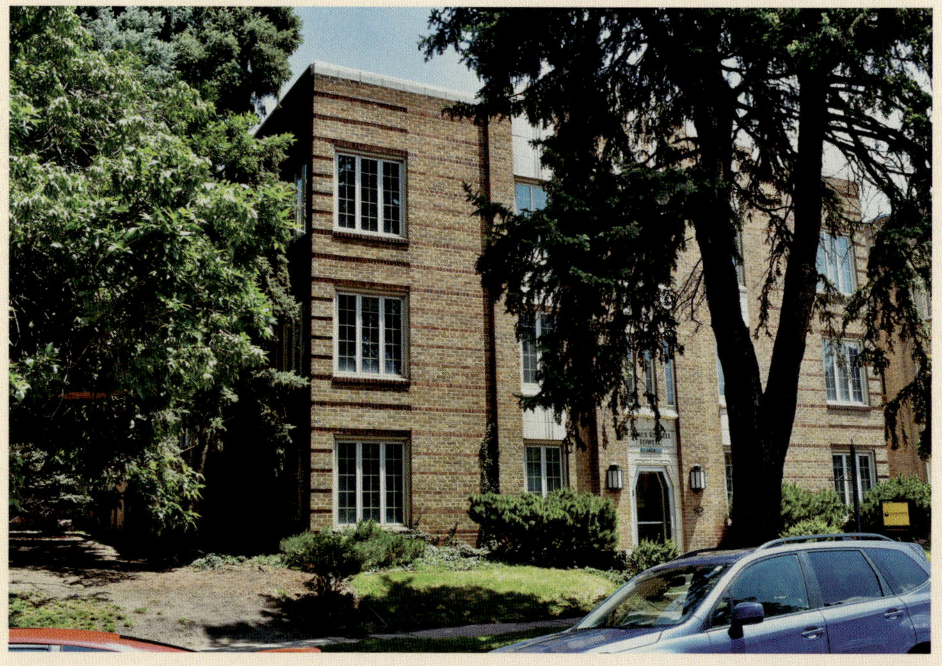

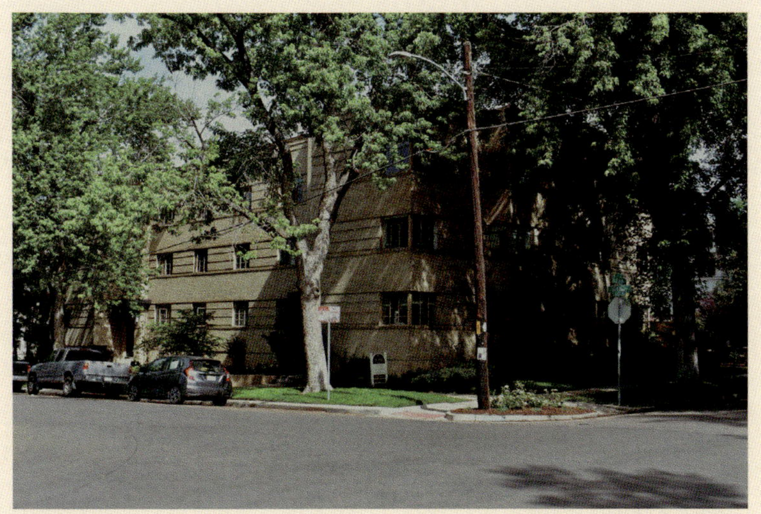

The Stanley Arms, a 1937 apartment building at East Tenth Avenue and Lafayette Street, exemplifies the Art Moderne style, but more importantly, this was where Florence Rena Sabin (1871–1953) and her sister Mary lived. Born in Central City, Florence was "the best known woman scientist of her era," per a National Institutes of Health biography. She was the first female professor at Johns Hopkins University; her statue represents Colorado in the US Capitol's Statuary Hall. (DPL, X-25314.)

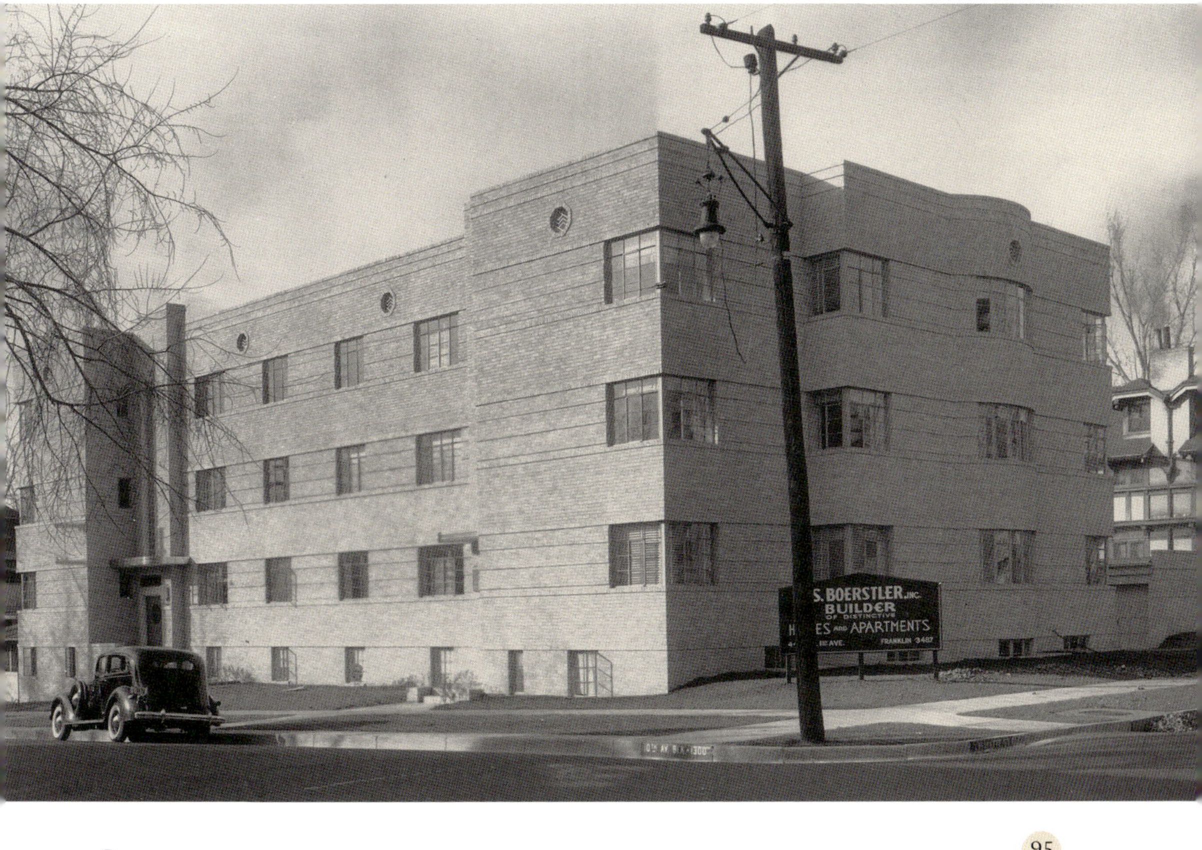

Consistent with our mission to preserve history on a local level, this book was printed in South Carolina on American-made paper and manufactured entirely in the United States. Products carrying the accredited Forest Stewardship Council (FSC) label are printed on 100 percent FSC-certified paper.

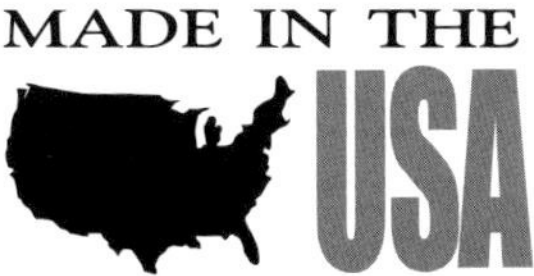